RUSSELL SPARKES has worked in the City of London since graduating with an honours degree in Philosophy, Politics and Economics from Oxford University in 1976. During his career he has worked with a leading merchant bank and major pension funds and insurance companies. He is currently employed as a fund manager with one of the largest ethical fund managers in the UK.

Russell Sparkes has followed the subject of ethical investment since the early 1980s, and has written articles on this and on business ethics for various professional journals. He is a Director of the UK Social Investment Forum, the body promoting and advising on ethical investment in the UK. A practising Christian, he is concerned to integrate Christian values in the world of finance. He is married with two daughters.

The Ethical Investor

RUSSELL SPARKES

with a foreword by the Bishop of Oxford

HarperCollins*Publishers*

HarperCollins*Publishers*
77–85 Fulham Palace Road, London W6 8JB

First published in Great Britain
in 1995 by HarperCollins*Publishers*

1 3 5 7 9 10 8 6 4 2

A catalogue record for this book is
available from the British Library

ISBN 000 627863 9

Typeset at The Spartan Press Ltd,
Lymington, Hants
Printed and bound in Great Britain by
HarperCollinsManufacturing Glasgow

Contents

Acknowledgements

For many years the Ethical Investment Research Service (EIRIS) has produced a regular newsletter called 'The Ethical Investor'. While this book and that newsletter share the same title, it should be noted that there is no other connection between them.

Writing this book involved a considerable amount of research and I would like to thank all the individuals who kindly spared time and effort to help me try and make it as accurate as possible: Mark Campanale; Giles Chitty; Lord Clinton-Davis; Pat Conaty; Lee Coates; David Craine; John Drummond; Mark Goyder; Mark Hayes; Antony Hardy; Francis Higgins; Chris Holmes; Charles Jacob MBE; Sue Jenkins; Serge Lourie; Pat Meehan; Geoff Mulgan; David Owen; Bill Seddon; Peter Silvester; Anne Simpson; Robert Taylor; Tessa Tennant; Lucy Varcoe; Perry Walker; Sue Ward; Peter Webster; Canon Bill Whiffen; Rev Crispin White. I would also like to thank my editor at HarperCollins, Giles Semper, for his encouragement in the early days of the book, and his help in clarifying my ideas.

Lastly, I would like to thank my wife Rosemary without whose constant support and quiet hard work the manuscript would never have been completed.

Foreword

Until recently the prevailing attitude towards the economic order was to regard it as a morally neutral sphere in which there is money to be made or lost. This attitude, the culmination of the movement which began in the seventeenth century, if not earlier, would have been unthinkable to the majority of Christians in previous ages. Now however, there is a welcome return to considering investment in other than purely financial terms. Ethical investment is an idea whose time has come.

I very much welcome this book as the first comprehensive treatment of the subject, from its theoretical foundations through to practical considerations of how you actually go about investing ethically.

Russell Sparkes shows how ethical investment has been a powerful lever for political change. But no less significantly he shows how ordinary investors can carry through their most deep seated convictions into the financial sphere. As human beings we all have moral convictions of one kind or another. Now it is possible to apply those convictions in a consistent and systematic way. If you have watched your mother die painfully of cancer and are totally opposed to smoking, it is now possible to invest your money in a way which does not kill other people in the same way. If you have been appallled by the figures of thousands of children dying every year through some of the hundred million anti-personnel mines around the world, it is possible to invest your money in such a way as to have no part in the production of such weapons. If you believe passionately in the conservation of our environment and fair treatment for developing countries in their trade relations, again it is possible to ensure that your treasure is where your heart is. Nor does this necessarily lead to lesser returns, as Russell Sparkes shows.

This book will be invaluable to the growing number of people interested in theory, history and practice of ethical investment.

Richard, Oxon

14th December 1994

CHAPTER ONE

What is Ethical Investment?

In the case of ethical investment it is not so much a choice between good and bad as a choice between various 'goods' or various 'bads'. We cannot hope to escape these real dilemmas . . . the fact is that we must live in the real world. I am reminded of G. K. Chesterton who said that 'if a job is worth doing it is worth doing badly'.[1]

RICHARD HARRIES, BISHOP OF OXFORD.

The new field of ethical investment

If the 1980s was a period of blatant consumerism whose slogan was 'shop until you drop', the 1990s rejected this ethos in favour of a more restrained approach. There was increasing awareness of the fragile ecosystem that supports all life on Earth, and also of how modern technology was integrating the world into one single economic unit. The discovery of a hole in the ozone layer over Antarctica resulted in the chemical companies and refrigeration manufacturers of Europe and North America being obliged to phase out production of the cfc chemicals which were regarded as the prime cause of ozone depletion.

On the positive side the rise of 'green consumerism' meant increased demand for products made without wasteful and possibly dangerous chemical inputs; witness the success of 'organic' vegetables, or the 35% in increase over five years in the sales of herbal medicines in the European Union to a staggering £1.2 bn by 1992. Most retailers were badly hit by the UK recession of 1990–3, but the sales of Body Shop continued to rise as customers were attracted by its simple formula of environmental conservation, Third World development and absence of cruelty to animals. Even politicians seemed to be rejecting the aggressive individualism of the Thatcher years in favour of greater awareness of community values.

Yet is there more to investment than making as much money as possible? In the 1980s Wall Street shouted that 'greed is good', but we now know that the idea that everybody can get rich is an illusion, and the 'Yuppie' period of the 1980s seems as distant and strange as the Roaring Twenties. Increasingly people want their money invested in ways that benefit the community or the environment, or, at the very least, they do not want it invested in companies that pollute the rivers and actively destroy the rainforest, in companies that make profits out of human suffering in the Third World or through addictive and destructive drugs such as tobacco. Repeated surveys (the last was by Mintel in 1991) have shown that around 40% of the public want their money invested ethically. Interestingly enough, most of those in favour said that they would make ethical investments even if they knew in advance that the returns would be lower than on conventional investments.

In view of this public demand it is not surprising that *ethical* or *socially responsible* investment has become the fastest growing sector of the investment management field. The first ethical unit trust, Stewardship, was launched by the insurance company Friends Provident in June 1984. From scratch and in just ten years socially responsible unit trusts and linked products grew to £800 m. Nor should the £4 bn

The Growth of Ethical Funds since 1984

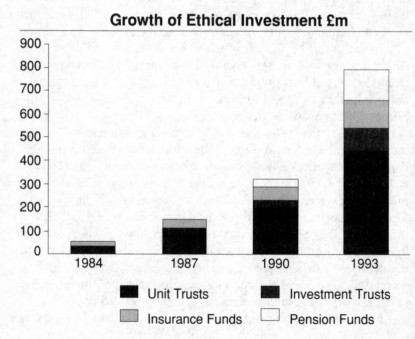

Growth of Ethical Investment £m

Legend: Unit Trusts · Investment Trusts · Insurance Funds · Pension Funds

of funds managed by Anglican and Methodist investment bodies under ethical guidelines be forgotten. The diagram shows the impressive growth of investment funds run on ethical lines since the launch of the Friends Provident Stewardship Trust.

The detailed numbers lying behind the chart are as follows:

(at year end)	1984	1987	1990	1993
Number of funds	2	11	30	42
Total size £m	54.6	143.1	317.2	801.5

The growth rate over each three-year period was remarkably constant at 35% a year compound.

Another sign of public interest in this field has been the increased media coverage that it received. Financial journalists have been interested in ethical investment for some time, but from the second half of 1993 onwards there were frequent articles in the *Financial Times* and in the financial sections of the heavyweight press, as well as major reviews in magazines like *Money Management* and *Professional Investor*. The latter is the trade magazine of the investment management industry, and in response to demand from fund managers themselves, in January 1994 it announced its commitment to publishing regular articles on ethical/green investment.

This book is focusing most of its attention on investment in company shares, often known as equities. From a financial point of view, all the evidence suggests that putting savings into equities is the best way to preserve them from the ravages of inflation. For ethical investors there is also the problem that most building societies and banks are not interested in taking any ethical conditions on the money deposited with them. The relatively few that do, such as the Ecology Building Society and the Co-operative Bank, are discussed in Chapter Nine, Ethics in Banking.

Another reason for buying equities, and perhaps the best, is that owning a company share gives the buyer a share in the ownership of a business. Shareholders technically appoint the directors of a company to run it on their behalf, and have the right to hire and fire them. Thus shareholders are the only people who can *force* a company's management to act in a responsible way. Socially responsible funds have traditionally had a bias towards shares in smaller companies. This was partly for negative reasons, as most large companies are conglomerates with some unacceptable activities, and partly for more positive reasons. It is much easier for an ethical fund to build up a significant stake in a smaller company, which assures that the management listens very carefully to what the managers of that fund tell them.

Ethics and investment

It is probably time to clarify what is normally meant by 'ethical investment'. It does not mean a moral campaign to clean up the Stock Exchange, or raise the standards of those who work in the financial field, much as this may need doing. Ethical investment is straightforward, and simply means an investment philosophy that combines ethical or environmental goals with financial ones. When the first ethical unit trust was launched in the UK in 1984 it emerged out of considerable work done by churches such as the Methodists and Society of Friends (Quakers) on what they regarded as areas that churches simply should not invest in on moral grounds: arms manufacture, the production of alcohol or tobacco, gambling and oppressive political regimes. Along with the Methodist Church, Quaker charities such as the Rowntree Trust played a large part in setting up EIRIS (Ethical Investment Research and Information Service) in 1983. These origins explain why the term 'ethical invest- ment' and the use of such *negative criteria* (avoiding the areas you do not like) became so widely established in the UK, rather than the American term 'socially responsible investment' which is probably more descriptive.

However, from the point of view of the potential investor, there are plenty of funds to choose from, and for many investors the first step in ethical investment is to set out industries that they want nothing to do with. 'Ethics' in this context usually means relating to the suffering, death or abuse of human beings, although an increas- ing number of people apply it to animals too. It seems self-evident that it is morally wrong to make profits out of the arms trade with its ever more sophisticated ways of killing and maiming people. Like- wise the profits from addictive and destructive habits such as cigar- ette smoking which unnecessarily kills thousands of people each year or gambling which causes huge misery, as can alcohol abuse. 'Oppressive regimes' may require a little more thought. In some parts of the Third World dictatorial regimes still exist (Amnesty International has a list of thirty countries) where ordinary people live in fear of their lives. Such governments may encourage Western multinational corporations to set up there which pay low wages and make huge profits as a consequence. These profits are *ethically tainted*. Western companies also find the Third World a dumping ground for things that are no longer acceptable in the US or Europe. This can be literal dumping, as in the case of hazardous waste, or the more insidious promotion of dangerous products.

Smoking is declining throughout the Western world, but heavily advertised and growing rapidly in Asia and Latin America. As Keith Ball of Action on Smoking and Health recently said: 'It's obscene that a major cause of death is being pushed on these African countries'[2] Inquiries by the US House of Representatives in 1994 examined whether tobacco should be regulated as a drug by the US Food and Drug Agency (FDA). The FDA's case to regulate tobacco was strengthened by reports from its head David Kessler that tobacco companies added chemicals, such as ammonia, to increase the nicotine absorption of cigarettes, and hence their addictiveness. Kessler stated baldly: '. . . the findings lay to rest any notion that there is no manipulation and control of nicotine undertaken in the tobacco industry.'[3] If the FDA does regulate tobacco, this is surely the first step towards making cigarette smoking as extinct as the cocaine which Sherlock Holmes quite legally smoked in the 1890s.

Ethical investment has not stood still, and its first ten years saw increasing awareness of the dangers of pornography, nuclear power and animal exploitation. An increasing focus on pornography did not reflect a sudden awakening to the evils of the sex trade, but rather an increased awareness of how pervasive they were. Most 'men's magazines' are privately owned, but pornography comes in a variety of ways such as the satellite channels that make most of their money from 'adult films', not to mention the exploitation of women through Page Three photographs in ordinary newspapers. The task for ethical fund managers, aided by EIRIS, was accurate research to identify companies involved in this.

The production of nuclear materials is another item that was added to most prohibited lists. Many writers have shown that even from the beginning 'peaceful' nuclear power generation was tied up with the production of plutonium for military purposes (see, for example, Walter Patterson's *The Plutonium Business*). Most of us suspect that the cumulative exposure to low levels of radiation is far more dangerous than governments admit, as the clusters of leukaemia sufferers around nuclear power stations such as Sellafield suggest. (The Canadian expert Rosalie Bertell estimated in 1985 that nuclear power worldwide had caused some sixteen million casualties, and this was before the Chernobyl accident![4]) Finally, the exploitation of animals has become something that an increasing proportion of ethical investors find unacceptable. This has had the practical effect of reducing the amount of cosmetic and food products that are tested on animals.

The press has tended to focus on the negative aspects of ethical investment, but it is worth stressing that right from its beginning with Friends Provident Stewardship, most funds have had positive aims of benefiting the community. In the United States 'socially responsible investment' grew up in the late 1960s when students questioned the investment of their universities' funds into companies that profited from the Vietnam War. The Americans have had better success in getting across the positive side of the subject. As Amy Domini, one of the pioneers of responsible investing, wrote in 1984: 'The positive approach complements the avoidance approach. Those adopting it seek investments in companies that enhance the quality of life. These companies produce goods or services of high quality and have good relations with their employees and the communities in which they operate. This approach assumes that all these positives indicate the probability of a superior investment return – which it does.'[5]

A small but growing area of ethical investment is *alternative investment*. Pension funds, charities, and unit trusts are legally restricted in what they are allowed to do if the financial return is doubtful, so alternative investment is normally done by individuals. For example, CAT is a company based in North Wales that has promoted renewable energy sources such as wind turbines and solar power since 1973. In 1990 it issued 500,000 new £1 shares to fund development of its site and allow it to demonstrate wind and solar power in operation to the thousands of visitors it receives. In 1991 Shared Interest raised £800,000 to fund sustainable Third World enterprises. This money was lent on to such charities as Traidcraft and Oxfam, Canada to enable them to buy more Third World produce and simple manufactures made in an ecologically sound way. The way 'social businesses' like Shared Interest, Traidcraft and the Charities Aid Foundation are blurring the distinction between commercial operations and the voluntary sector is discussed in Chapter Thirteen, The Social Economy.

What sort of ethical investors are there?

A good sample of most people's concerns was a research project carried out in 1992 by Chris Cowton of Templeton College, Oxford, using a sample of 125 people from an EIRIS questionnaire. Using cluster analysis, he found that about half of the sample fell into two clear groups (i.e. about 25% each) which he called 'political' and 'religious'.

Areas of concern	Total %	Political %	Religious %
Advertising	40	0	31
Alcohol	39	3	63
Animals	46	39	3
Defence	89	76	84
Gambling	47	12	56
Newspapers	5	3	0
Nuclear power	66	58	28
Overseas interests	26	9	0
Political contributions	46	30	16
Size of company	13	9	6
South Africa	96	85	100
Tobacco	70	9	94
Financial Institutions	56	46	16

Source: EIRIS[6]

These findings were supported by research done by the NM Conscience Fund at the end of 1993. It sent out a questionnaire to owners of units in its fund which revealed that 87% of them had bought in view of the stated ethical investment policy and only 7% had done so on the grounds of investment performance. Unit holders were asked to rank positive and negative criteria on a scale of 1 to 5, where 1 meant unimportant and 5 very important.

Positive Criteria	Score	Negative Criteria	Score
Environmental Awareness	4.67	Oppressive Regimes	4.72
Employee Welfare	4.24	Armaments	4.55
Community Involvement	3.54	Animal Exploitation	4.36
Charitable Donations	2.62	Tobacco	4.05
		Gambling	3.17
		Alcohol production	2.66

Brian Wilkinson, NM's Head of Marketing, said: '. . . these results show that ethical investment goes further than just "green issues". Environmental awareness is important, but so too is the avoidance of companies which profit from totalitarian governments, the arms trade, or animal exploitation.'[7]

Ethics and ecology

While the early UK ethical investment funds were influenced by the ethical principles of the churches, the 1990s saw more interest in ecological issues with a number of funds set up which concentrated their activities on environmental matters. It should be noted that two quite distinct types of *environmental* funds were set up. Some just saw the growth in green consumerism and environmental services generally as a way of making money. Others could be truly described as *green funds* with a commitment to sustainable development. Fund managers like Tessa Tennant of NPI/Merlin sought out companies that were positively benefiting the environment through the manufacture of such things as better control of pollution or more energy-efficient devices, and simultaneously, in a process of *constructive engagement*, encouraged the managers of ordinary companies to have greater awareness of green issues. Unfortunately, the use of the word 'environmental' in a fund's title did not say which type it was. (Green Investing is described in detail in Chapter Five.)

In 1987 John Elkington and Tom Burke wrote *The Green Capitalists*, a study of how consumer demand was forcing even heavily polluting industries such as the chemical industry to clean up their act, but lamented that: 'Many of the investments necessary for the pursuit of environmental excellence are inhibited by the preoccupation of the financial institutions with quarterly or half-yearly returns. Industrialists, increasingly under pressure from both their customers and the general public, may well understand the necessity of responding to the demand for higher environmental standards, but find it hard to persuade their financial masters, who remain loftily isolated from all pressures.'[8] The rapid growth of green funds helped industry to respond to those pressures. Six years later in September 1993 it was fitting that Tom Burke, by then a special adviser to the Secretary of State for the Environment, hosted a meeting at the Prince of Wales's charity Business in the Environment, which set up a Fund Managers' Environmental Forum to educate *all fund managers* about environmental issues, and not just those running green funds.[9]

Some people have argued that 'green' investing is intrinsically different from the older 'ethical' type. I think this is mistaken. Both are motivated by the belief that investment means more than making as much money as possible. In practice virtually all funds whether they use the term 'ethical', or 'ecological' cover both aspects, although the emphasis may be on one side or the other. EIRIS's Executive Secretary Peter Webster made the following comment: 'A neat division between "green" and "ethical" . . . does not work. In fact it can be unhelpful. An apparent choice between two labels obscures the need to ask what is meant by "green" or "ethical". It may also suggest that "ethical" is somehow "ungreen", when in fact green issues are an important part of the approach of most ethical investors. And are there really large numbers of people who care passionately about green issues, and not at all about anything else?'[10]

Tessa Tennant of the NPI research unit is probably the City's leading thinker on the whole subject of green investing. She argues that there is no real difference between ethical or environmental investing: 'The two are part and parcel of the same thing – investors avoiding tobacco companies on ethical grounds will almost certainly choose to avoid them on environmental grounds if they are apprised of the fact that for every 300 cigarettes made from Third World tobacco, one tree is burnt . . . Socially responsible investment should take into account both ethical and environmental issues'.[11] Tessa Tennant gets support from an unexpected source: '. . . today the ecological crisis has assumed such proportion as to be the responsibility of everyone' – Pope John Paul II, New Year Message, January 1990.[12]

For many people environmentalism is truly a moral crusade, and one that is a part of a wider view of how the earth's resources should be used. To take but one example, is it morally applicable or practical for the United States, having destroyed 90% of its indigenous woodland, to pressurize poor Brazilians to stop their own economic development programme in order to save the remaining 45% of the Brazilian rainforest? This was well put in a book published in 1994 by Charles Rubin, *The Green Crusade*:

> One critic has called 'environmentalism' an essentially meaningless term because it does not distinguish any distinct concern or point of view ... But a sympathetic student of environmentalism is closer to the mark when he suggests that environmentalists are 'the vanguard of a new society'. Being an environmentalist, in other words, means being part of a political or moral crusade for a better world. Environmentalism (in America) is heir to the anti-slavery and temperance movements and thus a part of the ongoing saga of evangelical reform that has characterized American history ... We know it wants to save the earth. We forget just how much, in the spirit of its predecessor, it seeks to save us from ourselves.[13]

Shareholder action

Shareholder action or shareholder activism occurs where groups of shareholders get together to raise public awareness of something that a company is doing, and try to use their influence as shareholders to persuade and maybe compel the company to change its ways. An example might be the campaign in the early 1980s led by the World Development Movement to force the Brooke Bond tea company to give better pay and conditions to the workers on its tea plantations. In the UK, companies are obliged by law to hold an annual general meeting for their shareholders once a year. The management is forced to answer questions from shareholders who can also put forward resolutions governing the conduct of the company. Shareholder activists have found that the fear of being embarrassed at the AGM is a powerful tool to persuade the management of a company to modify its behaviour, as it did in the Brooke Bond case.

Shareholder action has always been an integral feature of ethical investment in the US. Indeed, Ralph Nader's action in forcing General Motors to discuss workers' rights and consumer issues at its 1970 annual meeting was part of the process leading to the creation of social investment in the US. It has had less success in the UK. There are a number of reasons for this. Firstly, it is much easier to force an American company to discuss a proxy resolution (the US equivalent of the British shareholders' resolution) at its annual meeting than it is to get a resolution on the agenda of a British AGM. Secondly, in the UK about 80% of all shares are owned by the big investment institutions, whereas in the US private investors are much more important, and hence the threat of shareholder activists to persuade individuals to sell their shares is a much more powerful weapon. However, the growing significance of ethical investment in the UK means that socially responsible funds will increasingly be able to put such issues on the agenda.

Activists often work together with ethical funds on issues of mutual interest. A good example occurred in 1985 when Social Audit published a list of charities and medical organizations which held shares in tobacco companies. Many of the latter felt so embarrassed that they felt forced to sell their tobacco holdings immediately, so causing a significant decline in tobacco shares on the stock market. The British Medical Association was also stung into setting up a tobacco-free ethical fund for its members. In 1990 to 1991 the Peatlands Campaign co-ordinated a campaign of groups such as Friends of the Earth and ethical fund managers to force Fisons to change its policy of peat extraction. The possibility of customer boycotts and critical shareholder resolutions, caused the company to reconsider. This campaign received support from the highest levels of society: 'If we would like other countries to stop regarding their rainforest as "useless jungle", we would do well to set an example by not treating our peatland habitat as "useless bog"' HRH the Prince of Wales.[14] In 1993 Greenpeace Business worked with green fund managers successfully to prevent the London flotation of Barito Pacific, an Indonesian timber company suspected of massive deforestation.

The biggest impact of socially responsible investors and shareholder activists together was on US investment in South Africa. Following the 1985 declaration of the State of Emergency in that country, a campaign to force US investors to sell their South African holdings resulted in an increase in the amount of investment funds using it as a social screen surging from $40 bn in 1983 to $200 bn in 1987. Not only did this campaign force some of the biggest investors in the US to sell all their direct investments in South Africa, but they were also obliged to sell shares of American companies that were regarded as supporting the apartheid regime through strategic industries such as arms and computers. This campaign had the result of forcing some of the biggest companies in America, such as IBM and General Motors, to reduce their activities in South Africa, and this sustained financial pressure certainly played its part in forcing the apartheid regime into negotiating with the African National Congress in 1990–3. South Africa is such an important subject in the development of ethical investment that Chapter Eight is devoted to it.

Some people may be nervous of shareholder action on the grounds that it sounds rather too close for comfort to political campaigning. Yet as long as the aims are shared with those of socially responsible investment, shareholder action seems just another way of achieving them. Amy Domini has no doubts. 'What does shareholder activism have to do with ethical investing? Everything. When you invest positively, you make a statement about what you consider vital . . . But that is not enough. If the drive for corporate responsibility is to have real force, two things must happen. First, more shareholders must become aware of their duty to influence corporate action . . . Second, corporations which have not responded to shareholder concerns must be compelled to face these issues.'[15]

Ethical investment in practice

For most people buying shares directly themselves takes more time and effort than they can afford, and they will let a professional investment manager take care of the details. There is also the risk that if someone owned shares in only one or two different companies and there was then a problem with one of them, a large part of his or her savings could be lost. Buying a well-diversified unit trust eliminates this problem as it normally contains between fifty and eighty different holdings. Nevertheless, investing directly does have the big advantage that the *investor chooses* the criteria that he or she feels is important. For example, a vegetarian might want to avoid investing in any companies involved with meat production or animal experiments, but want to support companies that promote health-foods. People thinking of investing directly themselves need to think carefully about financial matters and to assess the areas of concern to them. Advice on how to carry out a personal 'ethical audit', and on how to find the information necessary to make an informed judgment of the suitability of a particular company is given in Chapter Two, Doing it Yourself.

As was mentioned earlier, socially responsible investment has been the fast-growing sector in the UK fund management field since its 1984 launch, which shows the pent-up demand from the public to be able to invest in equities with a clear conscience. But how is this money managed in practice? How does an investor in one of the thirty ethical unit trusts now available know that they are going to manage his/her money ethically? The first step is the investment criteria, which should be clearly spelled out. The table below shows some typical areas of concern:

INVESTMENT CRITERIA

ETHICAL INVESTMENT		ECOLOGICAL INVESTMENT	
Avoid	Support	Avoid	Support
1) Arms Trade	1) Good employers	1) Nuclear	1) Energy conservation
2) Tobacco	2) Help minorities	2) Ozone depletion	2) Recycling
3) Gambling	3) Help disabled	3) Acid rain	3) Eco-labelling
4) Oppressive regimes	4) Encourage Third World	4) Big water polluters	4) Waste minimization
5) Nuclear	5) Big donations to charity	5) Harm to rainforest	5) Natural Products
6) Pornography		6) Harm to wildlife	
7) Animal exploitation			

The next safeguard is the statement of Investment Policy and Objectives that by law unit trusts have to publish. Anyone who invest-ed in a fund and found it that was in breach of its objectives could later sue it for misrepresentation. The Policy and Objectives statement is an excellent way to get a feeling for the main aims of the fund.

POLICY OBJECTIVES OF SOME OF THE LARGER UK FUNDS:

Fund	Size	Launch Date
Friends Provident Stewardship	£145.1 m	1984

Objectives

To invest in UK companies whose products, services and operations are considered to be of long-term benefit to the community both here and overseas. Investments in companies involved with the armaments, gambling, alcohol and tobacco industries are avoided as far as practicable as also are companies with interests in South Africa. Analysis goes beyond products and covers such issues as employment practices, attitudes towards local communities, natural resources, pollution control and the political and social environment in which companies trade.

Fund	Size	Launch Date
CIS Environ Fund Cooperative Insurance	£22.1 m	1991

Objectives

Investment is limited to companies which are likely to benefit from measures taken to improve the environment, human health and quality of life ... The core of the portfolio consists of shares in companies involved wholly or in part in the manufacture of products, industrial processes or the provision of services associated with improving the environment and the enhancement of human health and safety.

The next safeguard that ethical investors have is that many funds are supervised by a panel of external experts who ensure that the company sticks to the policy set out in the objectives. This panel is known by such names as the *Advisory Committee* or the *Committee of Reference*. The experts are normally well-known names in fields like social policy, charity work, or environmental expertise. Friends Provident's advisory committee includes Charles Medawar, Director of the Public Interest Research Centre, and Charles Jacob MBE, 'the father of ethical investment' in the UK. CIS Environ has Lord Clinton-Davis, a former Labour Minister and EU Commissioner for the Environment, and the broadcaster Valerie Singleton. The

TSB Environmental Fund has the well-known biologist and environmental activist David Bellamy. The NM Conscience Fund, which was taken over by Friends Provident at the end of 1993, had the unique feature of inviting all its unitholders to a meeting once a year where they were able to grill the fund manager about his actions. This was a good idea which could be copied by other ethical funds.

Analysing a company in detail is normally carried out by the fund management team of the investment manager concerned, with the help of research produced by stockbrokers. The City has become increasingly aware of the importance of environmental issues. Top stockbrokers James Capel found that their *Green Book*, a major review of companies operating in the environmental field, proved to be their most popular research report. About half the socially responsible funds use the advisory services of the Ethical Investment Research Service (EIRIS) to help them screen potential investments. EIRIS services are also available to the public to help them check their own investments. As an example of how ethical screening works, the following EIRIS report on animal issues may be useful. The report found that twenty-five out of the top fifty companies on the Stock Exchange would be unacceptable to anyone worried about the abuse of animals.[16]

ANIMAL EXPLOITATION

Company	A	B	C	D	E
Argyll Group		X			X
British Airports		X			
BAT Industries			X		
BOC	X		X		
Bass			X		
Boots	X	X	X		
British Airways		X			
British Petroleum	X		X	X	
Cadbury Schweppes			X		
Courtaulds			X		
Glaxo Hldgs	X				
Grand Metropolitan			X		X
Guinness		X			
ICI			X		
Inchcape		X			

Company	A	B	C	D	E
Kingfisher		X			
Marks & Spencer		X		X	
P & O Shipping		X	X		
Reckitt & Colman	X	X	X		
Sainsbury		X		X	X
Shell			X		
Smithkline Beecham	X		X		
Tesco		X		X	
Unilever		X	X		X
Welcome	X				

The crosses X are black marks in the following areas:
A manufacture pharmaceuticals or medicines using animal testing.
B sell or manufacture soaps or cosmetics using animal testing.
C provide animal testing services.
D derive turnover from intensive farming or slaughterhouses
E derive a substantial part of their turnover from meat processing.

Most of these screening methods are still fairly vague, and individual funds do vary in how stringently they treat them. For example, some funds refuse to invest at all in a company that has activities in an area their objectives prohibit. The majority of ethical fund managers will invest in a company as long as it only has a small part of its turnover in such a forbidden area, while actively trying to persuade the company to sell it or otherwise improve its performance. Most socially responsible investment managers use a kind of judgmental *ethical credit rating* to help them decide whether to invest or not in a given company. For example, Sainsbury as shown above might get two black marks for its animal products policy, but its store development programme is generally regarded as more environmentally friendly than other food retailers such as Tesco, while the company gives big donations to charity and has a good record on workers' rights. On balance most ethical investors find it an acceptable holding. How ethical funds put it all together in practice is a large and complex issue which is treated in more depth in Chapter Three, Ethical Unit Trusts in Practice.

Does it work financially?

The other key question is whether ethical investors have to accept lower returns on their investments than they would get from conventional alternatives. In other words, do they have to pay for their principles? The good news is that the evidence suggests that over the long term ethical investment has produced a return as least as good as comparable ordinary funds. Further, well-run and committed ethical fund managers like Friends Provident, or the Central Finance Board of the Methodist Church have generated a long-term track record of significantly above-average investment performance. This is documented in Chapter Six, The Rewards of Virtue.

In the US, where socially responsible investment has been around a lot longer than in the UK, the evidence is undeniable. The United States Trust Company is one of the largest investment management companies in America with a lot of what it calls socially sensitive accounts. As early as the 1980s its studies showed the good relative investment performance of ethical funds. (The S&P 500 is a measure of the broad US stock market, much as the FT All Share does in the UK.)

US TRUST PERFORMANCE STATISTICS

Year	Socially Sensitive Funds % change	Normal Funds % change	S&P500 % change
1980	+22.4%	+19.4%	+32.3%
1981	+ 8.4%	+10.7%	− 5.0%
1982	+27.7%	+26.2%	+21.4%
1983	+15.9%	+16.2%	+20.7%
Average over period:	+19.7%	+19.4%	+17.7%[17]

It is not surprising that ethical funds should outperform the competition. While in the short term share prices tend to be affected by interest rates and general financial fashion, in the longer term they are driven by general trends in corporate profitability. Companies that make money unethically tend to have to pay for it in the end, which reduces their profits and can in extreme cases destroy a company. A good example is the US asbestos industry which neglected employees' health for many years and was forced into bankruptcy proceedings eventually. On the other hand, there is no doubt that environmental protection and energy saving is a growth area and that companies in this field should therefore be able to show faster profits growth than industry as a whole.

There is increasing evidence that companies which work with the community, rather than seeing it just as an object in which to make profits, do better in the long run. In 1989 the magazine *Financial Weekly* published a study showing that forty-three British companies which were identified as good employers showed a profits increase of 109% (technically defined as earnings per share growth) over the previous four years. This was significantly better than the stock market as a whole whose profits increased by a mere 68% over the same period.[18]

CHAPTER TWO

Doing it Yourself

As the message from the market gets ever more insistent, ethical investment offers investors a way to communicate their ethical concerns alongside their financial ones; it keeps ethical questions on the corporate agenda; and it supports those within the companies and the City who want to see ethics playing a greater part in corporate life.[1]

PETER WEBSTER, EXECUTIVE DIRECTOR OF EIRIS, NOVEMBER 1993.

As Peter Webster says, ethical investment enables individuals to use their savings in a positive way to promote corporate responsibility, as well as in a negative way of avoiding activities distasteful to them. However, before considering ethical or any other kind of investment it is essential to consult an appropriate financial expert, such as an independent financial adviser (IFA), or financial consultant in a bank, who can assess the financial requirements of the individual and the best means of achieving them. The financial adviser will normally start by carrying out a *financial audit* of the client's monetary needs and resources and such financial planning will focus on things such as pension and insurance planning. Financial advisers have a duty to be cautious and therefore will tend to spread the risk of investments via pooled products such as unit trusts and long-term pension plans, and it is right that they should do so. (For advice on independent financial advisers specializing in ethical products see Chapter Four; for information on ethical unit trusts see Chapter Three.)

However, there are a number of reasons why people might want to invest directly in shares themselves:

1 *Autonomy* – the simple desire to explore how the City works for themselves, rather than leaving it to an expert.
2 *Precision* – investing in any pooled fund such as a unit trust involves submitting to general criteria. People on their own can design a

portfolio that exactly meets their own specific concerns which may come well down the list of priorities used by many ethical unit trusts, such as women's rights.

3 *Campaigning* – less suitable for an individual than for a pressure group, nevertheless owning shares, with the consequent right to attend the annual general meeting, is a well-known campaigning technique.

4 *Positive Investment* – many ethical unit trusts (Friends Provident Stewardship and some others excepted) tend to have more detailed negative criteria than positive ones. Direct investment enables investors to help positively companies, often small, working in areas such as improved environmental technology.

5 *Alternatives* – if a client requests that funds should be invested ethically, it is practically certain that the financial adviser will do this through socially responsible unit trusts and linked savings vehicles in order to achieve the financially necessary diversification of risk. In practice it would be legally difficult for an IFA to recommend an investment into social enterprises such as Traidcraft or Shared Interest and the same is true of other alternative investments such as the CATS wind power scheme in Wales.

6 *Tax* – there is a purely financial reason why people should invest directly in company shares – PEPs. Personal equity plans (PEPs) are a highly tax-advantageous way to invest. Each UK adult can invest up to £6,000 a year in a general PEP, and all dividend income and capital gains are tax-free. A general PEP may invest in unit trusts as long as 50% of the assets are held in the UK or Europe, but on top of the general PEP allowance, there is a further annual PEP allowance of £3,000 which must be invested in a single company. The costs of PEP compared to long-term savings plans are low, and the saver's money is accessible which is not true of pension plans.

A Personal Audit

The next step for the ethical investor is to find out what ethical factors are of real concern in order to carry them out in practice. It is important to list and evaluate them systematically, that is, carry out a personal ethical audit. If this is not done, there must be a real danger that having actually bought shares in a company the investor later discovers something wrong with it and has to sell it again. People often think of ethics as being purely negative – *thou shalt not* – but the great advantage of do-it-yourself investing is that the individual devises the rules and can seek out positive criteria. As mentioned above, this could be in the field of alternative investments, or it could be in companies working in the environmental protection field with positive attitudes to women, donations to charity, etc.

The most thorough ethical audit I am aware of was published in the CEIG document *Our Best Interest*[2] (OBI) which was available to the public from the end of 1993. It advocated an ethical credit rating on a score of 0 to 10. A score of 0 meant a mandatory ban, for example, this might mean no investment in companies with operations in South Africa, or companies which might test cosmetics on animals. A score of 1–2 meant a discretionary ban, probably vetoed but worth a detailed analysis – some people would argue that pharmaceutical companies which test new products on animals would fall into that category, as might companies selling nonmilitary equipment to the defence services or retailers with a heavy reliance on alcohol. At the other end, a score of 8–10 was 'excellent', and a recommended purchase. (The other scores were more relevant for institutional ethical investors who can try and change company behaviour – *constructive engagement*.)

A Product or Service	B Company Ethos	C Social Factors	D Environment
1 Alcohol production and retail	1 Good management – Cadbury Committee	1 Pay good wages	1 Greenhouse gases
2 Fur trade	2 Accounting – bad practices	2 Health and safety	2 Nuclear power
3 Gambling	3 Pay of directors ratio to employees	3 ESOPS	3 Ozone depletion
4 Military plus nonmilitary sales	4 Political ties	4 Worker consultation	4 Pesticides
5 Pornography	5 Newspaper links	5 Trade Union recognition	5 Waste disposal
6 Tobacco	6 Community involvement	6 Equal opportunities	6 Water pollution
7 Companies involved in safety and protection, or training and education	7 Respect for law	7 Sunday Trading	7 Animal Testing
		8 Advertising standards	8 Animals reared for food
		9 Oppressive regimes	9 Energy use
		10 Third World links	10 Recycling
			11 Environmental statements

There were four categories: the acceptability of the product or service, the evaluation of the company ethos, social factors and environmental performance. *Our Best Interest* went into these in great depth, but for the individual investor it is probably sufficient to mention the areas of concern.

In practice all these categories require two things: detailed knowledge of a company and considered judgment of what is and what is not acceptable. Take the example of sales to the military. OBI suggests three levels of acceptability: 3% of sales, 10% of sales or 33% of sales. The problem with this mechanistic approach is that a company which sells 30% of its total production of socks to the army might be vetoed, whereas GEC, which is one of the UK's largest arms manufacturers, is such a large conglomerate that defence sales are less than 20% of sales and could therefore prove acceptable. OBI therefore also recommends a ceiling on the absolute amount of sales to the Ministry of Defence. There is also a quality criterion – there might be an absolute veto on company groups which have sold arms either to oppressive regimes or to countries fighting civil wars or to countries engaged in a non-UN-sponsored armed conflict.

I am not suggesting that most individuals will want to go to this amount of work, rather that this is an interesting example illustrating the thought processes involved. However, for people who are passionately concerned about certain issues, this kind of detailed ethical investigation of companies is available from EIRIS, as described below.

The Financial Basics

Note that anyone in charge of other people's money, such as a club or small charity, is in a *trustee relationship*, and must take legal advice if considering investing on an ethical basis. Chapter Twelve, The Legal Framework, explains the concept of a trustee and the relevant legal questions to ask. Such investors should probably adopt a portfolio approach of holding a number of shares in different companies. It is sometimes stated in the financial press that you need £100,000 to have a portfolio of shares, but this is a misconception. A merchant bank or other investment manager is unlikely to welcome anyone with less than that to invest as a discretionary client, but that is a reflection of their own costs and their need to make a profit. For people willing to do their own administration, probably the minimum sensible holding in one company is around £2,000. Share dealing is cheap these days – there are plenty of discount brokers who charge a minimum fee of £20 for each transaction.

The essence of creating a portfolio is to spread the risk of a particular company or industry hitting hard times. For example, anyone who invested all their money in defence company shares over the last three years would have done badly as they were adversely affected by defence spending cutbacks. How many shares in different companies do you need to have a diversified portfolio? Surprisingly few according to the actuarial experts, at minimum seven or eight holdings, though double that to be really comfortable. In other words, the minimum to create a directly owned portfolio is £14,000, which a windfall or legacy could put within reach of many people. Note that this would have to be a *diversified* portfolio, with all the holdings in different industries. For illustration only:

1 A retailer
2 An engineering company
3 A natural resources company
4 A financial company
5 A publisher/information services company
6 A water utility
7 A high growth company, such as a cellular telephone company.

The next step is actually to analyse companies. Clearly, that is a distinct subject in its own right. *Beginner's Guide to Investment*, by Bernard Gray of the *Investors Chronicle*[3] is a useful introduction. There are a few basics worth mentioning, however. Investing in equities is essentially about one thing – growth in profits. As long as a company's sales and profits are genuinely growing, over the long term its share price is likely to move ahead.

The financial community and the financial press sometimes give the impression that investing in equities is a complex and time-consuming process best left to the experts who more than justify the fees they charge. This is mystifying nonsense. As long as people are prepared to do the work, and in the case of a portfolio ensure that it is diversified, there is no reason why they cannot invest on their own.

To start with, they will not be deducting 6% of their money as an initial fee on a unit trust, with a further 1% deducted each year as a management fee. In fact, in the United States during the 1980s 62% of private individuals saw the performance of their portfolios beat the main US stock market index, the S&P 500. Only 25% of professional money managers were able to do so. In the UK in the ten years to the end of 1993, the value of the bench-mark FT All Share Index rose fivefold in value, or 16.8% a year compound. Only 14% of so called growth trusts managed to exceed this.

The simplest and most natural way of investing is for someone to buy shares in a company they know and whose products they like. Generations of women have bought shares in Marks & Spencer because they enjoyed shopping there, and they respected the company's policy of buying British and its record of good staff treatment. Financially this has turned out to be a very good investment strategy. Some people may wonder whether this is not a naive, down-market way of investing. Far from it! Peter Lynch is regarded as one of the world's best professional money managers. In the ultracompetitive world of American mutual funds, the Fidelity Magellan fund which he ran consistently outperformed its rivals. Peter Lynch does not look at stock-market fashions, worry about the economy or use complex technical means of analysis. His investment philosophy, summed up in his book *One Up on Wall Street* is very simple, that investors make money investing in things they know and understand, what he calls the *power of common knowledge*.

As Lynch expresses it:

> In fact, the amateur investor has numerous built-in advantages that, if exploited, should result in his or her outperforming the experts, and also the market in general . . . I talk to hundreds of companies a year and spend hour after hour in heady powwows with CEOs, financial analysts, and my colleagues in the mutual fund business, but I stumble onto the big winners in extracurricular situations, the same way you could.[4]

He lists several companies he invested in, and whose share price rose several times in value, simply because he liked the product:

> Taco Bell I was impressed with the burrito on a trip to California; Apple Computer, my kids had one and then the systems

manager bought several for the office; Dunkin' Donuts, I loved the coffee.

Body Shop – A Case Study

It is all very well for Peter Lynch, a trained professional with all the resources of Wall Street at his command, but how is an ordinary person to even begin to analyse a company? A simple case study involving Body Shop illustrates some of the issues, as it is a company many ethical investors feel comfortable with. People working in the City and those in campaigning organizations such as Greenpeace will have access to vast databases covering financial and other facts, but I have limited myself to information easily available to the public.

The obvious first step was to walk into a Body Shop branch and ask what information they had available. The answer was that there was no financial information on the company available there, but I was given several leaflets on its products and philosophy:

1 Against Animal Testing
2 Trade Not Aid
3 Body Shop approach – Packaging
4 The Body Shop Tour

1 Against Animal Testing states that Body Shop: 'does not commission or test any product or ingredient on animals – we never
   have and we never will.' It goes on to state that Body Shop insists
   that any supplier of ingredients must have had a non-animal
   testing policy for at least five years before it is acceptable to Body
   Shop. The Five-Year rule is enforced by a team of researchers
   sending out a twice-yearly monitoring form to the suppliers of
   1,100 ingredients. It continues: 'We will continue our fight until
   there is a world-wide ban on this cruel and unnecessary activity.'
2 Trade Not Aid says that since 1987 Body Shop has operated fair
   trading agreements with local communities in developing countries as the company explores for natural ingredients in such areas.
   'The great challenge is to create small-scale trade links that are
   economically viable without impinging upon local traditions and
   ways of life.'

3 The Body Shop Approach – Packaging accuses the cosmetics industry of producing three main products: packaging, garbage, and waste. It therefore states that Body Shop uses minimal packaging and encourages customers to bring plastic packaging back for recycling. To encourage customers to save on packaging, it operates a refill service which saves the customer 20p on each bottle.
4 One of the themes of this book is that people who claim to be ethical investment managers have to prove their ethical integrity through clarity and disclosure. I was therefore very interested to see Body Shop invite customers to the Body Shop Tour, an inspection behind the scenes.

The next step was to get hold of the Report and Accounts of the company for the last few years to examine its financial progress. These showed that the company's profits grew very rapidly until its financial year 1992–3, when it was adversely affected by the recession and by the entry of Boots and some food retailers into the natural cosmetics market. (Like many retailers, Body Shop has a financial year ending in February.) However, in 1993–4 it overcame these problems with UK sales recovering, and continued strong expansion in the US, and pretax operating profits rose from £21.5 m to £28.6 m. To answer the question of whether Body Shop shares are a buy or a sell on purely financial grounds, I would compare the likely growth rate of the company's profits with the stock market rating of them. (This is normally the P/E ratio, the share price divided by the earnings per share. P/E s are explained in detail in *Beginners Guide to Investment*. Essentially, the better the growth prospects, the higher the P/E.) Hence commenting on the Body Shop's results for 1993–4, *The Financial Times* said: 'On a forecast of £33.5 m pretax this year, the prospective P/E is just under 20. The rating is nothing like it has been at in the group's 10-year stock market history, but is justified by current growth prospects.'[5]

A Company Ethical Audit

Body Shop hit the newspaper headlines in August 1994 with a number of articles arguing about the genuineness of its ethical stance. This was a good example of how difficult it can be for an ordinary investor to assess a company's ethical credentials. You are only likely to find good news about a company in its own Report and Accounts! The only way for the ordinary individual ethically to audit companies is to use the abstract of newspapers articles which is available in most libraries. This will give some of the articles which have been printed on a particular company, although mostly they are just arranged in some kind of date order, so the researcher just has to trawl through. (Large businesses may have on-line database systems such as Textline and FT Profile which search through all the stories which have appeared in the media on a certain company over a specified period of time. They are expensive, however, and unlikely to be found in most libraries.)

Looking out for articles on Body Shop in 1994, a selection of the most interesting subjects were:

1 April 1994 London *Evening Standard* controversy about Anita Roddick appearing in a commercial for American Express. Chairman Gordon Roddick wrote: 'The article "Saving the planet from hypocrisy" said Anita Roddick's appearance fees, paid by American Express, went into her pocket. In fact, they were passed on to two projects in Mexico. One to support healthcare for the Huichoi Indians in Guadalajara, and the other to the Mesquital Indians who featured in the ad.'[6]

2 May 1994 also saw an article that Body Shop Managing Director Anita Roddick was personally planning to open an 'alternative business school' in Devon looking at human, animal and environmental rights. She said: 'You can fly the flag of social change and still make a profit. All that Milton Friedman stuff about the only responsibility being to the shareholder's pocket can be dumped.'[7]

3 *The Times* commented on the results: 'Whether you accept Anita Roddick's born-again environmentalism at face value, or view it as a cynical marketing package, one has to admire Body Shop's commercial resilience.'[8]

4 In an interview in *Today* Anita Roddick stated: 'If I am proud of anything, it is the ability to ask questions and challenge the status quo, to ask why it's not possible to have morals and run a business, why its not possible to put something back in?'[9]

5 *Financial Times*, July 1994 Gordon and Anita Roddick sold 3.5 m shares of Body Shop to raise £8.4 m. Of this £2.1 m would be given to the Healthcare Foundation to help the development of an inhaler to alleviate colds and hay fever. The Foundation is a

charity set up in 1987 with Michael Grade and Richard Branson, and which produced the cut-price Mates condoms. Another £2 m was allocated to guarantee the bank funding of Millennium: *Tribal Wisdom and the Modern World*, a film on the sufferings of indigenous peoples around the world.[10]

6 Other information was an article in an American magazine discussing how in September 1993, Body Shop launched an AIDS awareness campaign in its US stores entitled 'Protect and Respect', while another source showed the Roddicks to have provided much of the finance to get off the ground the *Big Issue*, the newspaper for homeless people to sell rather than have to beg.

While the above does not pretend to be exhaustive, even compiling that much data took a lot of time and effort! People who do not have access to on-line databases also have the problem that there is a time lag of several months before research abstracts are available, so the August 1994 coverage of the Body Shop story would not be available until October at the earliest. There is also the problem that the ethical investor cannot be sure that the ordinary commercial press has picked up issues which would be of concern to him or her. (Since the critical debate on Body Shop was based on second-hand press reports of US material not available in the UK, it is not discussed here.) For all these reasons, many people delegate the work of ethical investigation to a specialist service – EIRIS.

An Ethical Research Service

The only place which provides such information and makes it available to the public is the Ethical Investment Research Service (EIRIS, pronounced 'iris'). EIRIS was set up in 1983 by a group of churches, the main impetus coming from the Quakers, Quaker charitable trusts and the Methodist Church. The aim was to produce the information required to apply ethical criteria to investment, to identify alternative investments for ethical investors and to promote a wider debate on issues of corporate responsibility. For example, EIRIS produced a detailed investigation of the Body Shop question and reviewed the company's operations in a number of areas where it had been attacked by critics. These included animal testing, charitable giving, corporate governance, environmental issues, franchises, and trade-not aid. EIRIS concluded: *'Overall we feel that Body Shop has been unfairly treated. But our clients will be thinking carefully whether any of the facts that do emerge from this story affect their view of the company.* [11]

EIRIS is a charity whose policy is determined by a Council of Management which includes such ethical investment notables as Philip Wade, Finance Officer of the United Reformed Church, Mark Hayes of Shared Interest, Trevor Jepson formerly of the Joseph Rowntree Trust, Bill Seddon, Investment Manager of the Central Finance Board of the Methodist Church, and Bill Whiffen, Secretary of CEIG, as well as Sue Ward, a journalist and pensions expert and Marlene Winfield, a policy analyst. EIRIS has been run since inception by Peter Webster, formerly a member of the Young Quakers whose demands for a more ethical investment policy by the Society of Friends in the late 1970s helped cause EIRIS to be created. Ten years later Peter Webster wrote: 'When EIRIS was launched in 1983 I think we were clearer about the research that people needed than we were about who might buy it. We hoped that there would be enough demand to replace our grant funding, and the hope was fully justified.'[12] Peter Webster need not have worried; whereas in 1986 grants still amounted to nearly half EIRIS's expenditure of £30,000, by 1992 expenditure had grown to £270,000 completely covered by the sale of its services. (Like many charities, EIRIS has found it useful to establish a trading company, EIRIS Services Ltd).

It should be noted that EIRIS does not make moral judgments about the companies it analyses – its expertise lies in the research. It does not give advice on the financial suitability of any investment. Some people have argued that EIRIS should be more critical and more activist like ICCR in the US. I think that this confuses two issues: you cannot be both an accurate and objective research organization, and a campaigning group. Nobody would expect Greenpeace to advance the arguments against global warming, or the World Wildlife Fund to provide facts in favour of drug testing on animals, yet this is what an objective research unit has to do. It is up to the individual investor then to decide, for example, that having heard the facts, he or she thinks that any kind of animal testing is barbaric and should be absolutely excluded from their portfolio. While EIRIS obtains the vast majority of its information from independent sources, if a company is criticized, EIRIS will always contact it to hear its side of the story (fact sheets were sent out to

1,009 companies in 1993). Companies who supply information to EIRIS have to feel sure that it will not misuse it, while investors have to know that the information produced is as accurate as it can be.

EIRIS offers three main services to investors:
1 An *Acceptable List* of all the Company Groups in the service's index which meet the criteria specified by the investor.
2 A *Portfolio Screen*, which analyses all the company holdings in a portfolio to ensure that they meet the ethical criteria specified.
3 *Factsheets*. EIRIS can supply a factsheet showing all the information in its database on a particular company.

The basic screening service of up to twenty shares costs £43.50, while combining that with a Mini Acceptable list costs £82.25. The Service also provides a quarterly newsletter, a free list of ethical IFAs, and promotes seminars on such subjects as how ethical investors should react to the changes in South Africa. There are also Briefings examining a particular subject in depth, such as water pollution, oppressive regimes, trade with the Third World, etc. The main advantage for the private investor is that EIRIS charges quite substantial sums to ethical investment firms for its research/database and screening services (as well as Peter Webster it has nine researchers), which it then makes available to individuals. For someone with, say, £20,000 invested in twenty companies, paying £43.5 to have them ethically screened does not seem expensive.

EIRIS basically uses intensive analysis of as much data possible to compile its Company Groups profile. Company reports and accounts are a starting point, along with newspaper reports and national surveys, market research, etc. EIRIS then sends each company in its survey an annual factsheet, as well as detailed questions on specific topics. For example, a large research project was carried out in order to assess how companies were (or were not) abiding by the statutory rules on water pollution following a National Rivers Authority statement in 1992 that *there has been a real and significant deterioration in the quality of some rivers in recent years.* EIRIS's Head of Research Karen Eldridge described the effort required:

'It was horrendous! We spent over 400 hours analysing and entering the data last year. We have to approach each of the ten NRA and seven River Purification Boards (RPB) individually for information. Then we check whether the consent holder is owned or controlled by a Stock Exchange group. Finally we have to tie up all the monitoring data with the relevant consent to see which of the consents have been exceeded.'[13]

'By the end of February 1991 we had reached some 6,858 conclusions about 800-odd company groups . . . Rather than classifying facts, we classify Company Groups. We create consistent factual bench-marks that help investors choose between them. Not a complete picture, but a clearly defined basis for decisions with many practical attractions.'

An emerging theme is the general business ethics of a company. By the end of 1994 EIRIS planned to provide such information under the general heading of 'controversy'. The mis-selling by life insurance companies of such products would seem one such example. Over 25% of EIRIS's clients screen out financial institutions because it is impossible to know how they use money. Peter Webster said that the new controversy service had been set up following requests from institutional clients for information on subjects like British Airways 'dirty tricks' against Virgin Atlantic Airways: 'A number of larger clients came across these things in the newspaper and asked if the allegations were true and why they had not heard about it from EIRIS.'[14]

Peter Webster gave what I thought was a very good summary of the philosophy behind EIRIS in August 1993:

'In practice the next ten years will depend upon people like you. It may not feel as though your tentative questions to a bank manager, or fund manager, or individual decision about a particular investment can change the world. But it is exactly these things which have made ethical investment a significant and growing trend.'[15]

CHAPTER THREE

Ethical Unit Trusts in Practice

Investment decisions cannot be separated from the social effect of those decisions. In effect there are two bottom lines, the financial and the social, and these need to be balanced.

JOAN BAVARIA, FRANKLIN RESEARCH, BOSTON USA, 1991[1]

. . . the formation of a trust to create an increased awareness of the responsibility of ownership . . . to provide a suitable avenue through which those members of the public already conscious of their social responsibility are enabled to invest in equity without disturbing conscience[2]

CHARLES JACOB, PROPOSALS RELATING TO THE FORMATION
OF THE STEWARDSHIP UNIT TRUST, SEPTEMBER 1973

The Range of Ethical Products

Chapter One showed the growth of socially responsible or ethical funds over the last ten years. At the beginning of 1994 there were forty-four green/ethical funds in existence, with over £800m invested. The UK had a much wider range of products with an ethical basis than anywhere else in the world, ranging from unit trusts to segregated funds, personal pensions and all types of insurance products. Some of these were pension and insurance plans which entailed a commitment to a long-term savings scheme, with financial penalties for early withdrawal. Unit trusts and investment trusts, on the other hand, have the great advantage that at a small financial cost they can be immediately bought and sold, and such trusts are therefore the obvious choice for the responsible investor requiring flexible long-term savings.

MAIN ETHICAL FUNDS: JAN 1994

	Launch Date	Size £m
a) Investment Trusts		
1) International		
Commercial Union Environmental	April 1992	18.4
Merlin International Green	Dec 1989	50.3
2) UK Based		
Friends Provident Investment Trust	Dec 1993	30.0
b) PEPS Only		
Henderson Green	May 1989	7.5
Homeowners Green Chip (1+2)	Nov 1989	9.8
Sharpe Ethical PEP	Jan 1994	0.2
c) Unit Trusts		
1) UK Based		
Abbey Ethical	Sept 1987	20.6
Allchurches Amity	Mar 1988	17.6
CS Fellowship	July 1986	4.8
Eagle Star Environmental	June 1989	12.4
Fidelity UK Growth	June 1984	75.4
Friends Provident Stewardship	June 1984	154.4
Friends Provident Stewardship Income	Oct 1987	43.8
NM Conscience	Oct 1987	12.3
Scot Equitable Ethical	April 1988	12.6
Sovereign Ethical	May 1989	8.3
TSB Environmental Investor	June 1989	21.4
2) International		
Abtrust Ethical	Sept 1992	1.0
Acorn Ethical	Nov 1988	3.5
CIS Environ	May 1990	24.7
Clerical Medical Evergreen	Mar 1990	14.5
Equitable Life Ethical	Feb 1994	15.0
Friends Provident N. America	Oct 1987	5.3
Jupiter Merlin Ecology	April 1988	12.1
NPI Global Care	Aug 1991	5.6

(The Henderson and Homeowners funds are only available as PEPs
– most UK-based funds and some overseas ones are also available in
PEP form.)

But how is the ordinary investor to make sense of, and to compare,
all these different funds? One way is to delegate it to an ethical IFA

(independent financial adviser) as described in the next chapter, but many people who are committed enough to want their money managed in a socially responsible way may well want to do some extra checking themselves. For both prospective ethical investors and for people who want to know in general terms how ethical funds work, I decided to describe in detail three unit trusts: Friends Provident Stewardship, CIS Environ Trust and NPI Global Care. They are generally regarded as well-run funds illustrating good general principles of socially responsible investment. (Green Investing is described in Chapter Five.)

There is one distinction which seems worth making. Ethical funds fall into two categories: *general funds*, which seek to combine a reasonable return with general socially responsible criteria, and *specialist* or *activist funds* which feel that it is essential to have no contact with certain activities whatsoever. The former approach might involve in a unit trust such as the Friends Provident Stewardship Trust, or the CIS Environ Trust avoiding around 40% of the UK stock market, whereas a specialist fund like the NPI Global Care fund excludes up to 90% of all UK companies. The former approach is unlikely to affect adversely investment performance – indeed the signs are that if properly done, *it can improve it*! The latter must detract from performance, but the investor has a higher degree of reassurance about certain issues. Investors in NPI Global Care *know* that their money is not being invested in any company which tests anything on animals, which is not the case for more general funds, but the 'ethical purity' is likely to come at some financial cost. (Some critics argue that such a high level of exclusion is a result of over-rigid interpretation of criteria, and is far beyond what most investors would wish.)

There are four questions which someone thinking of buying an ethical investment fund ought to mull over. The first is the ethical *investment philosophy and criteria* used to achieve it; the second is the *advisory committee* which monitors that the policy is being carried out and how it operates, the third *the resources* available to the fund, and last is the *investment performance* of the fund. The whole question of the investment performance of ethical funds is discussed in Chapter Six, The Rewards of Virtue. That chapter should enable anyone to assess the financial performance of an ethical fund. Some investors may feel that financial return is not important, but for most people it is a factor in the judgment of which fund to select – if only a secondary one.

The question of resources

The question of the resources available to a unit or investment trust is a vital one, and yet one that is rarely addressed. A City rule of thumb indicates that a unit trust needs a minimum of £10 m invested to make it viable, i.e. to justify the expense of employing a full-time fund manager with the database and administrative support he or she needs. At least an ordinary investment fund can use financial information that is generally available, and therefore share the cost of items like stockbrokers' research or financial news wires like Reuters with all the other funds run by the investment management company. Stuart Bell of PIRC is an expert on socially responsible investing, who in 1991 complained: 'One of the main problems is that the promotional images on which the ethical products are sold often give the false view of the stringency of the detailed investment policies pursued . . . compromises occur because, although funds tend to use their ethical bias as their main marketing point, they put relatively little effort into their ethical research. Research deficiencies may cause funds to fail to fulfil their promises.'[3]

Peter Silvester notes the sheer size of the Stewardship funds means more resources are available for researching companies: 'Unlike some of our smaller competitors, we do not, for example, apply a blanket ban to all companies appearing on the Ministry of Defence's list. If a company is just supplying overalls, or an electronic part for missiles which is also commonly found in all sorts of other applications, we would not necessarily exclude it.'[4] An ethical or green fund needs its own specialist information. At the minimum, its fund manager needs to carry out his own research on pollution, human rights, etc., which is time consuming and which needs delving into publications and databases whose cost the fund will have to bear on its own. The fund will probably use a specialist screening service like EIRIS and have to produce dossiers for the advisory committee. Indeed, use of such a service is a good test of the seriousness of an investment manager.

All of this costs money. Hence it is *more expensive* to run an ethical unit trust than its general equivalent. I discussed this in some detail in the March 1994 edition of *Professional Investor*, the journal of the investment management profession:

In short, ethical investment is becoming more complex and

difficult to do – it is becoming an asset class in its own right, and one that requires the allocation of adequate resources to do it well. This does not necessarily mean that ethical funds have to be run by a large group, only that there must be a commitment to the field, and an awareness that the required high staff overhead may have to be funded for a while before the funds become big enough to cover it – which if the performance is good they certainly will.[5]

Most independent analysts have estimated that the UK's total of 1,550 unit trusts is far too high, and that a process of consolidation is likely to reduce that number. We are just starting to see that happening in the ethical investment field. In October 1993 the Target Global fund was closed after six years, with only £3 m invested, while the NM Conscience fund, of a similar age, was recently acquired by Friends Provident. The NM Conscience fund investors are lucky that they have been acquired by a investment management company with a commitment to responsible investing – not everybody may be so lucky. As *The Times* reported:

> An investor has criticized Edinburgh Fund Managers for refusing to offer the option of free transfers when it merges an ethical trust into a non-ethical trust. Glynne Evans invested £500 in the Global Opportunities Fund when it was managed by Target Unit Trust Managers . . . she chose the trust not only for its ethical investment policy, but because a percentage of its management fees were to be donated to Save the Children. But Target's 13 trusts were sold to Edinburgh Fund Managers in January this year.[6]

Ethical Investment Criteria

The first step for a potential investor in an ethical fund is to get details of the fund itself. Appendix One lists all the responsible investment management companies in the UK. The marketing department will normally be pleased to supply the last couple of unit trust reports describing what the fund has done, plus some kind of policy statement spelling out the principles on which it is run. Anyone considering investing in such a fund might well get details of five or so different funds in order to compare them. As well as the three described in this chapter, other funds which have been positively mentioned by IFAs include: Scottish Equitable Ethical, Abbey Ethical and Clerical & Medical Evergreen – the latter is often mentioned for its total ban on animal testing.

The obvious place to start must be the Friends Provident Stewardship Unit Trust. Not only was this the first ethical unit trust, but Friends Provident accounts for over 50% of all socially responsible funds invested in the UK in terms of size! The company also offers the widest range of ethical products covering the whole range of unit trusts, pensions and insurance funds.

The Stewardship Trusts Investment Philosophy and Criteria

Dedicated to Principles

This Trust aims to invest, as far as is practicable, in companies whose products or services make a positive and healthy contribution to society . . . we seek out companies with healthy track records in labour relations, pollution control and environmental protection . . . We make every effort to avoid investing in the tobacco industry, in alcohol, and in oppressive regimes . . . nor in companies involved in the arms trade, gambling or exploitation of animals.

Dedicated to Performance

Our experience shows that this policy can achieve excellent long-term results. We believe that there is a good reason for this: concerned companies are usually operated by diligent, concerned managements, and this shows up in their financial performance. It's also true that 'socially conscious' companies tend to avoid adverse publicity, strikes and boycotts of their products.

Positive Criteria

1 Companies operating responsibly in the community.
2 A record of suitablility, quality and safety.
3 Environmental improvement and pollution control.

Negative Criteria

1 Degradation of the environment – water pollution, nuclear power, CFCs, etc.
2 Exploitation of animals – furs, intensive farming, animal-tested cosmetics.

4 Conservation of natural resources.
5 Open about its activities.
6 General management ap-
  proach to its staff, customers
  and the public.

3 South African trade.
4 Military contracts.
5 Repeated prosecution by the
  Health and Safety Executive,
  National Rivers Authority or
  Advertising Standards.
6 Tobacco or alcohol.
7 Pornography.
8 Gambling.
9 Financial institutions whose
  loans cannot be monitored.
10 Other unreasonable ex-
   ploitation of people generally.

In looking at the negative criteria the Committee takes into account the significance of the particular activity and also takes an overall view of the positive and negative criteria taken together.

The CIS Environ Trust works within a general philosophy of what it believes ethical investment is about, and then describes its own specific aims and criteria:

Philosophy
Socially responsible investment describes investing on the basis of certain noneconomic principles, in the hope of fulfilling long-term social objectives without necessarily sacrificing financial returns. It represents a desire to work through the existing business structure to achieve, on the one hand, a better world, and on the other, a closer identification between personal ideals and investment.

Aims
The CIS Environ Trust was therefore a natural progression in this (Co-operative) tradition ... (it) encourages and enables investors to profit from the growing interest in environmental improvement while avoiding the undesirable areas set out. *It is recognized that investors in the Trust will want to see a good return, and this is an important consideration in the range of investments selected.* (My emphasis)

Selection of Investments
a) Positive Criteria
Environ's main concern is to invest in companies considered to be making a positive contribution to the environment, human health and safety . . . It also invests in areas which are considered to improve the quality of life of the population . . . such as medical, scientific, and educational publishing, education and training, tele-communications.

b) Negative Criteria
1 Animal Testing
Companies which conduct tests on animals are to be avoided unless those tests are conducted for the benefit of human health (one of the Trust's positive criteria) or animal health.

2 Items With Military Applications
Suppliers of goods and services which have predominantly military applications are avoided.

3 Oppressive Regimes
Companies are avoided which have a significant amount of business in countries considered to have oppressive regimes . . . consideration may be given to cases where the activity of the company could be regarded as beneficial to the local population.

4 Tobacco
Companies concerned with the manufacture of tobacco and tobacco-related products are avoided.

5 Generation of Nuclear Power
Investments in companies involved in the generation of nuclear power are avoided.

Degrees of Avoidance
In no circumstances will involvement be allowed in a company where over 10% of turnover is derived from activities involving the areas of avoidance noted in sections 1–4 above, and in most cases exposure to these areas will in practice be much less than 10%. The avoidance noted under the section on nuclear power is stricter, with no involvement at all.

To me at least the above seems clear. The CIS Environ fund seeks to influence companies to improve their behaviour, rather than simply to sell any it disapproves of. It honestly admits that investors in the fund want to receive a decent financial return, and tries to take account of positive rather than just negative factors. It also recognizes that often there are genuine ethical dilemmas, as Marketing Manager David Mott explained: 'If you dig deep enough, you could find fault with any company. We think we have been successful in striking a balance between good investment returns and establishing criteria which the average, caring investor would be happy with.'[7] Trust Secretary Robert Taylor added: 'We do not attempt to allocate points ratings to companies, preferring instead to weigh positive and negative factors through discussion in order to reach a balanced viewpoint. It is this approach that we feel is distinctive to Environ.'[8]

The Criteria used by the NPI Global Care Fund is set out below, a page taken from the booklet explaining the fund.

What are our Investment Criteria?

Before launching the Global Care Unit Trust we prepared a set of detailed criteria which enables us to identify and therefore exclude companies operating in a number of areas which we believe are unacceptable to investors wishing to adopt an ethical strategy. These are classified into three categories:

- Impact on People
- Impact on Animals
- Impact on the Environment

Within these broad categories we identified a number of specific areas of concern and agreed what the strategy should be in each case. A summary of these areas, and of our stance in each case, is given below.

AREA OF CONCERN	TOTAL EXCLUSION	PREDOMINANT EXCLUSION
Impact On People		
Advertising		•
Alcohol		•
Gambling		•
Military Involvement		•
Oppressive Regimes		•
Pornography	•	
South Africa	•	
Breast Milk Substitutes	•	
Tobacco		•
Impact On Animals		
Animal Research	•	
Fur	•	
Meat/Dairy Production	•	
Impact On The Environment		
Greenhouse Gases		•
Mining		•
Nuclear Power	•	
The Ozone Layer	•	
Pesticides	•	
Tropical Hardwood		•
Water Pollution	•	

There follows two pages of detailed explanation of what the exclusion criteria mean in practice. To give three samples:

Advertising
Companies which have had three or more public complaints upheld against them by the Advertising Standards Authority (ASA) in the previous two years in a number of ASA categories.

Pornography
Companies which publish, print or distribute newspapers or magazines, or distribute films or videos, classed as pornographic.

Animal Research
Companies which manufacture pharmaceuticals, medicines, vitamins,

cosmetics, soaps or toiletries, unless they make it clear that their products and ingredients are not animal tested.

Investment Manager Chris Holmes confirms the restrictions on the fund. 'Taken together, the exclusion criteria mean that we cannot invest in over 90% of the FT All Share Index, which must mean that the performance of the fund will diverge from it.'[9]

The Advisory Committee

If the investment philosophy and detailed criteria are a guide to what a socially responsible fund is trying to achieve, the advisory committee is an indication of how likely it is to attain it. Despite their great importance little has ever been written about them. To redress the balance, I have included quite full details of the advisory committees of two funds. The NPI Global Care Fund has historically not had such a committee. Chris Holmes agrees that they are vital but explained to me: 'I want a good advisory committee, and have felt that up to now the Global Care Fund was too small to justify the kind of heavyweights we want. However, with our expansion into green investment following the Merlin team's move to NPI, an advisory committee will be set up in 1995 – it's one of the many things which I am working on now'.[10]

The Friends Provident advisory committee is known as the Committee of Reference. I spoke to Charles Jacob MBE, widely known as the 'father of ethical investment' for his trail-blazing work in exploring the legal possibility of setting up an ethical unit trust as early as 1972! As described in Chapter Seven, it was this work which led to the establishment of the first ethical unit trust by Friends Provident in 1984, while he also invented the 'Stewardship' name. It was only fitting therefore that I discussed the work of the Committee of Reference with him.

Friends Provident Stewardship Unit Trust – Committee of Reference

Charles Jacob, former Investment Manager, Central Finance Board, Methodist Church.
Joanna Lumley, actress, writer, trustee Zoo check.

Charles Medawar, Director, Public Interest Research Centre.
Roger Morton, Trustee, J. Rowntree Research Centre Trust.
Marlene Winfield, member board of EIRIS, Director of New Consumer.
John Whitney, former Director General of IBA, non-executive director Friends Provident.
Lyn Wilson, management consultant, non-executive director Friends Provident.

When the concept of Stewardship, the first UK ethical trust, was being developed, the requirements of both capital and 'conscience' were matters of individual concern. The final selection of investments was required to be in the hands of professional investment managers. Equally essentially, an independent qualified body appeared necessary not only to ensure that the advertised policy of the Trust was adhered to, but also to consider the ethical merits of shares available for investment. Thus the idea of a Committee of Reference was born, an approach since accepted by many of the ethical trusts subsequently issued.

The Stewardship Committee sees its role as a positive one. While investment in companies involved in such areas as armaments, gambling, brewing and tobacco is to be avoided as far as practicable, its main search is for companies whose products and services are considered to be of long-term benefit to the community both in the UK and overseas. The analysis of individual companies, however, goes far beyond products and services, and encompasses such issues as employment practices, attitudes towards local communities, natural resources, pollution control, and the political and social environment of countries in which companies operate.

The investment selection criteria, with their positive and negative aspects, cover over ten pages. It is not unusual for an agenda of 200 foolscap sheets to be presented every six weeks for consideration by the Committee. As a result the analysis of over 800 companies has resulted in less than half being acceptable for further consideration for investment. I doubt whether any other ethical fund is able to go into the depths of research that is required by Stewardship if only because the sheer size of the funds enables us to afford it. Much of the research is done by EIRIS although internal sources also contribute to the analysis.

I cannot stress too much that considerable discussion and consideration of company merits are necessary. Few situations can be defined as black and white, and the weighing up of 'positives' against negatives is necessary when considering shares in several sectors. Of course, our many investors also have many different interests, and concerns and problems can also arise in assessing the relative importance of different investment criteria. All correspondence from the investors is considered and dealt with by members of the Committee of Reference. Members are also 'on call' to deal with any new or changed situations which may arise between meetings so that the managers can make their investment decisions efficiently and without delay, first having received clearance of general acceptability from members of the Committee.[11]

The Friends Provident Stewardship vetting procedure is quite clearly unsurpassed in its detail and thoroughness. When the Stewardship Trust was launched the Committee of Reference was largely represented by Quakers, a possible weakness, but the Committee has now widened its horizons and its members represent a broader viewpoint.

The CIS Environ Fund emerged from two streams – the tradition of the co-operative movement that economic issues must work within a social framework, and the increasing awareness of the vital importance of environmental issues. Who better to discuss it than its advisory committee chairman, Lord Clinton-Davis. As Stanley Clinton Davis he was a minister in the 1974–9 Labour Government, and then served as the European Commissioner for Transport, the Environment and Nuclear Safety from 1985 to 1989.

CIS Environ Fund – Advisory Committee:
Lord Clinton-Davis, former European Commissioner for the Environment.
Antony Hardy, Investments Manager, Church Commissioners.
David Shreeve, Executive Director, Conservation Foundation.
Valerie Singleton, radio and television journalist.
Professor Douglas Wood, Manchester Business School, Professor of Corporate Responsibility.

The key thing, which must be paramount, is the interests of shareholders, the people who have been motivated by their beliefs to invest their money in the fund. I would agree with you that the Advisory Committee has a number of roles: to supervise the fund managers and make sure that they carry out the ethical and environmental claims made for the fund; to act as an ombudsman reflecting the concerns of individual shareholders, and to be an ultimate adviser when the fund managers are genuinely unsure – which in real life is not infrequent.

In practice things are rarely black or white – a company may have one activity you dislike but generally produce useful products in a environmentally friendly way. At the same time there are some things which we do not touch, like nuclear power. The Committee does have long discussions within itself, and with the fund managers, but ultimately we make recommendations and it is very rare for the managers to challenge those. We are a friendly Committee with a wide breadth of varying expertise – some people may think that media people are on committees just to be a figurehead or a name, but that's quite wrong in our case. We are lucky to have an investigative journalist with considerable experience of consumer affairs and a down-to-earth attitude.

We have a very organized structure, and I think that's the key. Two weeks before our quarterly meeting we get a detailed agenda plus minutes of the last meeting, and often my colleagues and I will ask Environ secretary Robert Taylor to produce further research material on companies. We also have external research provided by Manchester Business School. The fund managers attend the meeting and we have active discussions. We have an approved list of companies in which the fund managers can invest, and if they want to bring a new company onto the list the Advisory Committee has to approve it. We review both countries and companies, and ultimately we receive formidable dossiers. We have recently had a debate on China for example, where you have a huge and poor population trying to improve their standard of living, but you have to question whether they are doing it in a sustainable way, and also the human rights abuses in that country, and we eventually decided that the Environ fund should not invest there directly. I might add that the quality of our research material is very high, sometimes better than you get in the House of Lords!

I think that the Committee is part of the process where funds like Environ have a wider impact than just on their shareholders. You could say that funds like ourselves with positive environmental criteria are a stimulant to make industry take proper cognizance of environmental factors. Let me give you an example, the use of peat in gardens. We have made inquiries in a number of large store chains such as Tesco, Woolworths, etc., and caused them to re-examine their policy, and introduce peat substitutes. Our first aim is to work together with companies to help them achieve good environmental practice; if we cannot achieve this we will take them off our approved list, and this fact may well receive effective publicity where it counts – in the investment press. We listen very carefully to what Friends of the Earth and other campaigning organizations tell us. Recently there was a query from FoE about a packaging company, and since I happen to be Chairman of the Organic Packaging Council I was able to resolve it fairly quickly.[12]

The Environ fund clearly has an advisory committee of high calibre individuals with complementary skills. David Shreeve and Lord Clinton-Davis have a deep knowledge of environmental matters, while Lord Clinton-Davis also has an intimate knowledge of the world of politics. Antony Hardy brings the practical experience of the UK's largest ethical investor – his predecessor at the Church Commissioners, Peter Brealey, was the first chairman of the Environ Advisory Committee. Valerie Singleton contributes detailed knowledge of the media and consumer affairs, and Professor Douglas Wood theoretical rigour. (Note that while external research is produced by Manchester Business School, this is the Business Information Service, and quite independent of the department headed by Professor Wood.) Overall I rate the CIS Environ Advisory Committee highly – in fact, the breadth of the committee puts it on a par with the Friends Provident Committee of Reference in my opinion.

To sum up, an advisory committee is there to represent the unitholders (i.e. investors) and to protect the ideals they have subscribed to in buying shares in the fund. As such it has three quite distinct roles: to reflect the concerns of the unitholders who may write to them; to be a sounding board and ultimate point of reference regarding tricky ethical issues; and lastly to act as a supervisory body to ensure that the fund managers follow the ethical guidelines decided. They also have one other function – to signal that they are not happy with the way the fund is being run by resigning en masse. This dramatic act has only happened once, when a group of committee members all left a particular fund in 1989 at once, an action which sent a shock wave through the relatively small world of ethical investing. Steve Burkeman, the Secretary of the Joseph Rowntree Trust, and one of those who resigned from this particular fund, said later:

Like disinvestment, resignation is something one can only do once. Several of us did resign from the Ethical Investment Fund Committee because we felt we were not able to do the job unitholders were being told that we were doing. We insisted that the unit holders should be told, in an agreed form of words, why we had resigned. I have to say that I resigned with the greatest of regret – there were many good people involved in the fund, including the managers . . . However, in the end, it may be necessary for committee members to resign in order to ensure that ethical funds are living up to their public rhetoric.[13]

Ethical Integrity – the key test?

Another important question, which is rarely addressed, is the ethical nature of the investment managers themselves. This consists of two areas: the *culture of the investment management company* itself; and finally what I call *ethical integrity*. What I mean by the latter is that it is not enough to be ethical, in the suspicious modern world such claims need to be demonstrated. It is one area where I think ethical trusts could do better, and involves *transparency and greater disclosure*, just as ethical IFAs disclose commission although not yet legally obliged to do so.

Often decisions are difficult and involve trade-offs, and I think fund managers should try harder to communicate why they have made certain decisions. For example, the Friends Provident Stewardship fund has been criticized for holding Amersham International, which uses radioactive isotopes for medical research. CIS Environ has likewise been attacked for owning Huntingdon International, which tests some drugs on animals. I have no doubt that both funds have internally studied both these cases, and discussed them at great length, but outside unitholders do not know this for sure.

Where conviction is part of the reason for buying a fund, they should be told why, possibly by means of a regular bulletin to unitholders. Of course, legal reasons may preclude too much detail being produced on why a particular company is unacceptable.

The NPI Global Care fund probably has the best reputation for ethical integrity. It has a very clear statement of what it is trying to do, and its ethical integrity is bolstered by the fact that the investment of the fund is run by Christopher Holmes, who as Investment Manager of NPI is the head of its investment management team, and therefore has the power to carry out what he aims to achieve. The fact that investors can contact Chris Holmes and discuss concerns with him has been a major positive factor behind the positive reception of this fund. He has also, quite obviously, put a lot of thought into NPI's ethical venture:

> For me the management of the Global Care Unit trust is a very important though small part of my total work . . . radical ideas are expressed in our Global Care Fund. It is not perfect but it goes some way to respond to these concerns. It is a vast improvement over more conventional investments . . . if you talked to our General Manager or marketing team you would see that we all share a 'vision' of how a company like ours should be run. For many years the marketing department wanted to launch an ethical product, but the stumbling block was me. It took me about three years, a lot of reading of books (mostly American) on ethical investing, and a lot of deep thought before I was convinced that an ethical product could genuinely be run alongside a lot of normal commercial products.[14]

What is perhaps most distinctive about the Friends Provident Stewardship fund is the immense amount of time and trouble the company has taken to perfect its ethical screening procedures. As long ago as 1989 Investment Manager Peter Silvester was quoted as follows: 'It's taken five or six years to evolve, but the managers here have become adept at finding the companies that meet the positive criteria and avoid the negative criteria.'[15] Even then Stewardship had cleared 250 shares as acceptable.

As the pioneer, it is hardly surprising if Friends Provident has also seen itself as an evangelist for responsible investing. Peter Silvester again, this time at the end of 1993: 'While growth in ethical funds is impressive, we believe it is just the tip of the iceberg. Some people are holding back because they do not understand what an ethical investment is and how it can compete with a traditional fund. Once the arguments have been explained, they are hard to refute.' Nor did he feel that Stewardship missed out because of its tight guidelines: 'This is nonsense. Our committee has found more than 450 companies (the fund invests in 170) with a market capitalization of £140 bn which conform to our criteria.'[16]

In fact Peter Silvester is confident that such intensive analysis of companies pays dividends in terms of superior investment performance in the longer term. 'We're looking for companies that have good products, good practices and good markets. If you're doing that, you'll find you're in the right pool for healthy companies – we haven't found it any handicap at all when it comes to performance.'[17] 'The evidence is that most of our ethical funds have actually outperformed the rest of our funds, particularly on the pensions side.'[18] The ultimate test – the excellent long-term outperformance of the Stewardship funds over ten years, confirms his confidence, as described in Chapter Six.

The ethical audit

Regarding the *culture* of the investment management company, it is interesting that no major merchant bank has ever tried to launch a socially responsible fund. Presumably, they realize that potential investors just would not take them seriously. A similar fate appears to have overtaken the Eagle Star Environmental fund – while this makes no claim to be 'ethical', the fact that it is ultimately owned by the tobacco giant BAT Industries has turned many ethical investors and IFAs against it The life insurance industry has had a justifiably poor press recently owing to its poor selling practices. A list of life insurance companies fined over the last two years is shown below. It is noticeable that with the exception of NM Financial Management, which was subsequently sold to Friends Provident, none of them has any involvement in ethical products!

INSURANCE COMPANIES FINED
BY LAUTRO 1993–94

1993	1994
Canterbury Life	Aegon
Colonial Mutual	Crown Life
Interlife	LAS
NM Financial Management	Legal & General
Prosperity Life	Laurentian life
Liberty Life	Norwich Union
	Premium Life

Source: Lautro

In June 1994 the Office of Fair Trading produced a report, *Surrender Values of Life Insurance Policies*, demonstrating what poor returns many life insurance companies gave to people surrendering their policies. The *Financial Times* commented on the report as follows:

'The study shows that several companies that offer the worst early surrender values are also those which have been fined or disciplined by Lautro, the self-regulatory body for the life insurance industry, for mis-selling. They include Guardian, London and Manchester, Reliance Mutual, Legal and General, and Colonial Mutual. Other companies offering poor value to early leavers in at least two product types are Royal Life, AXA Equity and Law, Irish Life, and Pearl.'[19]

It says something for ethical investment that no insurance company offering such products appears on the above black list!

Likewise the commitment of Friends Provident and NPI to socially responsible investment derives from their common Quaker roots and is aided by the fact that, as mutual insurers, they do not have shareholders requiring constantly increased profits. Friends Provident is clearly proud of its Quaker roots going back to 1832. The range of its ethical products and the resources it devotes to the field are unparalleled, and the company has moulded the whole conception of what ethical investment should be. The Stewardship funds have had the full backing of the Board since inception, and as Peter Silvester told me at the end of 1994: '. . . as Investor Director I, plus my senior investment colleagues, have personally overseen our Stewardship activity from its start in 1984, and we still do!'[20]

The great co-operative tradition expressly lies behind the CIS (Co-operative Insurance Society), parent of CIS Unit Trust Managers who run the Environ Trust. CIS has only one shareholder – the Co-operative Wholesale Society. As it proudly states: *'The Cooperative Movement too grew out of 19th-century social experiments . . . the Movement has often used its economic activity as a basis for taking a stand on social issues, including trade with South Africa.'*[21] Environ sees itself as an environmental/ethical fund run by a financial services organization operating within general: 'Cooperative principles of unadulterated products and fair prices.'[22]

At the end of May 1994 it was announced that the Merlin research team, known for its environmental research, was moving to NPI. Chris Holmes explained: 'We have recognized significant opportunities for ethical/green products and services among UK pension and charitable funds and believe these opportunities will expand much as they have done in the United States. Tessa and her team have a first-class reputation in the ethical investment field, and I believe their skills will help NPI develop its range of ethical products.'[23] Given the high reputation of both NPI and the former Merlin team among ethical IFAs, the combined group could have the long-term potential, despite the relatively small size of their existing funds, to become a significant force in UK ethical investment.

CHAPTER FOUR

Financial Advisers to the Public

TRUST IS MORE IMPORTANT THAN COMMISSION. A
survey for Laurentian Life found that trust is more important than
commission when choosing a financial adviser. 50% of those surveyed
said that they would ignore commission and use the adviser they trusted
most when disclosure hits next year. Only 10% said that they would
choose the adviser solely on the basis of the lowest commission.

FINANCIAL ADVISER, MAY 1994.[1]

Few people probably feel that they know enough themselves about financial products to decide exactly what they need. For example, even if someone feels certain that they want to invest their money ethically, should they put this into a unit trust, an ethical savings account or a personal equity plan? The latter sounds good, as it shields an investment of up to £6,000 a year from income and capital gains tax, but what about the charges? How long does the investor have to commit his money? What happens if he or she needs it in a hurry? The previous chapter gave some examples of how to distinguish between various funds which call themselves 'ethical', but many people may not want to go through the bother of all this.

In fact, the correct starting point for any investor is to assess how protected he or she is if things go wrong, which normally involves some form of insurance. This is increasingly important as governments around the world cut back on social security benefits. A good financial adviser is invaluable in helping people who may well have limited means to discover the best mix of products for their particular needs. For example, someone with dependent relatives should almost certainly have term life assurance, which is very cheap, to pay out if the breadwinner dies. Self-employed people should consider permanent health insurance (PHI), which will pay an income if they become ill and unable to work. Then there is the whole question of pension provision.

For all these reasons the best solution for the potential ethical investor is probably to talk to a financial adviser who should be an expert on the technical aspects of savings, including tax, but also be aware of what are the current best performing ethical products available, both in terms of financial return and the general *ethical integrity* of the fund or investment manager. However, ethical integrity is probably the last thing that the public currently associates with salesmen of financial products, as the cartoon below by Roger Beale well illustrates:

It therefore makes sense to look in depth at the way investment products, mostly insurance related ones, are sold to the public. Firstly, because it shows weak professional ethics and secondly to be a guide to the uninitiated through what some may feel is a jungle of poorly informed salesmen. The obvious starting point is the new regulatory format which came into force at the beginning of 1988 and which had a massive impact on the way such products are sold in the UK. (People who just want advice on choosing an IFA should jump to page 60)

The Regulatory Framework

The sale of investment products in the UK is regulated by the 1986 Financial Services Act which came into force at the beginning of 1988. This introduced the *polarization requirement*, where any one selling such financial products had either to be the representative of one company or be completely independent and deal with the whole market. Of course, salesmen directly employed by one company always sold only that company's products, but independent financial advisers (IFAs) had always accounted for a significant part of the market. (Many people equate IFAs with insurance brokers, although the latter term is technically limited to those registered under the Insurance Brokers Registration Act 1977 and a member of the IBRC.) The polarization rule was coupled with one of giving *best advice*, which was not defined as being reasonable in the circumstances, but rather as the best product in the whole market place. A large *compliance procedure* was also required. There was also the *disclosure requirement* that commissions on the sale of insurance and pensions products should be revealed. Finally, the Act also established a complex mixture of regulation. The banks and insurance companies had always been regulated by the Bank of England, the Treasury and the Department of Trade and Industry, as well as the Fraud Squad for criminal breaches of the law. To this was added a number of self-regulatory bodies (SROs). Top of the pile and overseeing the others was the Securities and Investments Board (SIB), which had other SROs carrying out the work: Imro for the investment management industry, Lautro for the life insurance industry and Fimbra for independent advisers.

As independent experts predicted at the time, the 1986 Financial Services Act had the opposite effect from that planned by the government; instead of increasing customer choice, it reduced it. The Big Four banks: Lloyds, National Westminster, Barclays, and Midland all set up their own life insurance companies (Nat West after some hesitation), so that a customer entering their premises is only offered products from their own in-house life insurance company. Most IFAs are small businesses owned by one or two people and many of them found that the bureaucratic compliance demands of the Act, coupled with the legal requirement to show best advice, was simply too much trouble and involved too much expense. A large number decided to opt for being a tied agent of an insurance company, i.e. they would only sell that company's products so that they no longer had to worry about best advice. Since many of these small IFAs would previously have dealt with four or five insurance companies which they knew well and whose mix of products they thoroughly understood, it is hard to see how the customer got a better deal out of all this. Interestingly enough, the requirement to disclose commissions was resisted by the big insurance companies and Lautro allowed them to show commissions in such a way that only the experts, and few clients, actually understood.

What the charges really mean

There is an old adage that life insurance is sold, not bought, which means that few people would probably buy a policy if they were not persuaded to do so. This requires a lot of time and effort on behalf of insurance salesmen, so the story goes, hence they need to be rewarded on a commission basis. Since these products have a long life span – up to twenty-five years – the commission needs to reflect this. All of this is true up to a point, but few people really realize what a large bite is taken out of their money when they invest in a life insurance or pension product. The chart overleaf shows how much of an investor's £1,000 would be used up in commissions.

The chart shows how much of the investor's money would be left after first-year charges. This is a flawed comparison, since it assumes that the pension or endowment plan continues in operation. It is not really fair to compare a ten-year endowment policy, where all of the commission is charged in the first year, with a unit trust, since in practice if the policy ended after one year, the adviser would have to return a significant part of the commission to the life office.

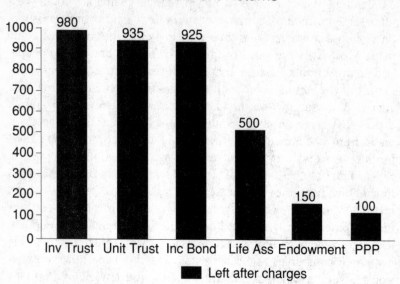

How Charges Reduce
Investment Returns

Left after charges

The chart shows how much would be returned after one year to investors paying £1,000 into different types of policies if the underlying portfolio remained unchanged. PPP = regular premium personal pension plan, transfer value.[2]

Still, on the basis of this comparison, £1,000 invested in such a policy would after one year have about £150 left after all charges, while a regular personal pension plan would probably have only £100 remaining.

The smallest bite would be taken by investment trusts, where £1,000 invested would leave £980 of the saver's money to be put in the stock market. Unit trusts, single premium pensions and guaranteed income bonds all take about £60 to £70 away from the £1,000 in commissions. The other point to note is that the complex charging structure tends to obscure where the money goes. For example, most people buying an endowment insurance product probably do not realize that for every £30 premium paid, only about £1 actually pays for life cover – the rest is used to build up an investment fund – and to pay commissions.

SHORT LAUTRO TEST THAT
A MONKEY COULD PASS!

Such was the headline in the *Financial Times* in March 1994. It was based on a comment made by Gillian Hurley, aged twenty, who had spent the 'worst time of her life' selling personal pensions and other life insurance products. After four weeks' training, she travelled around the South of England selling investment plans, yet she complained that despite having passed the training standards laid down by Lautro, she often did not know enough about the products which she was selling or their possible disadvantages to give 'best advice'. Since her earnings, in common with the industry, were worked out on a commission basis, she was under pressure to sell as many products as possible. 'I learnt to bluff my way through many situations where clients asked too many technical questions – dangerous considering I was toying with the financial future of many people. The product training I received was atrocious. (To satisfy the Lautro requirements) I had to take a half-an-hour test that a monkey could have passed.'[3]

About 150,000 people in total sell insurance and investment products. Less than half have worked in the industry for more than two years. It is worth noting that the Society of Financial Advisers is working to raise standards in the industry, and as Lee Coates suggests: 'if the public demand membership of SOFA for all advisers, then the committed advisers will join, thus raising standards.'[4]

The six years since the Financial Services Act was introduced have seen scandal after scandal. The late 1980s found many elderly people encouraged to buy *home income plans*, which in theory 'unlocked the capital' in their homes, but in practice were loans backed by investments in single premium investment bonds. In effect, what elderly investors thought was a safe investment led to large commissions for the salesmen, and for them the risk of losing their house. A *Which?* survey in August 1993 concluded that: '. . . too many advisers see your redundancy pay-off as the route to £££ commission for them, rather than financial security for you.'[5] *Which?* described some advice as 'simply appalling'.

Finally, in November 1993 came the bombshell that a study by accountants KPMG Peat Marwick for SIB discovered that out of 500,000 personal pension transfers from company schemes, *400,000 were incorrect!* In other words, that number of people were encouraged to come out of company pension schemes at significant cost to themselves in order to generate big commissions for sales-men. The effect of this is likely to result in millions of pounds of costs for the insurance industry and a serious blackening of the industry's reputation. While many insurance agents have lost their jobs, no chief executive of an insurance company has done what might be considered the honourable thing and resigned.

Another large blow to the industry's reputation came in March 1994 when one of the largest and most respected insurance com-panies, Norwich Union, suspended 800 agents – its entire life and pensions sales force. Norwich Union is a mutual company, i.e. it is owned by its own policy holders, and does not therefore have shareholders pressing for ever-increasing profits. Norwich was sub-sequently fined £325,000 by the insurance regulator Lautro which included costs. This was paid out of the profits fund, i.e. with the paradoxical effect that the fine was ultimately paid by the policy holders who might have lost out in the first place. The low esteem in which the industry is held could be seen when the PIA was set up. Its Chairman was Joe Palmer, former Chief Executive of Legal & General. A Labour member of the Commons Treasury Committee asked '. . . whether Mr Palmer should be seen in the category of people of the highest quality on whom the regulatory system depen-ded.'[6]

More regulation

In 1994 this plot thickened yet further with another level of regula-tion – the Personal Investment Authority (PIA). This was planned to replace Fimbra and Lautro in July 1994, but the whole system currently lies in confusion, with the refusal of the largest life insur-ance companies such as the Prudential or Standard Life to be regulated by it, and electing to report directly to the supervisory body, SIB. For most people this whole quarrel may seem of no interest, and indeed a guaranteed cure for insomnia, but it is in fact very important. Many independent experts, perhaps the majority, would argue that the current system of regulation of investment products in the UK has the worst of both worlds: it has the large, inflexible bureaucracy of a statutory system, combined with the support of vested interests and failure to deter wrong doing associated with the failure of self-regulation.

Logic would suggest that the current system of self-regulation has not worked well, and consideration should be given to its replacement by a fully fledged statutory body, as the Consumers Association has argued. The American equivalent of the SIB is the Securities and Exchange Commission (SEC). The SEC has a large enforcement arm, and it was its exposure of the 'arbitrageur' Ivan Bosky which brought the 1987 Guinness scandal to light. The SEC has in the past arrested traders who were suspected of insider dealing actually on the floor of the New York Stock Exchange and taken them away in handcuffs. This may not be pretty but it certainly deters others. There is another point – at least statutory regulation would be paid for by government. At present the system being 'voluntary' is funded by a levy on member firms – i.e. *it is ultimately paid for by the customer.* In this case, to create a new layer of authority is a bit like putting a fifth wheel on a car which will not start.

There is one other theme which should surely be emphasized, which is *transparency and disclosure.* It is an elementary proposition of economics that markets only work when consumers are informed or have the information to make choices. Yet in the insurance field up to now there has almost been an unspoken agreement between supposedly competing companies that they would not reveal the true costs of their products, so keeping the buyer in the dark. Ten years after the 1986 Financial Services Act insurance companies will, from the beginning of 1995, finally be forced to reveal the commissions they pay when someone buys a particular product. It is to be hoped that this will be in large print and prominent in the documents shown to potential clients. (Independent experts have calculated that being forced to reveal commissions will reduce life insurance sales by up to twenty per cent!) Disclosure of commissions is only the start – what about investment returns, surrender values, how many policies are normally surrendered, lapse rates etc? Glenn Morgan, lecturer at the Manchester Business School, wrote that market forces were unable to: '. . . force poor providers to improve their performance, or reward efficient companies. Consumers cannot see these differences because of lack of disclosure, and companies can get away with flouting standards because of a lack of vigorous enforcement . . . what is needed is regulation that will enable the customer to distinguish between good and bad companies.'[7]

Choosing an IFA

The majority of such excesses appear to have been carried out by salesmen, employees of certain insurance companies paid on commission. While certainly some independent advisers also behaved badly, on the whole IFAs seem to have come out of the affair relatively well. It was a feature of financial advisers who specialized in 'ethical products' that they were happy to disclose what commissions they received before this became mandatory in January 1995. Independent advisers also have the distinct advantage that they can recommend the full range of ethical products. Since the big banks only sell their own products, which do not include any ethical funds, anyone walking into a bank branch has the choice of buying a non-ethical product or going elsewhere.

Yet how is the ordinary person to know who to trust and who to avoid? A list of some independent financial advisers specializing in ethical products is shown in Appendix Three at the back of the book. Of course, it is not necessary to go to an IFA specializing in the ethical field to get advice on such products; any general IFA will have some knowledge of ethical funds if the client expresses a clear preference, although they may lack the in-depth knowledge of the specialist. A list of independent financial advisers in a particular area can be obtained from IFA Promotion – see Appendix Three for details. Many advisers are introduced through personal contact, and there are some basic questions which are worth asking before dealing with an IFA:

1 make certain that they really are independent advisers and not the tied representative of a life insurance company.
2 Ask how long they have been in business, and if accounts are available.
3 Ask if they have professional indemnity insurance and if they handle client money, and if the latter, how, i.e. via a third party.
4 Inquire whether they are fee-based or paid on commission. From January 1995 the latter must be fully disclosed by law. (There is a lot of debate in the financial press about the relative merits of fee-based and commission advice. Most IFAs believe that while in a perfect world fee-based advice would be the norm, in the current system 90% of people would rather pay by commission.)

Three Ethical IFAs

Another good test is the quality of the literature produced by the IFA. I think that this is particularly important in the field of ethical investment where the very growth of the field has encouraged some people to jump on the bandwagon. The leaders in the field have all obviously invested substantial time and effort in producing high quality material. An IFA who claims to be an authority on ethical investment but who can only produce a scruffy piece of paper on the subject deserves to be looked at with some scepticism. The three 'ethical IFAs' described in this section all pass this test. Barchester and Ethical Investors Group produce regular bulletins on responsible investment, while Holden-Meehan produce a regular glossy twenty page book *An independent guide to ethical and green investment funds.* The book, of which the 1994 copy was the fifth edition, is an annual review of all socially responsible funds. Available free from Holden-Meehan, this is the guide most often quoted in the financial press as their source material.

Anyone interested can obtain a list of all IFAs who offer advice on ethical investment from EIRIS. However, as it lists all advisers who claim expertise in this field, to be on EIRIS's list does not necessarily entail a particularly deep commitment to ethical investment. (In order to be included on the EIRIS list IFAs have to fulfil one of three criteria: that they put more than £100,000 of business in ethical funds, or they put more than 40% of their business in ethical funds, or they have bought the EIRIS guide *Choosing an Ethical Fund.*) In fact, while EIRIS's commitment to be making as many people as possible aware of ethical investment is to welcomed, the last criterion appears too loose and could be profitably replaced with one about experience in the field. Those who have spent a minimum of two years working for an industry leader like Barchester or Holden-Meehan and then set up their own company probably have much more expertise and commitment to ethical investment than some larger, more established firms.

To get a feeling of what an ethical investor should hope to find in an adviser claiming to be an expert in responsible investment, I interviewed three IFAs generally regarded as outstanding in the field: Giles Chitty of Barchester, Pat Meehan of Holden-Meehan and Lee Coates of Ethical Investors Group What struck me about all of them was a very high level of professional competence coupled with a keen and long-standing commitment to green/ethical invest-ment. The knowledge that all of them possessed not just of ethical funds, but of the investment management companies and the fund managers themselves, was impressive. It is noteworthy that all three are based outside London, although Holden-Meehan are also re-presented in London.

Possibly the IFA most totally committed to ethical investment is Lee Coates of the Ethical Investors Group (EIG), a company which he set up in August 1989. EIG, based in Cheltenham, is unique in that it accepts only ethical business, i.e. all of its £2.7 turnover (total new business) is in ethical investment products. Some rivals have derided this strategy as a recipe for starvation, but the fact that the company is approaching its fifth anniversary suggests otherwise. Lee Coates also demands a high level of professional expertise and business ethics within the sale of life assurance products. He is only one of 800 IFAs in the country with a Member of Society of Financial Advisers (MSFA) qualification, as well as being an As-sociate of the Chartered Insurance Institute (ACII). Before found-ing EIG Lee Coates spent six years with two major life assurance companies, Abbey Life and Friends Provident, but was frustrated by what he perceived to be the low level of expertise in the industry. Subsequent events have shown his pessimism to be justified. Friends Provident were also introducing their ethical investment products, but he found that IFAs were not interested 'I don't want police-bashing hippies as a client' was one response.

The other unique thing about EIG is that Lee Coates pays himself a salary of £16,000 a year and gives the rest of the profits of the business to a variety of charities such as Friends of the Earth and Greenpeace. In 1993 EIG generated an income of £150,000, of which £27,00 was given to charity. Over the first five years £65,000 has been given to charity. EIG has also been the UK pioneer of vegetarian and cruelty-free funds, while Lee Coates has written to a number of companies inquiring about their treatment of animals etc. Lee feels passionately about both ethical products and professional integrity, and is so enthusiastic that (as he himself admits) it is hard to stop him in full flow. Clearly he was destined for the top as an insurance salesmen, if he had wanted to. He is sceptical about the professional ethics of the industry:

The trouble with life assurance in this country is the commission system, so that the only thing most companies are interested in is as many sales as possible, irrespective of what the client needs. A lot of salesmen are just in it to make as much money as possible, just for pure greed. I thought of becoming a fee-based adviser to get round this problem, and charging £80 an hour, but the problem is that this is elitist; a rich solicitor will happily pay this, but a lot of ordinary people who read the *Guardian* and are really concerned about the environment don't understand that they are paying more anyway in commission, and will turn away and go to an ordinary adviser. The only answer for the insurance industry to dig itself out of the hole it has got into is to have a lot higher level of training and qualifications for its salesmen. At the moment, almost any fool can pass the tests.

I am sceptical about how many of the 'ethical funds' really are looking at these ethical issues in any kind of depth. For example, a lot of them own the drug company Glaxo on the basis that its products are 'humanitarian', but in fact it is on Greenpeace's list of the 'Filthy Fifty' biggest polluters in the UK, while it is believed to be still practising vivisection. I have argued at some length with Friends Provident about the subject of factory farming. They said to me some time ago that since they had 80% of the ethical investment market they must be doing it right, but I noticed that at the launch of the Friends Provident Ethical Investment Trust this had fallen to 52%!

As an adviser I find that many clients want ethical funds with clear guidelines, they want to be sure that they do not hold any companies whose activities they do not agree with. It may be all right for a church or charity fund with broad objectives to have the 'least bad' company in a sector such as, say, food retailers with their ecologically disastrous superstores, but my clients just don't want to invest in these areas at all. There should be many more ethical funds available – I have nagged Standard Life and Norwich Union about this, and one has made vague noises about thinking of doing so at some point, although there is little action so far.[8]

The oldest and biggest IFA specializing in green/ethical products is Barchester Green Investment, based in the lovely cathedral city of Salisbury. Barchester was set up in 1985, right at the beginning of ethical unit trusts in the UK. Originally it specialized in sales to the clergy, hence the name from Anthony Trollope's novels of rural clerical life. The company's total turnover in 1993 of £8.7 m, with 85%, or £7.4 m in ethical products, make it the market leader in the UK. There are two partners, Giles Chitty and Geoff Griffiths. I talked to Giles. He is a quiet, thoughtful man – when you ask him a question, he thinks about it for a minute or two before answering, to get it just right. For Giles, ethical investment is part of a way of life. For many years he was a top business executive with a large multinational company, then it all changed:

Like many people I suppose I had a mid-life crisis in my thirties. I was working in Indonesia, and I saw this beautiful country being destroyed to make way for Western-style industry. I just had to leave. I came back to the UK and for six years lived at the Findhorn Foundation in Scotland, where I was able to live in a community where people really mattered. Then with some other people I set up The Financial Initiative, the first and so far the only social venture capital fund in the UK; this produced acceptable financial returns in the long run, but it was a long haul, so when I was invited to join Geoff in expanding the ethical emphasis of Barchester, following the launch of seven new ethical funds, I was very pleased to do so. I see green/ethical investment as a part of a process of education and communication. The modern economic system is heading towards disaster, but the rising tide of ethical and green funds makes companies aware of their obligations, and also gives investors the power to make their concerns felt.

At the same time, our job is to give the best financial advice possible. That is why we don't only sell ethical products – there are times, such as when someone is coming up to retirement, when they need a traditional with-profits scheme and there simply isn't an ethical product available. Actually, it is getting technically harder and harder to give best advice. The insurance and pensions industry seems deliberately to make its products more and more complicated and harder and harder to understand. I'm meant to be an expert, and it can take me three to four hours really to understand a policy's complicated charging structure. I just don't believe that the ordinary salesman, let alone the client, understands what they are buying or selling. If there is one thing which I would force the industry to sort out, it's clarity and transparency – people should know what they're buying, and what they are paying for it.

As regards the 'best' green ethical funds, the performance has actually been very consistent. We set up our own broker fund, Best of Green, in 1991 which has now got over £7 m invested in it, and this has consistently invested in seven underlying trusts: Friends Provident Stewardship, as well as their North American and Income funds; Jupiter Merlin Ecology, Scottish Equitable, Clerical Medical Evergreen, and NPI Global Care. Funnily enough, when Clerical and Medical set up the Evergreen fund, they only had environmental screening criteria – I pointed out to them that most serious green investors see this as a moral issue, and would therefore like them to add ethical criteria – and they did! With other leading green IFAs (such as Holden-Meehan) we set up the GIFA (Green Independent Financial Advisers) Forum to help promote awareness of green/ethical investing to a wider audience, and at the same time, to push the insurance companies to make more ethical products available. While of course we are competitors, we collaborate to get higher standards and better products to recommend to our clients, and to get the green message across, and that is why the new unit trust portfolio we have set up does not have the Barchester name, since we want to encourage other GIFAs to use it.

The departure of Tessa Tennant and her whole environmental research team from Jupiter to NPI is a major development. This could be the beginning of a long-term move by NPI towards what I call a 'congruent ethical investment institution'. Such an institution would get round the problems faced by all the current ethical fund providers of having one ethos for the fund and a different ethos for the running of the whole company.[9]

The sale of investment products is a fiercely competitive business, and few IFAs probably have the generosity of spirit which the above example shows is typical of Barchester. Anyone going to an adviser will find that most of the initial session consists of a *fact-find*; the IFA needs to know about an individual's existing savings schemes, his tax position, his family circumstances, his health, job security, aims in investing, etc., before he can even begin to advise on what savings products are appropriate. Giles Chitty's partner Geoff Griffiths wrote in late 1993 to IFA Promotion (IFAP), who write a standard questionnaire which is used as a fact-find by more IFAs than any other, suggesting that they should include the following question: *Do you have strong views about the way your money will be invested with regard to armaments, tobacco, repressive regimes, animal exploitation, etc?* The Director-General of IFAP, Joanna Hindle, agreed with Barchester that the public should be made more aware of the availability of ethical products (Mintel surveys show about 40% of the public would buy them if their adviser discussed them), and since the beginning of 1994 the above question has appeared on the IFAP questionnaire.

It could be argued that a person's social views should be an integral part of any 'fact-find', and it would seem likely that more and more IFAs will include such questions over the next few years, which will accelerate the growth of socially responsible investment. Holden-Meehan's Social Issues Questionnaire is shown at the end of this chapter.

Many IFAs run broker funds, so they are probably worth a brief explanation. Essentially, they are a fund of funds, i.e. they do not invest directly in the stock market themselves, but invest in what they regard as the best unit trusts or other funds. The client normally pays a small fee, and in return he or she is able to switch from one fund to another without paying crippling initial fees. To give an example, an intermediary wanting to create such an ethical broker fund might include Friends Provident Stewardship as a good all-purpose ethical UK equity fund, Merlin Ecology Fund as a specialist global green fund and NPI Global Care as a specialist global ethical fund. People needing income would have to use Friends Provident Stewardship Income, as it is the only ethical high income fund, while the Ecology Building Society might be used as a home for cash. Note:this is only a theoretical example, and is not meant to suggest that anybody should use it as the basis of their own portfolio.

For young, long-term investors the adviser would probably invest most money in the growth unit trusts, while older people requiring income would put the majority of their money in the income-producing funds. If people's circumstances change, due to such events as birth, marriage or redundancy, this gives the IFA more flexibility than he/she would otherwise have. (This is a simplified example excluding all the tax and other contractual arrangements which the IFA would have to consider in real life.)

There are two disadvantages to broker funds which are worth noting: firstly, that an extra 0.5% is normally added to the standard unit trust fee of 1.5%, and secondly that such funds have income and capital gains tax deducted at the so-called composite rate. This means that they are not tax efficient for people who are not liable to income tax.

Holden-Meehan is the largest firm of advisers which carry out a significant amount of business in ethical investment. Total sales in 1993 were £12.7 m, of which 45% was ethical, i.e. £5.7 m, making it the second largest ethical IFA after Barchester. The firm has six partners, of which two are particularly identified with ethical investment: Amanda Davidson in London and Pat Meehan based in Bristol. Pat feels very strongly that ethics in investment advice necessitates starting with the client and his/her needs – which are paramount. While he is a keen advocate of responsible investment, he also feels that there are times when ethical products are not the best, and therefore there are times when they have to be advised against.

It is typical of Holden-Meehan, I think, that Pat is the only person to challenge me on a statement I had made that at the end of 1993 ethical funds amounted to £800 m in total. They had done independent calculations coming to £755 m. The difference was whether a Fidelity UK Growth fund should be included – but to me it is a good illustration of Pat's determination to get it right. He also has strong views on the future of the industry:

The investment and pensions market is becoming more and more sophisticated and so are compliance requirements. We think that the only answer is an extensive computer system, and we have invested heavily over the last five years to achieve this. As well as a comprehensive database the system allows us to review all of our clients' financial needs and to use the computer to illustrate how varying certain assumptions alters the projected returns. For example, suppose a thirty-year-old man starts a pension plan and saves so much a month, then making various educated assumptions about interest rates and the average growth rates of equities, he can end up with a pot of money worth say £2 m when he retires in 2025, which will pay him a growing pension of £183,000. Sounds great, but what is that going to be worth in 1994's money? If you input the average inflation we have seen in the last thirty years, then his £183,000 pension when he retires is only worth £13,500 in 1994 purchasing power. If his final salary when he retires is £40,000 in 1994 money, then he is going to face a big drop in his income on retirement, which he ought to be made aware of, and persuaded if possible to raise his contributions now.

That's just an example, but I think it shows that for us 'responsible investment' means being responsible to the client's needs as well as to society. We see ourselves as long-term financial planners, with the technology enabling us to tailor the product to the client's requirements. Our *Guide* surveys twenty-one of the largest ethical unit trusts, and we profile five of them that I regard as having real integrity: Friends Provident, Merlin Ecology, Scottish Equitable, Clerical Medical Evergreen, and NPI Global Care. Probably my favourites are Friends Provident Stewardship, which dominates the UK ethical investment market with a successful ten-year record, and the NPI Global Care fund with very clear criteria. The latter is managed by NPI Investment Director Chris Holmes, so you can see commitment from the top. Their recent recruitment of the Merlin Research Unit backs this up and may make us reconsider the Merlin Ecology fund as a recommendation.

Our ethical-managed stockbroking service allows individuals and organizations with at least £100,000 for investment to benefit from economies of scale, and to draw up specific criteria on a client-by-client basis. A charity may want to address specific ethical criteria without taking the broad brush approach of the packaged ethical unit trust. A cancer-prevention charity may only be interested in screening out tobacco products, for example. We are hoping that this type of approach, which helps draw up the criteria and demonstrates the effects of them on investment, will lead to a changing of attitudes in particular by charities. There are times when there are no appropriate ethical products for a specific client's requirements, and if this is the case then we explain the position clearly to the client.

I do think that responsible investing is going to take a much bigger slice of the total investment market over the next ten years. A recent Mintel survey suggested that 40% of clients would like at least some ethical investments, but currently only 1% of IFAs offer this service. Our experience, which we know has been

confirmed by others, is that the average client who knows he or
she wants ethical products is an educated one with a reasonable
level of income and knowledge. Holden-Meehan have been involved in setting up and maintaining the GIFA group. In our view
it is important that standards are kept up in the sector by sharing
information and pushing the product providers to innovate. After
all, it is the advisers who talk to investors on a day-to-day basis,
and we should be regarded as the best form of market research.[10]

THE HOLDEN-MEEHAN SOCIAL ISSUES QUESTIONNAIRE

We ask that you complete the questionnaire, keeping in mind that in
the process of being a socially responsible investor, you will doubt-
less find some other issues of more concern to you than others. This
is not inevitable but appropriate, since focusing on one or two issues
is more apt to allow a well-targeted investment process. Please circle
the number that best describes your level of concern in an issue:
1 Very concerned; 2 Concerned; 3 Somewhat concerned; 4 Not
concerned.

Investment Concerns

A)	Companies involved in South Africa	1	2	3	4
B)	Unfair Labour practices	1	2	3	4
C)	Environmental Abuse	1	2	3	4
D)	Nuclear Power	1	2	3	4
E)	Arms Manufacture	1	2	3	4
F)	Alcohol	1	2	3	4
G)	Tobacco	1	2	3	4
H)	Vivisection	1	2	3	4
I)	Political Donations	1	2	3	4
K)	Gambling	1	2	4	
L)	Financial Institutions	1	2	3	4
M)	Other (please specify overleaf)	1	2	3	4

Positive Factors
Please indicate your level of concern to invest in those companies
which demonstrate a positive business activity that exhibits socially
and environmentally commendable methods in the following categories:

A) Waste Management	1	2	3	4
B) Environmental Protection	1	2	3	4
C) Alternative Energy	1	2	3	4
D) Recycling of Resources	1	2	3	4
E) Purification/Filtration	1	2	3	4
F) Energy Conservation	1	2	3	4
G) Environmental Friendly Retailing	1	2	3	4
H) Water Treatment	1	2	3	4
I) Please Specify	1	2	3	4

CHAPTER FIVE

Green Investing

The ability to manage environmental performance is rapidly becoming just as essential an ingredient of business success as managing costs or assets. Companies will need to improve, and to be seen to improve, their environmental performance year on year.

MICHAEL HESELTINE, SECRETARY OF STATE FOR THE ENVIRONMENT,

1991.[1]

The environment – a non-issue?

As the above quotation suggests, business and the environment was a major political theme at the beginning of the 1990s. At that time the Green Party received 15% of the vote in the European elections, Mrs Thatcher commissioned *Our Common Inheritance*, a strategy document for environmental policy, and the world's politicians all went to Rio. Yet only a few years later, the politicians and the media had cooled off. The newspapers put stories about pollution on the inside pages and in smaller columns than they had five years before. Yet the issues had not gone away.

Indeed, by 1994 there were increasing signs that the British Isles were beginning to feel the effects of global climatic change. In January 1994 the Department of the Environment published a review showing that ozone layers over the UK in the winter of 1992–3 were the lowest since records began in 1979, and about 25% below earlier levels. It is to be hoped that Scotland in particular does not eventually share the experience of Puentas Arenas, a city at the tip of Patagonia where at the end of October 1989 an 'ozone hole' lingered over an inhabited area for the first time in history. An American research team from Johns Hopkins University noted several cases of animal eye diseases and severe human sunburn, unusual in such a cold climate. A local nurseryman noted that plants in a greenhouse were healthy, but similar plants exposed to the sun wilted and died. The leaves on a eucalyptus tree suddenly turned yellow and dry: 'This tree's been here for twenty-five years, and it's the first time this has happened. It's got to be radiation, there's no other reason.'[2]

The summer of 1994 will also go down in memory as the one when Southern England experienced Los Angeles-style smog for the first time. Pollution levels were above World Health Organisation levels and hospitals recorded a record number of admissions for severe asthma attacks. Is it a coincidence that the Department of Health found that asthma cases more than doubled from 1979 to 1991? A *New Scientist* study estimated that car pollution could be killing 10,000 people a year, more than the coal smogs of the 1950s. Yet despite the ever increasing scientific confirmation of global warming and its increasing impact on our daily lives, the subject receives less and less media attention. According to Jonathan Porrit: 'One reason might be the emergence of the so-called contrarians, predominantly right-wing groups who devote their lives to rubbishing the consensus about global warming. There are dozens of such organizations in the US, many of them funded by the businesses which stand to lose most as the world moves about to do something about global warming . . . eminent meteorologist Sir John Houghton commented, "the quality of their work is simply pathetic".'[3]

At the 1992 Rio summit many political promises were made. The UK Government pledged to stabilize carbon emissions at 1990 levels by the year 2000. The vehicle chosen to do this was the Energy Saving Trust, with the idea that the electricity and gas industries should identify ways to cut carbon dioxide emissions, with the cost of this being financed through customer's bills. In May 1994 the whole programme was thrown into confusion with a statement by the gas regulator refusing to allow these costs to be levied on consumers. By mid-1994 the Energy Saving Trust had received £25 m of the £2 bn funding it required to reach the government's targets for the year 2000. The Trust's executive director said he was 'just trying to keep the show on the road.' The House of Commons's 1994 audit of the government's environmental effectiveness found it had failed to keep more than twenty-seven of its environmental commitments, and that there was considerable slippage in implementing others.[4] The *Financial Times* described the 1994 White

Paper, *Taking Rio Forward*, thus: 'The document is notably devoid of new or inspiring initiatives, and it lacks the force needed to convince the reader that it will resolve the increasingly difficult contradictions between the government's environmental aims and its policies in other areas'.[5]

The role of green investors

Yet if politicians are backsliding, *green investing*, as in the case of South Africa, allows people to express their concerns via the financial markets and force industry and governments into action. In the US forty proxy resolutions on the environment topped the list of social issues in 1993; thirty-two American companies were asked by their own shareholders to endorse the CERES principles. The ICCR reported that environmental resolutions received 20% of shareholder votes, much higher than social issues usually get. It is estimated that there are over 13,000 non-governmental organizations (NGOs) actively campaigning on environmental issues. These range from the huge like Greenpeace, Friends of the Earth and the Worldwide Fund for Nature, to special-interest groups like the Soil Association promoting organic foods, or Surfers Against Sewage. The European Environment Bureau in Brussels coordinates 150 environmental groups in putting pressure on the EU.

Green investors can and do work with such NGOs sharing information and expertise. Take, for example, the subject of toxic waste exports. The 1990 Basel Convention on 'The Control of Transboundary Movements of Hazardous Wastes' banned the export of toxic wastes from richer countries to the developing world, with the exception of export for 'recycling'. This weasel word allowed a booming trade in hazardous waste to develop. David Owen of Ecofin noted:

> How to cut costs during a recession: export hazardous wastes to Third World countries by claiming they are being sent for recycling. In 1993 Britain exported 105,346 tonnes of such waste, an increase from 85,000 tones in 1992, 72,500 in 1991 and 30,000 tonnes in 1990. Considering that the recession is known to have subdued hazardous waste generation, the unavoidable conclusion is that they are exploiting a loophole in the Basel Convention . . .

Not only are there no checks to ensure that recycling is, in fact, taking place, but these wastes are being sent to South East Asia at a time when governments freely admit that no modern waste treatment and recovery facilities exist.[6]

Greenpeace built a formidable campaign round this issue, involving the media and with active support from Chris Smith, Labour's environmental spokesman. Greenpeace demonstrated misdesignaton of toxic waste. One example was in Brazil where exported zinc furnace dross, described as 'micro-nutrients for fertilizer production', was in fact an extremely harmful cocktail of heavy metal poisons such as lead, mercury, cadmium, etc. Initially, the UK Government rejected calls to stop illegal exports of toxic waste on the grounds that it was 'cultural imperialism' to prevent Third World countries from importing the stuff. The churches took up the issue following an October speech in 1993 from the Pope that 'it is a grave abuse and an offence against the solidarity of humanity when industrial enterprises of rich countries profit from the weak economies and legislation of poorer countries by exporting dirty technologies and wastes which degrade the environment and health of the population'.[7] The Anglican Church followed up with a plea in *The Times* in March 1994 signed by the Archbishop of York and seven other bishops: 'We urge the Government to reconsider its position, and to support the proposed ban on all exports of toxic waste from OECD countries.'[8] In May 1994 the UK Government caved in, agreeing to a Danish proposal that the EU ban all toxic waste exports, although not until 1997.

Relations between industry and environmentalists need not be confrontational. The Business Council for Sustainable Development is a Geneva-based association of forty-four large international companies which submitted a report to Rio called 'Changing Course', urging other business leaders to adopt principles of *eco-efficiency* and *technology co-operation*. The former simply means a stated corporate goal of increasing added value while minimizing resource use and pollution. Technology co-operation commits companies with leading-edge clean technologies to share them. Yet the environment is a vast and complex subject, and perhaps the greatest benefit of 'green investing' is that it funds the creation of research units such as NPI and Ecofin. These have the technical ability accurately to monitor the environmental practices of individual companies and discuss those findings with their managements, and to make public their findings. As such they can lead public opinion and guide industry to a greener philosophy of operation, as the CERES principles well illustrate.

The CERES Principles

In late 1988 the American Social Investment Forum met with various environmental groups to form CERES (Coalition for Environmentally Responsible Economies), which then launched a set of ten principles to guide industrial companies to better environmental performance. The CERES principles came out at the same time as the Exxon Valdez disaster and they were initially known as the Valdez Principles. They state:

By adopting these principles we publicly affirm our belief that corporations have a responsibility for the environment and must conduct all aspects of their business as responsible stewards of the environment by operating in a manner that protects the Earth. We believe that corporations must not compromise the ability of future generations to sustain themselves. We will update our practices continually in the light of advances in technology and new understandings in health and environmental science. In collaboration with CERES we will promote a dynamic process to ensure that the principles are interpreted in a way that accommodates changing technologies and environmental realities. We intend to make consistent measurable progress in implementing these principles and to apply them in all aspects of our operations throughout the world.

1 *Protection of the Biosphere*. We will reduce and make continual progress towards eliminating the release of any substance that may cause environmental damage to the air, water, or the Earth or its inhabitants.
2 *Sustainable Use of Natural Resources*. We will make sustainable use of renewable natural resources, such as water, soils, and forests. We will conserve non-renewable natural resources through efficient use and careful planning.
3 *Reduction and Disposal of Wastes*. We will reduce and where possible eliminate waste through source reduction and recycling. All

waste will be handled and disposed of through safe and responsible methods.

4 *Energy Conservation*. We will conserve energy and improve the energy efficiency of our internal operations and of the goods and services we sell. We will make every effort to use environmentally safe and sustainable energy sources.

5 *Risk Reduction*. We will strive to minimize the environmental, health, and safety risks to our employees and the communities in which we operate through safe technologies, facilities and operating procedures, and by being prepared for emergencies.

6 *Safe Products and Services*. We will reduce and where possible eliminate the use, manufacture or sale of products and services that cause environmental damage or health or safety hazards. We will inform our customers of the environmental impacts of our products or services and try to correct unsafe use.

7 *Environmental Restoration*. We will promptly and responsibly correct conditions we have caused that endanger health, safety or the environment. To the extent feasible, we will redress injuries we have caused to persons or damage we have caused to the environment, and will restore the environment.

8 *Informing the Public*. We will inform in a timely manner everyone who may be affected by conditions that might endanger health, safety or the environment. We will regularly seek advice and counsel through dialogue with persons in communities near our facilities. We will not take any action against employees for reporting dangerous incidents or conditions to management or to appropriate authorities.

9 *Management Commitment*. We will implement these principles and sustain a process that ensures that the Board of Directors and Chief Executive Officer are fully informed about pertinent environmental issues and are fully responsible for environmental policy. In selecting our Board of Directors we will consider demonstrated environmental commitment as a factor.

10 *Audits and Reports*. We will conduct an annual self-evaluation of our progress in implementing these principles. We will support the timely creation of generally accepted environmental audit procedures. We will annually complete the CERES Report which will be made available to the public.

The CERES principles are not just a statement of philosophy – they are actually used by a number of large American corporations which have committed themselves to adopt them. May 1994 saw the biggest yet sign-up to CERES – General Motors!

Towards sustainable development

'Sustainable development challenges the entire industrial and commercial system to restructure itself, based on a completely new set of assumptions and beliefs about the ways we must conduct our economic affairs'. John Davis, *Greening Business.*[9]

The ideas behind the CERES principles can be summed up in one phrase – *sustainable development.* Without this concept, we are left with the situation as one citizen of a highly polluted town in New Jersey told the BBC's environment programme *Costing the Earth*: 'The big chemical companies made a fortune dumping waste here, and now they're gonna make another fortune cleaning it up.'[10]

Herman Daly is a distinguished economist who has developed the concept of steady state economics. He puts it this way: '. . . economic growth is held to be the cure for poverty, unemployment, debt repayment, inflation, pollution, etc . . . in short the panacea. This is growth mania. When we add to GNP the costs of defending ourselves against the unwanted consequences of growth, and happily count that as further growth, we then have hyper-growthmania. When we deplete geological capital and ecological life support systems and count that depletion as net current income, then we arrive at our present state of terminal hyper-growthmania.'[11]

In his books Herman Daly has created an Index of Sustainable Welfare (ISEW), which adjusts traditional gnp numbers to account for changes in social welfare and environmental quality. Longer-term costs of environmental damage are taken account of, as are changes in the distribution of income. The New Economics Foundation published in the spring of 1994 a chart of British economic growth (gnp) and ISEW since 1950. From 1950–75, gnp and ISEW moved in step, but since then the latter has been declining while the former shows steady progress.

UK GNP and Sustainable Growth 1950-1990

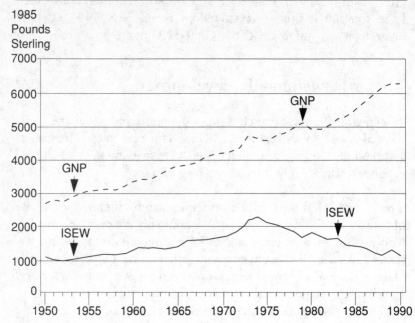

1985
Pounds
Sterling

Against this background, what is the task of green investing? Threefold I think. To force industry generally to think about environmental matters, to offer investors green investment vehicles, and most importantly of all both to help and push companies in a specific and technical way towards this goal. Tessa Tennant of NPI is one of the UK's leading thinkers on green investment issues. She defines it this way:

> By sustainable development we mean practices that meet the needs of the current generation without jeopardizing, through environmental degradation or social disharmony, the ability of future generations to meet their needs . . . finance has a key role to play in defining the parameters of industrial development. This may be achieved by investing in environmentally sound business and helping to raise standards or withdrawing investment from companies intent on environmental destruction.[12]

Promoting the word

Most surveys indicate that British industry is woefully slow in waking up to its environmental responsibilities. For example, the

British Institute of Management's 1991 Report, *Managing the Environment*[13], found that only 52% of organizations possessed an environmental policy. A 1991 survey by Dewe Rogerson of leading British fund managers found that they thought 80% of British companies had failed to develop a coherent environmental policy, concluding: 'Fund managers are concerned about the environment, and the balance of opinion among them is that a company's environmental strategy is an important factor when they take investment decisions.'[14] A 1992 Mori poll of 400 investment analysts found almost half of them were worried that the companies they analysed did not pay enough attention to the environment.

Groups like EIRIS and PIRC have, however, tried hard to make industry aware of what investors want to know. In May 1992 an EIRIS survey found that out of 783 companies only fifty had a public environmental statement meeting its criteria. EIRIS also surveyed investors in ethical/green funds to see which issues they were most keen to avoid.[15] Firstly, in terms of single issues, and secondly, adding them together:

Single Issue	% vote	Weighted voting	% vote
1 Nuclear power	32%	1 CFCs	59%
2 CFCs	25%	2 Polluting water	50%
3 Polluting water	21%	3 Greenhouse gases	48%
4 Greenhouse gases	20%	4 Hazardous chemicals	47%
5 Hazardous chemicals	20%	5 Nuclear power	46%
6 Tropical hardwoods	18%	6 Tropical Hardwoods	45%
7 Pesticides	10%	7 Pesticides	22%

PIRC too launched its own environmental code in 1991:

PIRC – UK Environmental Investment Code

As investors, we recognize that corporate performance and the value of our investments are increasingly affected by environmental factors. In pursuance of a prudent and environmentally responsible policy, we will encourage and support companies that demonstrate a positive response to environmental concerns. The fund calls on companies:

1 to make a commitment to achieving environmental excellence
2 to institute regular monitoring of their environmental impact
3 to establish procedures which will lead to incremental improvements in environmental performance
4 to comply with all current environmental legislation and seek to anticipate future legislative changes
5 to make available to shareholders regular and detailed reports of progress.

At the time of the launch Stuart Bell, PIRC's Research Director, commented that: 'the code will allow pension funds to use their muscle to raise environmental standards.'[16] In fact, at the same time as launching the code, PIRC acted as the City end of a successful campaign with Greenpeace and Friends of the Earth to stop the Fisons company damaging wetlands through peat extraction. Alan MacDougall of PIRC explained: 'The Fisons case shows it is practical for investors to get companies to respond. In fact investors provided the only effective form of pressure in that case.'[17]

Two years later PIRC carried out a survey of 600 of the largest companies, which indicated that even at this level things were still poor. Only a small number of companies had adopted environmental policies, and of those only 20% made these available to the public. Financial reasons were often behind this foot-dragging. PIRC's Anne Simpson concluded: 'The research shows that most companies consider improving environmental performance will cost money – and for that they will need investor support.'[18] However, on a positive note, the support of the local authority funds for the Code had been steadily building. Stuart Bell commented: 'Now we have built up a head of steam – we've got local authority pension funds behind us worth £16 bn.'[19]

Disclosure: the key factor

An environmental policy is a good first step, but what investors increasingly require is accurate and consistent information on a company's progress in achieving its goals. In other words, a 'green audit' to go with the traditional financial audit. Gradually accountants, finance directors and green investors are working together to hammer out what might be required. A landmark was the appearance of Professor Rob Gray's book, *Accounting for the Environment*[20] written in association with the Chartered Association of Certified Accountants on the problems of environmental audits. A practical example comes from the Hundred Group of Finance Directors of leading companies, whose 1992 statement *Environmental Reporting in Annual Reports* recommended that reports should:

- give sufficient information on the nature of operations to permit major environmental impacts and risks to be identified
- include disclosure of environmental policy, with guiding principles, priorities and key environmental issues for individual areas of operations
- identify realistic and where possible measurable targets for progressive improvements against substantial environmental issues
- contain claims that are capable of substantiation.

The *Financial Times'* Accountancy Column in April 1994 called for greater disclosure saying: 'A concerted strategy is needed to narrow the gap between what the investment community wants from companies, and what companies feel under an obligation to provide.'[21] It demanded the following deliverable items:

- clean-up provisions and contingent liabilities
- green accounting policies
- statements of corporate environmental policy
- the results of internal environmental audits

The government has promoted BS7750, the British Standard as environmental management which requires companies to have publicly available environmental policies, specific targets and internal environmental audits, and has also encouraged two major initiatives. *Business in the Environment*'s main function has been to assemble chief executives of companies with progressive environmental policies to encourage and assist other companies to do the same. At the end of 1993, saying that 'the BiE board see the financial community as an important influence on companies like their own', BiE announced a major project to:

1 raise awareness amongst fund managers, trustees and research analysts of the business case for taking environmental issues into account

2 provide practical tools to help them ask the right questions of companies

3 identify the gaps in environmental information available to investors.[22]

The other initiative is ACBE (Advisory Committee on Business and the Environment) a joint venture of the Department of the Environment and Department of Trade and Industry, whose Chairman is Nat West Chief Executive Derek Wanless. ACBE warned in 1993 that: *'Environmental liability will bring about fundamental changes to the financing process and the ability of some businesses and industries to raise capital.'* ACBE set up a special Financial Sector Working Group whose first report in 1993 stated that *'. . . the Group is very clear that it wishes to see all companies publishing environmental reports. Action is now required to achieve this . . . some standards will be required, and verification may be appropriate; legislation may be necessary.'*[23] It went on to affirm that:

- the London Stock Exchange should consider adopting standards of environmental disclosure as one of the requirements of its listing particulars
- the Securities Institute and the Institute of Investment Management and Research should establish standards of environmental awareness amongst their membership. Both bodies should give environmental awareness and best practice a high priority in their criteria of factors in assessing investments. They should encourage high standards of environmental performance and disclosure amongst listed companies.

In June 1993 the EU published its Eco-management and Audit Scheme (EMAS), which comes into force in March 1995. EMAS is a code promoting continuous improvement in the environmental performance of industrial activities by providing a framework in which companies must establish and implement environmental policies and produce a comprehensive environmental audit to be produced every three years, examining such factors as emissions per site, energy efficiency, etc. While adherence to EMAS is voluntary, green investors and risk assessment units of banks and insurance companies are likely to put great pressure on companies to sign up. Companies with good environmental disclosure will, over time, find investors and bankers more receptive than companies which appear to have something to hide. Mark Campanale of the NPI research unit described it thus: 'Investors are beginning to learn the techniques of environmental analysis and understand the information written in them. Increasing interest and knowledge will eventually make disclosure by companies on environmental matters with clear communication to financial stakeholders the norm rather than the exception.'[24]

The environment as a business opportunity?

There can be no argument that environmental services are big business and the long-term potential huge. Indeed they are. The global market for environmental equipment and services is worth about $200 bn currently (£140bn) according to both the OECD and the US Environmental Protection Agency (EPA), with expectations of the market at the end of the decade ranging from $300bn (OECD) to $600bn (EPA). The former's detailed estimates are shown below:

OECD – FORECASTS OF REGIONAL ENVIRONMENTAL SPENDING 1990–2000

	1990	2000	Annual Growth rate
North America	84.0	125.0	6.0%
Asia Pacific	26.2	42.0	6.2%
Europe	54.0	78.0	4.9%
Former Communists	15.0	21.0	4.0%
Africa & South America	21.0	34.0	6.9%
TOTAL	200.0	300.0	5.5%

It is generally accepted that the fastest growing areas are waste management, air pollution control and water treatment. While some of this is high-tech, a lot of it is day-to-day business like waste disposal. Green consumers are playing an increasingly important role; a 1991 Mori poll found that 44% of consumers found environmental friendliness very important and a significant feature in their purchasing behaviour. This does not just have a direct effect on retailers like Body Shop and B&Q, but indirectly via a company's general reputation.

Clearly, the main driving force behind this growth is rapidly growing environmental legislation coupled with the consequent risk of large financial penalties for polluters. The US has led the way with various forms of Superfund (described later). Yet there is more to it than this. The European Environmental Agency (DG XI) has the current role of collecting and filing data, as by 1996 all the member states must file their first batch of uniform environmental reports. DG XI's stated aim is to have a regulatory function after that date. Few people are aware of the amount of environmental directives flowing out of the European Commission in recent years:

	1985	1986	1987	1988	1989	1990	1991	1992	1993
No:	20	24	27	28	28	30	38	42	44

The UK regulatory flagship for the environment was the 1990 Environmental Protection Act (EPA–UK). This introduced a system of licensing for waste disposal, and a *duty of care to do so*. It also introduced the concept of *integrated pollution control* (IPC), covering air, water, and waste emissions. IPC was weakened by the concessionary clause '*best available techniques not entailing excessive costs*' (Batneec). The Act also lost a lot of credibility, however, when proposals under Section 143 to introduce a register of contaminated land similar to the EPA in the US were abandoned after protests from the property industry that it would make such land difficult to sell. Case law in the UK came close to establishing Superfund-type liability in the 1993 case of Eastern Counties Leather vs Cambridge Water before being overruled in the House of Lords.

It is not true that tight regulation hampers business; Germany's 1990 Environmental Liability Law is generally regarded as the toughest in Europe with its thorough code of regulation and liability for industries which could cause environmental damage. The German DIW economic institute found that tight environmental standards had helped develop a globally competitive environmental technology industry. Germany had gained a 20% global market share in environmental technology, exporting 40% of its output and employing 550,000 people. Germany does not just shine in environmental engineering however. It is also the leader in eco-packaging with its 'Blue Angel' badge, based on a UNEP scheme. Currently some 3,600 products have been awarded this award, guaranteeing that an independent jury has found it ecologically satisfactory. Examples are phosphate-free detergents or asbestos-free brakes. Germany has also shown Europe how to achieve very high recycling targets. Under the German 1991 Packaging Ordinance, producers of waste packaging are legally obliged to take it back and recycle it. The only exception is to pay a fee to the Duales System Deutschland, an independent recycling agency. Products are then given a 'green dot', and households have two rubbish bins – one for general waste, and a 'green bin' for products covered under the dual system. France has a similar system run by municipalities, but Britain has avoided legislation and opted for self-regulation. An attempt at a unified European Packaging and Waste Directive was vetoed by the EU Council of Ministers in August 1994.

The birth of environmental investment

The late 1980s saw increasing awareness that environmental services were becoming big business. One of the City's leading stockbrokers, James Capel, produced a 'green index' of thirty companies involved in environmental services, and a mammoth seventy-page annual review of the sector – *The Green Book*. Everything looked good, but in fact the summer of 1989 marked the peak of environmental investing, just like the peak of the Green vote. The Capel Green Index, having risen from an initial 100 in January 1989 to 147 in August 1989, then fell back to a low of eighty-seven in November 1990 before slowly rising again. Over the five years from its inception at the end of 1988 it steadily underperformed the FT Allshare Index.

	1988–90	1990–92	1993	5 Years to end 1993
J. Capel Green Index	−6.1%	+39.6%	+16.1%	+52.1%
FT All Share	+20.4%	+41.5%	+27.7%	+117.7%

What went wrong? In retrospect, the green euphoria pushed up share prices to levels which could not be sustained, particularly as there were not many quoted companies with genuine environmental exposure. The so-called 'green companies' were seen to be fast-growing and immune to recession and therefore deserving of a huge premium (a P/E of 19 compared to 11 for the UK market average). There was little discrimination as to what 'environmental' actually meant, or with some deserving exceptions, little hard analysis of what the growth prospects actually were. As David Owen described the time later: '. . . there was a somewhat undignified rush to attach "green" labels to any stock in the hope of its gaining an environmental premium. Much of this "research" was more concerned with image, resulting in shops, food manufacturers, and banks being dubbed "environmental". This clashed with what I understood to be the sector.'[25] In November 1990 Tessa Tennant complained: 'It is also apparent that there is some confusion as to what constitutes a green stock. For example, Merlin does not consider that the waste management sector is green per se. Indeed, the sector has a notorious cow-boy record . . . the poor definition of the methodology for managing green funds has become increasingly apparent.'[26]

In fact environmental spending proved not immune to economic downturn. The optimism also ignored obvious trends. Take, for example, the biggest single environmental industry in the world – the US market for collecting and disposing of municipal solid waste worth $35 bn (£21bn) in 1993. It was known in the late 1980s that there was a big switch going on in the US from burying waste, *landfill*, to recycling. From 1989 to 1992 the proportion of rubbish sent to landfills fell from 84% to 76% meaning lower volumes and prices for the industry. Yet despite the fact that companies such as Waste Management or the British-based Atwoods depended on US landfill for the bulk of their revenues, analysts did not lower their rosy growth forecasts for such companies to allow for this switch.

Another factor was that many companies in the US and UK made the fatal mistake of believing governments! The idea was that tighter environmental controls would drive small private operators and municipalities out of business. Many large companies in the early 1990s therefore invested heavily to ensure their plants met higher standards. When recession came, and standards were not enforced, they were undercut by 'cowboys'. David Owen describes their reward: 'After the 1990 Environmental Protection Act and the Government's then stated intention to comply with several waste EC waste management directives, the more responsible British waste management companies invested heavily in upgrading their plant, sites and support systems . . . they were rewarded with last year's cowboy's charter.'[27]

There may be another reason why environmental investment has generally produced a poor return over the last few years. The subject is so complex and all-embracing that only specialists devoted to the subject are likely to succeed in steering their way through the minefield. Every year the *Wall Street Journal* lists the best and worst of the thousands of mutual funds (unit trusts) on sale in America. In the bottom fifty in 1993 were some interesting names:

Fund	Size $m	1993 Performance	Ranking from bottom
UST Environmental	2.3	–7.2%	8
Invesco Strat Environ	40.0	–4.7%	17
Kemper Environ	41.6	–3.5%	22
Fidelity Sel Environ	54.5	–0.6%	50
Average US equity fund		+12.5%	

What was interesting about this was that there were no names of US investment houses specializing in green investing, such as Franklin or Calvert, appearing in the above list. In fact, just as semiconductors or biotechnology are regarded as specialist areas in the US which need expert analysts to invest in them, so the same is probably true of environmental investing. Looking at UK funds which describe themselves as 'environmental' or 'green', the picture is similar. The poor relative performance of companies operating in the environment sector dragged down these funds, but nevertheless the good relative performance of the Merlin funds is evident.

Fund	Sector	1993 rank	1992–93 rank
Eagle Star Env Opps	UK	4	3
TSB Environmental	UK	4	4
C &M Evergreen	O/S	4	4
Merlin Ecology	O/S	3	3
CU Environmental	Inv Trust	4	N/A
Merlin Intl Green	Inv Trust	2*	N/A

* six months only (The above uses quartile rankings, '4' is bottom 25% etc.)

Two green fund managers

In the UK there are only two investment research units specializing in environmental research and nothing else: the Merlin (NPI) research unit and Ecofin. Merlin was set up in 1988 as the City's first green research unit, mainly due to the vision and energy of two people: Derek Childs, a senior fund manager from Warburgs, and Tessa Tennant. The latter graduated in Human Environmental Sciences before working for the Green Alliance for six years, and had spent some months with one of the world's leading socially responsible investment managers – Franklin Research of the US. Sadly, Derek Childs died in October 1991, but Tessa built Merlin into an unquestioned position as the City's leading expert on environmental questions. It should be noted that in May 1994 the whole team left the fund management company Jupiter Tyndall to join National Provident (NPI), with the former keeping the Merlin name.

As well as Tessa Tennant, the NPI unit consists of three other researchers/fund managers, the most prominent being Mark Campanale who joined Tessa in February 1989, having worked in Africa following a master's degree in Agricultural Economics as well as a period of freelance consulting on environmental and ethical investment issues. The team generally has contributed to BS 7750 and worked with Rob Gray on green accounting. Tessa Tennant herself has become one of the small group of people actually shaping British environmental policy. She is an adviser to ACBE and a key figure in Business in the Environment's City initiative, as well as a member of the RSA Environment Committee.

She had a distinct philosophy right from the start. As put forward in 1990:

> . . . the idea is green consumerism. It was just a handful of people in the green movement who recognized the potential power of purchasing campaigns if they switched from the traditional rather negative approach of boycotting products to a more positive selection of environmentally superior goods and services . . . Our approach is not so much to see one sector as green and to avoid more contentious areas like chemicals and mining, but rather to seek out the most environmentally responsible companies within each sector.[28]

In 1990 the unit produced a substantial paper setting out its own criteria, *The Assessment Process for Green Investment*:

- Environmental issues are wide-ranging and the impact of a particular company on the environment will clearly depend on the nature of the activities. For example, the questions which are appropriate to ask of a food retailer will be very different to those asked of a paper manufacturer. However, there are some common themes:
- Products, processes, property and infrastructure management which save material and energy resources. Key words include: *energy conservation, process control, waste minimization, eco-labelling, recycling, transport, supply chains.*
- Emissions to the atmosphere, water or land. Key words include: *ozone depletion, acid rain, greenhouse effect, river, marine and ground-water pollution, contaminated land.*
- Activities which can harm sensitive areas such as the rainforests, special wildlife habitats and human settlements. Key words include: *Mineral extraction, logging, large-scale dams, monoculture plantations, agrochemicals, land rights.*
- Management which pays regard to ethical principles and to the needs of employees and local communities. Key words include: *BS7750* and *BS5750, Codes of Ethical conducts, share-ownership, animal testing, fair-trading overseas, political donations, charitable donations.*

The other specialist green investment group is Ecofin, formed in 1991. It resulted from a group of people working in the investment field deciding that there was an opportunity to create a 'research boutique' supplying information on environmental companies to the investment community, just as there are in such diverse areas as banking and computing. Best known in the UK is probably David Owen, a Founder Director and Head of Research. He has a D.Phil in ecology, and from 1989 to 1991 had set up and run a pan-European environmental research unit for the French investment bank Paribas. He is also on the steering committee of the Institute of Chartered Accountants Research Group. Ecofin started out as a supplier of research both on general environmental questions of interest to industry and financial institutions, but also produces detailed analysis of companies operating in areas like waste management or water supply. Its coverage is some sixty equities active in the field across Europe. In April 1993 Ecofin moved into investment management with a \$40m specialist fund, The Environmental Investment Company, with the idea that 'growing public concern will lead to increasingly stringent environmental legislation and more active enforcement of the legislation, which, in turn, will lead to significant real growth in spending on environmental products and services.'[29]

David Owen puts it like this: 'Since environmental concerns also embrace the threat of environmental liabilities and increased compliance costs and pressures upon non-compliers, the overall activities of qualifying companies need to contribute a "net environmental gain".'[30] Ecofin distinguish six sectors making up the environmental services sector:

1 Waste management, minimization and recycling
2 Waste provision and treatment, effluent removal and treatment
3 Prevention of air pollution, including alternative energy sources
4 Environmental consultancy and labs
5 Environmental monitoring and control
6 Derelict land restoration.

Ecofin created the Ecofin Environmental Index in 1992 covering companies in both the UK and Europe, and in January 1994 launched a global index of 210 environmental companies in conjunction with First Analysis Securities of Chicago. David Owen is optimistic about a revival of the sector's fortune's but points out: 'the onus for the investment community will be to provide a firm grasp about how each company is affected by liability issues and the regulatory climate. The green paint has flaked away to reveal several areas needy of fundamental analysis.'[31]

It is hard to deny that the long-term prospects for companies operating in environmental services should be good. If green investors are much more demanding, so much the better. David Owen again: 'the sector's hard times from 1990–94 mean that qualitatively based corporate image-making exercises no longer wash. Companies are expected to deliver.'[32] There were signs in 1994 in the US at least that the industry downturn was over, with companies like Waste Management outperforming the US stock market for the first time since 1989.

The environment as a financial 'black hole'?

'Environmental liability is the single most important issue affecting the property/casualty industry insurance over the next three to five years.' Kidder Peabody 1994:[33]

In the 1930s and 1940s a site called Love Canal in upstate New York, near Niagara Falls, was used as a disposal site for chemical waste stored in steel drums. The site was later covered over, and housing and a school built on top. In the 1970s the chemicals started to leak. Analysis showed the presence of over eighty toxic chemicals, including ten carcinogens, and a high incidence of birth defects, liver failure and various cancers. The area was declared a Federal Emergency, and the population evacuated. Love Canal was just one example of a series of communities poisoned by America's industry legacy. In 1980 the US Congress therefore passed the Comprehensive Environmental Response, Compensation and Liability Act, generally known as Superfund. The name derives from the creation of the Hazardous Substance Response Trust Fund 'Superfund' to fund clean-up. The Environmental Protection Agency (EPA) was charged to create a National Priorities List (NPL) of the most hazardous sites; 'potentially responsible parties' (PRPs) either had to pay for clean-ups themselves, or reimburse the Superfund for having done so.

However, Superfund itself was only meant to cover temporary spending, and its real basis was the 'polluter pays' principle, written in very stringent legal terms: *no-fault, joint and several, and retroactive*. What 'no-fault, and retroactive' means is that the liability for cleaning up a site exists even if the disposal was legal at the time and irrespective of the degree of care applied. 'Joint and several' means that anyone connected with the site is liable, even if totally different from the original polluter. Not only the current owner, but banks and insurance companies with a contractual relationship to the site. Since the original polluters may have been small companies incapable of paying, or indeed long gone out of business, this clause has resulted in a spate of lawsuits targeted at 'deep pocket' companies viewed as financially strong who may have had only a slight connection with the site. Companies in turn have every reason to try to fix the liability on their insurers.

How much could this all cost? At the end of 1993 some 36,000 sites were registered on the EPA system, of which 1286 sites had been placed on the NPL of most hazardous sites. So far the EPA estimates clean-up costs per site at $30m, and it believes that there will be 2100 sites on the NPL by the year 2000, making a total of $66bn (£44bn). However, outside experts believe that the actual number of hazardous sites needing to be cleaned up could be 3000 to 4000, with average costs of perhaps $50m per site, i.e. a total clean-up cost of $200bn. In addition, there are the enormous likely legal costs as parties dispute liability, plus third-party damages to people injured by pollution. (It is thought that total personal damages from the US asbestos industry could total $80bn alone.) The American insurance rating agency A. M. Best estimated in the spring of 1994 that the US insurance industry would need to set aside $260bn (£180bn) to meet future environmental and pollution claims. Since industry reserves total only $12.5bn currently, there is obviously a huge problem. Best described this as a financial 'black hole': '. . . environmental liability, both Superfund liability and all other hazardous waste liability, represents the single largest threat to the property and casualty insurance's financial health for the next several decades.'[34]

Environmental bankers?

'Environmental risk is just another aspect of risk management. All the usual risks are there: market, financial, capital cost, liabilities actual and contingent, reputational and strategic.' Hilary Thompson.[35]

The banks have found that they are second in line after the insurers in being regarded as 'deep pockets' in regard to environmental liability. This can even arise if they receive a contaminated site as 'collateral' for a loan which has failed to be repaid. All the major banks have therefore set up environmental risk assessment units. Since 1990 the National Westminster Bank has had an environmental management unit (emu) which builds environmental risk into its loan-pricing structure with a model that looks at the industries a company is operating in, and then allocates a category of risk to each. It stated that:

We have already started to formulate an informal policy towards the environment as a result of the deals that we have chosen to reject and those we have adopted. For example by preferring to finance double skinned oil tankers as opposed to single skinned . . . by financing projects where environmental risks are deemed to be within environmental tolerances, we are effectively shaping environmental practice on a case by case basis.[36]

As head of NatWest's environmental management unit Hilary Thompson reports directly to senior management and is generally regarded as being one of the UK's top experts on banking environmental risk. She takes a positive long-term view: 'The "pot of gold" will not just be for environmentalists. Cleaned-up land gains in value, and cutting waste often means more production for less money. New products will be developed – already water companies are selling globally the technology developed in cleaning up Britain's beaches. It should not by any means be assumed that "green" products will be more expensive.'[37] Although the unit was initially set up to assess the bank's risks on pollution claims, its influence has grown to affect senior management's thinking on the whole question of the environment. NatWest's 1993 environmental report was the first by a financial institution. The bank's Chairman Lord Alexander of Weedon is a member of the Prime Minister's Panel on Sustainable Development, and is also Chairman of *Business in the Environment*'s Programme Committee, while Chief Executive Derek Wanless has a similar role at ACBE.

The US is leading the way in environmental credit rating. The Investor Responsibility Research Center (IRRC) in Washington, funded by several hundred institutional investors and corporations, has used EPA data to build a huge environmental database on America's top companies and issue green ratings. Just as no investor would dream of buying a corporate bond without checking the company's credit rating, so in the future they are likely to use such environmental ratings. As IRRC's Jonathan Naimon puts it: 'Investors who fail to . . . assess environmental risk in a systematic way . . . may be setting themselves up for lower returns. Once the financial community realizes companies are having to spend hundreds of millions on this issue, the market reacts immediately.'[38] The Swiss company Eco-Rating is pioneering such an approach in Europe, an idea also promoted by the *Financial Times*'s Environmental correspondent David Lascelles. However, the plentiful environmental dating supplied by the EPA in the US is at present lacking in the EU.

Exxon, pension funds and the environment

'The Exxon trial takes us into an era where payouts can be on a scale capable of ruining companies as a result of a single act of pollution.' Jeremy Leggatt, Greenpeace.[39]

The Exxon supertanker *Exxon Valdez* ran aground in Prince William Sound in March 1989, spilling 11m gallons of oil into Alaska, one of the most precious areas of natural beauty in the US. Exxon was not helped by its laid-back approach to the affair – Chairman Larry Rawls declined to visit the site, saying that it would make no difference to the clean-up operation. Elizabeth Holtzman was then Comptroller or head of New York City pension funds (Nypers) 1990–93. With $52bn in investments, this was the second largest pension fund in the US.

We felt that when corporations treat the environment badly, they treat their investors badly by exposing their investments to enormous liability and negative publicity. We are such large investors that we cannot quickly sell holdings in problem companies, therefore it makes sense to exercise the power of ownership when faced with environmental negligence, and press for changes. Our primary job is to protect the assets of our beneficiaries, that's our fiduciary responsibility. But that responsibility includes protecting our portfolio investments from being damaged by corporate environmental carelessness.

We owned six million shares in Exxon, and after the *Exxon Valdez* disaster I organized a meeting with ourselves and other big pension funds and the Exxon management to express our concerns. We then went further in recommending that companies should adopt the CERES Principles, and when Exxon declined to publish an environmental report, we filed a proxy resolution instructing them to adopt the CERES principles. Note that we only file such resolutions as a last resort, and subject to four criteria:

1) the company must be associated with a severe environmental accident like the *Valdez* spill.
2) the company must be the subject of legal action for environmental injury, and therefore liable to pay fines.
3) the environmental damage must involve a specific community.
4) an assessment of whether the company's financial performance is poor.

To sum up, as long-term investors pension funds should practice responsible investment – avoiding environmental risk is part of their fiduciary duty. As shareholders they are responsible for examining their investment portfolios, and responsible investment is informed and intelligent investment.[40]

Elizabeth Holtzman's caution was proved to be justified in June 1994. A US federal court in Anchorage, Alaska, found the company guilty of recklessness over the oil spill caused by the *Exxon Valdez* tanker disaster. The recklessness verdict opened the way for the jury to assess punitive damages of $5bn, in addition to the $3.5bn damages Exxon had already paid, $1.1bn in federal and state charges and more than $2bn to clean up the contaminated coastline. Exxon's legal fees were also an additional burden. The day the verdict was announced, the price of Exxon shares fell sharply on Wall Street knocking $5bn off the company's stock market value.[41]

Mark Campanale recently wrote: 'ICI's disclosure in February 1993 that it was creating provisions of £148m to cover the cost of remediating soil and ground water in the US should not really have surprised the City, given the extensive range of environmental legislation already in place in the US.'[42] Yet surprise the City it did, and its share price declined as the news broke. In the US, the share price of the insurance giant Aetna dropped 10% in a day when it revealed a $100m environmental loss reserve with its second quarter figures for 1994. In the light of this, it seems only a matter of time before investment managers focus on environmental liability as they do on other possible negative features. It may well be that with the exception of experts like NPI and Ecofin, professional investors simply lack the capacity to do so. Tessa Tennant thinks so: 'The City understands that the environment is important for business, but has a total lack of interest in building up the necessary information base. Investment managers have lagged behind their peers in banking and insurance, but there will be a racheting up of the response.'[43]

The City may well have no choice. In America the interpretation of a trustees' fiduciary duty has been extended to poor performance by investment managers (see Chapter Eleven). In the long term an investment manager who suffers a significant loss through environmental problems may well be sued for not carrying out sufficient environmental 'due diligence'. Hugh Devas is a solicitor with the British law firm Rowe & Maw: 'Decisions to invest in industries which are then subject to (environmental) attacks will also be heavily criticized, and we may indeed see test cases brought by pension fund holders against fund managers on the environmental grounds. Today's fantasy may become tomorrow's fund managers nightmare.'[44]

Richmond's British example

The borough of Richmond in south-west London has had positive environmental policies for well over ten years, and has been distinctive in actively promoting environmental education in schools. In 1992 the government set local authorities the target of reducing the amount of domestic waste produced by 25% by the year 2000, but Richmond believes it will achieve this by the end of 1995. Councillor Serge Lourie is the Chair of the Investment Panel and keen to put environmental issues on the agenda:

Over the last two years we have felt that we should invite companies in which the pension fund invests to discuss their environmental policies with us. After taking legal advice, and discussions with PIRC and a specialist environmental fund manager, we decided that it would not be appropriate for us to instruct our fund managers, Gartmore and Schroders, on how to invest the £120m pension fund, for example to exclude a particular company from investment on environmental grounds. We might in future express our concerns about a particular company to them, however.

What we could do was to become 'active shareholders', discussing directly environmental policies with the senior managements of companies in which we invest. I have been impressed with the seriousness with which the corporate sector has responded to our inquiries. So far we have seen four companies: Blue

Circle, Anglian Water, NORWEB, and Asda. All of them sent main board Directors along, and in the case of NORWEB a joint Managing Director, while all of them also provided substantial information on their attempts to improve their environmental performance. Recently we visited top management of Asda at their London headquarters and discussed issues such as packaging and recycling, and also broader subjects like the location and energy efficiency of superstores. We subscribe to PIRC's environmental code, and whereas before we let the fund managers vote our shares, now we vote them via the NAPF service, so it's a matter of corporate governance as well as the environment. In the long term we believe that companies committed to high environmental standards will be better investments than those which are not.[45]

Richmond's example is a good one which will surely be followed by other councils. However, in the long term it would seem only a first step. The specialist advice of a NPI or Ecofin will be needed to give expert advice on what environmental liabilities or good environmental practices actually mean in financial terms and thus make the connection between 'fiduciary responsibility' and 'environmental risk' as described by Elizabeth Holtzman.

British investment funds and the rainforest

"OK, it's a slavery-based economy with no regard for ecological or humanitarian values. Anything else to recommend it?"

The early 1990s saw a flood of capital pour into what were called 'emerging markets', including the enormous sum of £26bn in 1993. Few people probably thought what their money was actually doing to the rainforest in Brazil or Indonesia, or to the indigenous people living there. A rare exception was an Indonesian timber company called Barito Pacific which launched a £250m-share issue in the summer of 1993. Greenpeace Business led a campaign involving fifteen environmental and human rights groups to stop the issue. The campaign, coordinated by one of the City's leading environmental research teams, sent letters to 275 fund managers warning of the company's policy of unsustainable logging, often on land belonging to indigenous peoples. Following this campaign, Salomon Bros and Schroders withdrew as underwriters to the share issue.

Expectations of an environmental victory were premature, however, and may have received a shock on Easter Sunday 1994, when the BBC's *The World This Weekend* news programme sent its experienced journalist Roger Harribin to Indonesia:

For hundreds of miles from San Marinder the forests have already been felled, and many species lost. The sort of lowland rainforest that used to guard this river are among the richest habitats in the world . . . Now the destruction has spread as far as the village of Matalibaq, home to the indigenous Bahau people who had their own kingdom before the Indonesians took over this island. Timber concessions on fifty square miles of Bahau land have been granted to a billionaire businessman, whose company Barito Pacific Timber is backed by British pension fund investors. Barito has forest concessions of 5.5 million hectares. That's an area bigger than the size of Switzerland.

Just upstream from Matalibaq, pop music blares out at a village for three hundred families of Barito's labourers. It looks like an old-fashioned Butlins camp, but on a clearing hacked out of pristine rainforest. Its families have been brought here as part of Indonesia's controversial transmigration programme, to resettle people from islands overcrowded by population growth. They have to walk three hours to work in sweltering temperatures, they are paid just a pound a day, and they haven't been given the smallholdings Barito promised them here. Barito's publicity brochures don't boast of clear cutting forests for settlements like this.

If you're a pensionholder with Legal & General or Schroders, there's no way of you knowing you're saving for your old age on the back of Bahau people in Borneo. Environmentalists lobbied fund managers to boycott Barito at the time of their international share launch last year, but both firms invested pensionholders' money anyway ... But do pensionholders want to make their money this way?[46]

The *Observer* picked up the story, noting that 'British pension firms are hastening the extinction of some of the world's rarest animals by investing in companies felling the Indonesian rainforest ... The investments were made despite environmentalists' warnings that Barito was fined millions of dollars in 1991 for illegal logging.'[47]

Some people may object that these are very poor countries, and that environmental damage is a necessary but inevitable consequence of the development required to lift them out of poverty. However, as the Barito example showed, such 'development' often reduces traditional peoples to penury with short-term profits going to a small elite. The result is the destruction of the natural environment, and, as many Third World charities have discovered, one of Asia's biggest growth businesses – the sale of young girls into child prostitution. As Tessa Tennant put it: 'the challenge for green and social investors is not to stop investment into emerging markets, but to ensure capital goes to those companies committed to the principles of sustainable development.'[48]

Global Warming – financial ruin?

'The insurance industry is first in line to be affected by climate change. It is clear that global warming could bankrupt the industry.' Frank Nutter, Reinsurance Association of America.[49]
'When historians finally conduct an autopsy on the Soviet Union and Soviet Communism, they may reach the verdict of death by ecocide.'[50]

The evidence does not bear out claims that global warming is 'hot air'. The Intergovernmental Panel on Climate Change (IPCC) was formed in 1988, its 1990 report *Climate Change* stating that it was *certain*: a) that there is a natural greenhouse effect which already keeps the Earth warmer than it would otherwise would be. b) emissions resulting from human emissions are substantially increasing the atmospheric concentrations of the greenhouse gases: carbon dioxide, methane, cfcs, and nitrous oxide. c) these increases will enhance the greenhouse effect, resulting on average in an additional warming of the Earth's surface. Ice cores surveys indicate that carbon dioxide levels in the atmosphere, remarkably constant at 275 ppm (parts per million) since the end of the Ice Age 15,000 years ago, have risen steadily since the industrial revolution reaching 354 ppm at the end of 1990. The same is true of other greenhouse gases such as methane and nitrous oxide. The IPCC went on to predict that by the year 2025 average temperatures could be 1 degree C higher, implying an average global sea level eight inches higher.

Munich Reinsurance is the world's largest reinsurer and has to pay damages when natural catastrophes occur. The company has found that such disasters have significantly increased in both frequency and cost over the last ten years, and 'show every sign of accelerating in coming years.'[51] The company's extensive database shows the cost (note it is in inflation-adjusted dollars). The apparent

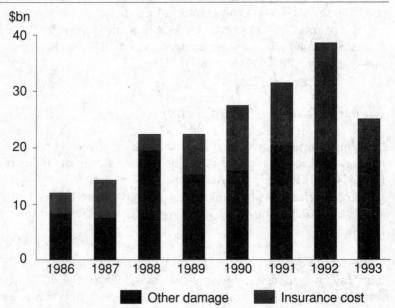

Natural Disaster Costs

reduction in 1993 was not due to a lower level of disasters, merely that many of them occurred in the former Communist bloc where there was little insurance cover.

'The insurance industry has awoken at a most senior level to the threat posed to its future by climatic change. It is only a matter of time before the banks and pension funds start to conclude the same . . . "a pot of gold" for environmentalists – institutional finance being directed preferentially towards environmentally sustainable businesses.' J. Leggat, Greenpeace.[52] Or, as the magazine *Institutional Investor* put it: 'Political pressures, the need to build on old industrial land, and the increasing sensitivity of pollution measurement are rapidly pushing environmental liability into the mainstream of investment decision.'[53]

CHAPTER SIX

The Rewards of Virtue

*In general the message seems to be that (*ethical*) constraints do not damage your wealth.*

THE WM COMPANY, CONSULTING ACTUARIES[1]

The question of investment performance is a key one for ethical investors. If, as opinion polls suggest, 35% of investors in socially responsible funds are willing to do so in the expectation of receiving a lower rate of return, this is not true of the other 65%. People in a trustee relationship are also inhibited from considering ethical investment if ethical restrictions are deemed to have a negative impact on investment performance.

It is sometimes implied in the financial press that investment returns must be reduced by having a smaller pool of investments to choose from. There are a number of theoretical answers to this type of question which are worth discussing briefly before moving on to examine what experience indicates. People with little knowledge of finance should not duck this chapter on the grounds that it is too difficult for them; there is no mathematics involved, and it will enable them to understand the technical arguments used for and against ethical investment. These are:

1. that any non-financial restriction on investment selection must reduce *diversification*, and hence returns.
2. that responsible investors are forced to avoid large conglomerates, and concentrate on smaller companies which over time grow faster – the *small companies* effect.
3. that exclusion of certain companies on grounds of moral or environmental repugnance anticipates later legal action and financial problems – the *anticipation effect*.
4. that properly done ethical/green investment needs a higher level of knowledge about the companies invested in than ordinary

investment managers possess – *the information effect*.

5 that the positive criteria used by such funds help them target well-run companies – a *positive selection* effect.

Diversification and Divergence

It has sometimes been argued in court cases about the legality of pension funds and charities imposing some ethical restrictions on their fund managers that this reduces diversification (true) and that this in turn must reduce investment performance (false). To clear up the question of diversification, it is clearly unwise to have all your eggs in one basket. The Nuffield Foundation provides a terrible example of what can happen, as described by Robert Hazel, Director of the Nuffield Foundation. 'In 1943 the Trust was given 10m shares in Austin Morris Motors by the founder of the trust, Lord Nuffield, who was also the owner of the motor company. These shares were then worth £500m (about £20bn in 1994 money). When the British car industry collapsed in the early 1970s, the Trust lost 80% of its assets.'[2]

Yet as explained in Chapter Two, you do not need to hold all the 700-odd shares in the FT All Share Index to diversify away the risk of one particular company going bankrupt. Financial theory says that under twenty holdings will diversify away most of that risk, technically known as stock or *specific risk*. Note that for an investor prepared to take risks, diversification may not be a good thing – the more share holdings a fund has, the less likely it is to be outstanding. As the veteran American investor Gerald Loeb put it: 'Diversification is a necessity for the beginner. On the other hand, the really great fortunes were made by concentration. The greater your experience, the greater your capacity for running risks . . . the less you need to diversify.'[3]

When considering the question of investment performance, it is normal to compare a fund manager with the bench-mark of either a stock market index or compared to a survey of other fund managers. The universal bench-mark in the UK is the FT Actuaries All Share Index which contains some 740 companies (excluding investment trusts). It might be argued that restricting a portfolio from investing in any sector such as defence, tobacco or breweries must reduce the ability to outperform such an index. There are two answers to that, one theoretical and one practical. The theoretical answer is that the more restrictions you put on a portfolio, the less its performance is likely to track that of an index. There is no logical reason why the returns from an investment fund allowed to put its money in any UK company should not closely track that of the FT All Share, and restrictions on up to 25% of the market should not greatly impair its ability to do so, but beyond that the restrictions would be likely to make the performances diverge significantly.

Note that this does not say whether such divergence would be good or bad, but that it would simply be likely to exist. Professional investment managers in the UK are compared by how they do relative to the All Share Index, and therefore highly unwilling to take a big risk that they may significantly diverge from it. It might be thought that professional investment managers have the facility to move into areas of the stock market which are doing well and sell those which are doing badly, and that their ability to do so would be adversely restricted by ethical constraints. Unfortunately, the idea of superior insight by investment professionals does not stand up to examination. Modern financial theory is called the Efficient Markets Hypothesis, which essentially means that the professionals cannot beat the market. Probably the best book on this subject for non-experts is *A Random Walk Down Wall Street*, by Columbia Professor of Finance Burton Malkiel.[4] In it he demonstrated that over a fifteen-year period, 70% of US pension fund managers had a performance 1.3% below that of the 12.1% annual return achieved by the main US bench mark index. In Chapter Two, I mentioned that over ten years 86% of UK growth unit trusts failed to match the performance of the FT All Share, while a recent survey of UK pension funds by the WM actuarial service found that the average fund underperformed the All Share Index by 0.7% a year, i.e. similar to the US results.

Hence the idea that ethical investment may impair investment returns by not allowing fund managers to move profitably into and out of certain sectors falls down. All the evidence suggests that they cannot do that in the first place!

Ethical Indices

It seems plausible that there may be an anticipation effect whereby ethical or green investors would recognize practices or problems earlier than other investors, and that these problems would then turn into financial costs. Ethical investment was born partly out of consumer rights, and consumer boycotts of things like fur coats have effectively eliminated an industry. The same may be true in the long term of the tobacco industry, not to mention the eventual collapse of the US asbestos industry as the true human and environmental costs hit home. In practice, however, it is hard to demonstrate this, if only because most companies are conglomerates which do not easily fit into clear-cut sectors. In 1989 the American consulting firm Barra analysed the effect of imposing ethical investment limits on certain sectors of the FT All Share for the previous five years to end October 1988.[4] This found that portfolios which excluded just tobacco, nuclear power or financial shares did slightly worse than the market as a whole, but that excluding just South Africa or defence enabled a portfolio to outperform. A portfolio using all the above ethical exclusion screens marginally outperformed the FT All Share by 0.06% a year, actually quite a good result.

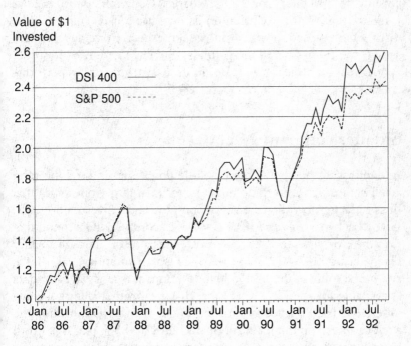

In the US the Domini Social Index is a carefully constructed index of 400 companies which would pass most ethical investment screens. It is modelled on the normal US stock market bench mark, the Standard & Poors 500, and actually includes 255 companies which are present in the former. The Chart above shows, for the almost seven years to the end of 1992, a close correlation between the two indices with a definite tendency for the DSI slowly but consistently to outperform.

Dr Robert Schwartz is one of the father figures of socially responsible investing in the US. He told a London audience in 1984: 'Performance in the management of assets is a function of the accuracy of judgments about the overall market, the future course of interest rates, and the ability to sort out industries with negative or positive potential in order to select investments that appreciate over time. In this fundamental approach, and with the availability of companies in every industry, I believe performance will not be hindered by restrictions on selected categories of investment.'[6] According to Friends Provident's Charles Congdon, there is little evidence that sector exclusion on its own has a clear impact: 'The distribution is about what you would expect from any random sample of fully discretionary funds. So far, therefore, it would appear that an ethical bias is not in itself instrumental in performance one way or the other.'[7]

Smaller company effect

In contrast to the above, there is little doubt that in the long term small companies tend to do much better than larger ones, and that this is a factor providing a positive boost to ethical investment funds. Going back to *A Random Walk Down Wall Street*, Malkiel found that over the sixty years to 1988, on average the value of shares in smaller companies grew by 12.3% a year, compared to an annual 10.0% rise in the value of the S&P 500 index. Similar if less extensive data is available for the UK, where the Hoare Govett smaller company index rose 18.4% a year from 1955 to the end of 1991, beating the average return on the main All Share Index by 4.5% p.a. It is worth noting that smaller companies tend to be much harder hit than big ones when a recession happens, and in fact UK smaller company shares did very badly in 1989–92. So much so in fact that for the ten years as a whole to the end of 1993 the Hoare Govett index actually underperformed the All Share, having been substantially ahead for the five years to the end of 1989.

Since most larger companies are some kind of conglomerate with interests in various industries, they are much more likely to fall foul of ethical exclusion clauses than smaller companies which tend to be much more 'pure plays'. For this reason most responsible investment funds have a definite bias towards smaller companies. The Barra survey mentioned above found that the 'smaller company effect' generated a return of 0.81% a year above that of the FT All Share Index, i.e. without that effect the returns from ethical investment would have been below that of the market.

In the late 1980s both smaller companies and ethical unit trusts did well. But the correlations were not precise, and it would seem wrong to attribute the good returns from ethical funds entirely to 'the smaller company effect', as Charles Congdon agrees:

> It may be cynically argued that much of the good performance was achieved courtesy of the 'smaller companies' effect; that ethical criteria forced funds willy-nilly into smaller companies, a sector which coincidentally produced strong outperformance in the late 1980s . . . There is only limited truth in this. Certainly most ethical funds will tend to have a bias towards smaller companies . . . The performance of the smaller companies sector is an important issue, however, because it does not correlate exactly with that of the total index. Over the long term, smaller companies as a species will tend to outperform their larger counterparts.[8]

Theoretical arguments can be taken only so far. My feeling is that there is no doubt that a smaller company effect exists, and also a small sector exclusion effect. What I suspect has been overlooked by most critics is the *information* and *positive selection* effects. If this is true, the performance of the larger ethical funds should show a clearly better track record than smaller funds. And this is the subject of the next section.

Ethical Unit Trusts in Practice

The only real way to assess whether ethical investment has a positive or negative impact on investment performance is to look at ethical funds in practice. In March 1994 I wrote an article in *Professional Investor*[9], the journal of the fund management industry, which was the first systematic attempt to analyse such funds. Since investment managers of non-ethical funds have been known sometimes to denigrate responsible investing, some of the conclusions of that article are reproduced below on the grounds that it can be used by non-professionals to force ordinary fund managers to consider the case for ethical products.

The key point to remember when looking at investment performance is to compare apples with apples, and pears with pears. What this means is that most funds have a specific job to do, to invest in, say, the UK stock market or in the Japanese stock market. The only way to assess the achievement of an investment manager is to see how his performance compares with that of the market area in which he works and his success relative to other funds active in the same field. For example, if the Japanese stock market plunges 30%, and UK equities rise in value 10%, all Japanese funds are likely to do worse than all UK funds. If the average Japanese fund has fallen in value 25%, then someone whose fund is down only 20% is doing a good job, while likewise a UK fund manager whose fund has risen only 7% when the average fund is up 11% is doing badly.

For this reason, investment managers tend to be judged relative to their peers. An above-average performance is good, below-average is poor. A technical form of average called the *median* is used, and relative performance is divided into *quartiles*. The top quarter of funds are called the *first quartile*, the next quarter ranging from a ranking of 26% to the 50% average mark, the *second quartile*, while the *third quartile* covers funds ranked ranging from 50% to 75% of all funds. Statistics on the investment performance of all unit and investment trusts can be found in two magazines published monthly: *Money Management*, and *Planned Savings*. Investors should be wary of unit trusts which have done spectacularly well in one year, as this may well mean that they have adopted a high-risk policy which worked well in the past but could be a disaster in the future. The best way of assessing the financial performance of a unit trust is over a minimum of three years, and preferably more.

Looking at the investment performance of actual ethical unit trusts was made difficult by the fact that the sector's rapid growth limits the number of funds with a statistically valid track record. There were, however, nine trusts with a minimum three-year investment performance ranking to the end of 1993, and their track record is shown below:

PERFORMANCE (QUARTILE RANKINGS)
UK EQUITY GROWTH SECTOR

	Size £m	1991	1992	1993	3 Years	Agg Score
Abbey Ethical	20.6	1st	3rd	2nd	1st	0.337
Allchurches Amity	17.6	3rd	2nd	4th	4th	0.426
Eagle Star Envir Opps	12.4	1st	1st	4th	1st	0.375
Fidelity UK Growth	75.5	2nd	1st	1st	1st	0.181
Friends Provident Steward	154.4	2nd	3rd	2nd	2nd	0.309
NM Conscience	12.3	1st	3rd	4th	2nd	0.422
Scot Equitable	12.6	2nd	3rd	4th	3rd	0.403
Sovereign Ethical	8.3	2nd	4th	3rd	4th	0.433
TSB Environmental	21.4	1st	3rd	4th	2nd	0.386
Sector Ave % change		+7.4	+10.0	+20.7	+62.4	
No. of funds			146	144	132	

Data derived from that published in *Money Management* magazine.
The aggregate score is a measure of the mean percentile ranking adjusted for the standard deviation.

With three first quartile funds (out of nine) over three years, and three second quartile funds, it was clear that ethical/environmental funds yielded their investors superior returns. This was particularly true on a weighted basis (reflecting the varying sizes of the different funds), since the six outperforming funds included five of the largest funds, and the six in total amounted to 87% of the sample at the end of the period, or 92.6% at the beginning of the three years under review. If an investor had invested on a weighted basis at the beginning of 1991 in these nine funds, by the end of 1993 this would have risen in value by 66.2%, compared to a 62.4% increase in the average UK growth trust over this period. The Friends Provident Stewardship Trust was such a large part of the UK ethical unit trust universe that it made sense to analyse its performance separately. At the beginning of 1991 the FP Stewardship Trust had a market capitalization of £89.6m, which amounted to 59.9% of the nine UK ethical funds then in existence. Over the three years its value increased by 65.1%, so it can be seen that it did not unduly skew the results.

There were two other points worth noting. Unit trust investors and their advisers are increasingly interested not just in the position of funds in performance league tables, but also in the volatility of those positions. The aggregate score in the above table measures both of these. It is noteworthy that the larger funds had a more consistent performance than the smaller ones. The Fidelity UK Growth Trust was outstanding, although it must be admitted that its ethical constraints were considerably less than its peers, nor was it marketed as an ethical fund any longer. The Friends Provident Stewardship Trust had the second highest aggregate score reflecting the Stewardship fund's fairly steady position in the middle of the second quartile. While the Abbey Ethical fund and the Eagle Star Environmental Opportunity fund both produced better absolute returns over the period than the Friends Provident Trust, they fell behind it because of their greater volatility.

The second interesting feature was that the smaller trusts appear to show a distinct deterioration in relative performance as each year progressed, which was not apparent in the three largest funds : Friends Provident, Fidelity and Abbey Ethical. This seemed strange given the heavy bias of most ethical funds to smaller companies. UK smaller company funds recovered in line with the economy in 1993, with the average UK smaller companies trust increasing in value by 31.8%, 11.1% more than the average UK growth trust. The increasing outperformance of the larger funds may reflect the explosive growth of information about environmental costs and liabilities in the last year or so, as well as the increasing variety of demands from ethical investors that their funds be managed in an ethical way. Since the press have become quick to jump on any fund that they suspect is using ethical/environmental investment purely as a marketing tool, ethical investment is becoming more complex and difficult to do. It is becoming an asset class in its own right, and one that requires the allocation of adequate resources to do well.

In sum, this would appear to indicate that there is indeed a very clear *positive selection* effect. Indeed, the evidence suggests it is the actual *process* of selection, if carried out thoroughly, that is the real reason why ethical investment has produced superior investment, rather than a concentration on the *products* excluded, as the press has tended to think. Ethical and ecological screening is an essential part of any ethical fund manager's life, and one that is very time-consuming and becoming more so. As long ago as 1989 Peter Silvester of Friends Provident was quoted as follows: 'It's taken five or six years to evolve, but the managers here have become adept at finding the companies that meet the positive criteria and avoid the negative criteria.'[10] A sign that the thesis of superior returns is due to the intensive research required, as much as the pure exclusions, was given by the above when he described the good performance of the Stewardship funds in December 1993 prior to the launch of an ethical investment trust. 'We get the performance because we've had to spend more time researching than most people do nowadays. We have looked at companies in much greater detail to get to know them.'[11]

Over the long term

The real test of any investment formula is over the long term, at least five years. In 1990 the WM Company of consulting actuaries produced a research paper *The Implications of Ethical Constraints on Investment Returns*.[12] This examined the investment performance of 126 charity funds for the five years to end 1989, of which forty-four were restricted by ethical constraints from investing in companies active in South Africa, tobacco, alcohol or gambling. The results were interesting:

UK Equity Investment Performance	1989	5 Years to 1989
All charities	+35.0%	+19.5%
Ethical charities	+36.5%	+19.9%

Clearly, the ethical investment restrictions had no negative impact, in fact, they appeared to give a positive boost to investment performance.

The Central Finance Board of the Methodist Church works under tighter ethical restrictions than other institutional investors handling charity and pension fund money. Chairman Charles Davis in the 1993 Report and Accounts noted how the fund had beaten the FT Index in 1992: 'I consider this another very good performance in view of the ethical restrictions under which our team work. As far as the FT100 Share Index is concerned there are 18 stocks in which we would not invest on ethical grounds which comprise over a quarter by value of that index.'[13] The CFB Investment Fund was part of a survey produced by CAPS. For the five years to the end of 1993 these were the figures:

	1993	5 Years to end 1993
a) UK Equities & Convertibles		
CFB Investment Fund	+30.6%	+18.8%
CAPS Median Fund	+28.5%	+18.5%
FT All Share Index	+28.4%	+18.1%
b) Overseas Equities		
CFB Investment Fund	+46.0%	+18.7%
CAPS Median Fund	+41.3%	+16.3%
FT World Index (x UK)	+24.9%	+ 9.5%

For the ten years to end February 1994, the main CFB Investment Fund increased in value by an annual rate of 18.1% compared to the 16.6% annual increase in the FT All Share Index. Although comparisons with other fund managers were not made, this was a very good result and would surely have been a first quartile result if it had been.

June 1994 saw the tenth anniversary of the launch of the Friends Provident Stewardship Trust, the first UK ethical unit trust. Its performance record was justifiably celebrated by the company. Over ten years it outperformed 71% of all funds in the UK equity growth sector. An initial £100 investment in Stewardship was worth £393 ten years later. The low volatility of the Stewardship fund was described earlier. However, as the aggressive performers which top the one year performance league tables tend to fall back the next year, Stewardship's steady performance translates into a very good performance over the long term.

The performance of the pension trust linked to Stewardship may be described as excellent – over ten years it outperformed 95% of all other funds in the Micropal UK equity sector. Its value increased by

476% compared to an average return of 302%. This result on its own is sufficient to refute the argument that ethical investment must have a negative effect on investment performance – if it did it would simply not be possible for the Stewardship unit-linked pension trust to be in the top 5%. As Peter Silvester stated: '. . . These results clearly show that with experience and skill, Stewardship ethical investment can produce competitive returns for investors allied to high standards of ethics and integrity.'[14]

CHAPTER SEVEN

History and Campaigning Groups

> *. . . the key to the power of ethical investing is the recognition that corporations and institutions are owned and managed by people. Ethical investing insists on their humanity. It denies them the luxury of pretending to be impersonal economic forces. It requires a recognition of responsibility for one's actions, and it demands that others assume responsibility for theirs. As an instrument for change, both personal and social, ethical investing is unequalled.*
>
> AMY DOMINI[1]

Amy Domini is an American investment counsellor who found that both she and her clients increasingly demanded that investments combined moral criteria as well as financial objectives. Her book with Peter Kinder, *Ethical Investing* (1984), being a landmark on the subject. Some people might say that the insistence on moral principle is one of the distinguishing features of America at its best and that it is not surprising that the modern combination of finance and ethics aimed at the public began there.

American Beginnings

Socially responsible investment (SRI) began in the late 1960s/early 1970s when a number of different concerns came together. One was that of the churches and universities about profiting from big business's involvement in the Vietnam War. Of course, this period saw violent demonstrations on many US campuses about the war and the draft of young men to fight in it. American universities and religious bodies questioned whether they should own shares in companies supplying war materials and whether they should use their power as shareholders to force change. These questions culminated in a major conference at Yale in 1970. Fifteen years later, Dr Robert Schwartz reminisced: '. . . the first socially responsible shareholder resolution, submitted in 1969, questioned the morality of Dow's production of napalm . . . (but also) the galvanizing issue in the US was the issue of disinvestment of holdings in companies doing business in South Africa. This was a church- and university-led effort.'[2] The sustained pressure, and eventual success, of ethical investors on South Africa is covered in Chapter Eight.

The churches were very much in the lead at this time. When in 1971 a group of Methodist clergy, worried about the Vietnam War, discovered that there was no investment fund available to avoid profiting from the war, they simply set one up – the Pax World Fund. Pax is an open-ended mutual fund which: 'through its investment objectives aims to make a contribution to world peace through investment in companies producing life-supportive goods and services.' It does not invest in arms, tobacco, or gambling, but seeks out: 'nonwar-related industries, firms with fair employment practices, companies exercising pollution control, and some international development.'[3]

In fact, the US churches also formed one of the first ethical investment pressure groups, the Interfaith Center on Corporate Responsibility (ICCR) in 1973. Its Executive Director, the Rev Timothy Smith, has no doubts of its role in bringing the Church's concerns to the heart of corporate America: 'God's power and judgment touch all aspects of human life . . . it is urgently important that the Christian voice be heard in the boardrooms of America's corporations as we work to build an economic future based on justice and hope.'[4] In 1992 he looked back and noted how both sides had learned from this process: 'For about 20 years now religious bodies have been involved in trying to raise questions of conscience and social justice with the business community. We have learned much by doing so, both in style and how one does this ministry most effectively, and also learned a great deal from people in the business community with whom we have talked. I think probably at this point we have got the grudging respect of many in business.'[5]

At the same time there was a growing feeling that big business was ignoring consumers' interests in order to maximize profits. 'Consumer activists' such as Ralph Nader and his 'Nader's Raiders' produced evidence to this effect, such as the book, *Unsafe at any*

Speed in 1966 illustrating the poor safety record of US automobiles. This was coupled with critical proxy resolutions at General Motors' general meeting. Amy Domini sees this as another crucial starting point: 'The social proxy movement actually began with Campaign GM . . . a Nader organization targeted General Motors because it was then the largest industrial corporation in America. It offered nine resolutions to GM for submission to its shareholders at its 1970 annual meeting. These resolutions dealt with the needs of minorities. workers and consumers.'[6]

Not everybody was happy with this trend, and Milton Friedman, the father of monetarism, had his say: 'I have called the doctrine of corporate social responsibility "a fundamentally subversive doctrine" in a free society and have said that in such a society, there is one and only one social responsibility of business – to use its resources and engage in activities to increase its profits so long as it stays within the rules of the game, which is to say, engages in open and free competition without deception or fraud.'[7] Despite Friedman's opprobrium, socially responsible investing grew steadily in the 1970s and early 1980s. In 1972 the Dreyfus Third Century Fund was launched to encourage social progress and change. Dreyfus is one of the largest mutual fund managers in America, and the fund focused on two areas: environmental protection and improvement and social factors like health and safety at work, and equal opportunity employment. It then devised a complex evaluation system of ranking these factors. However, it had no absolute investment exclusions, leading Tim Smith to describe its criteria as: 'big enough to drive a nuclear weapon through.'[8]

Growth of US ethical funds

In the late 1970s the traditional investment management house of Franklin Management received increasing requests for social investment services. In response to this, one of its senior fund managers, Joan Bavaria, set up a new company, Franklin Research, to specialize in SRI research and fund management. Note that this was a discretionary fund management service rather than a mutual fund company. In other words, fairly wealthy investors came to Franklin with their own social investment criteria and the company then devised the appropriate individual portfolio for them. The company publishes a monthly newsletter called *Insight* on ethical investment matters and is known for the thoroughness of its screening procedures.

Franklin's *Social Assessment Ranking* uses eight broad measures of 'corporate citizenship', such as employee relations, environmental record, equal opportunities, energy, the nature of the product, etc. Companies get a rating of 1 to 5, for example on employee relations:

1 Company is a unique leader in its employment practices as made evident by innovative employee participation, competitive compensation, women and ethnic minorities in management positions.
2 Company has strong commitment to workers, maintains healthy work areas, etc.
3 Company has average employee relations with no reports of strikes, safety violations, etc.
4 Company's employee relations are below acceptable standards in one major areas (labour disputes, employee safety, discrimination.)
5 Company has serious ongoing employee relation problems as made evident by strikes, current national labour boycotts, safety violations, etc.[9]

New funds continued to be launched in the 1980s. In 1982 the Calvert Social Investment Fund was launched, offering ethical money market and equity investment funds. Calvert's aim was to 'provide an economic return to its investors and an economic and social return to society that will contribute to the quality of life for all.'[10]

It had four main social investment criteria for any company investment:

1 deliver safe products and services in ways that sustain the natural environment.
2 manage itself with participation throughout the organization in defining and achieving objectives
3 Negotiate fairly with its workers and provide opportunities for women, the disadvantaged, and others for whom equal opportunities have often been denied.
4 Foster awareness of a commitment to human goals, such as creativity, productivity, self-respect, and responsibility.

In 1989 Amy Domini was a founder partner in Kinder, Lydenberg, Domini & Co, the first stockbroking firm specializing in social

investment research and corporate responsibility issues. In 1990 the
Domini Social Index (DSI) was created, the first ever stock market
index based on social screening. The DSI includes about 400 of the
top 1,000 companies in the US, and as shown in Chapter Six, the
investment returns compared to the benchmark S&P 500 Index
have been impressive.

DOMINI SOCIAL INDEX SCREENS

Exclusionary Screens	Qualitative Screens
South Africa	Product quality and customer relations
Alcohol, tobacco, gambling	Environmental performance
Armaments	Corporate citizenship
	Employee relations

At the end of 1994 there were around $15bn invested in thirty-five
socially screened mutual funds, amounting to some 2.5% of all US
equity mutual funds, including $2.0bn in the Calvert Group alone.

US SOCIALLY RESPONSIBLE MUTUAL FUNDS

Calvert Group	7 varying screened funds
Catholic Brothers Investment Services	7 screened funds
Covenant Fund	
Domini Social Index	
Dreyfus Third Century Fund	
Green Century Fund	2 screened funds
Lincoln National Social Awareness Fund	
New Alternatives Fund	
Parnassus Funds	4 screened funds
Pax World Fund	
Pioneer Group	3 screened funds
Rightime Social Awareness Fund	
Shield Progressive Awareness Fund	
Working Assets	4 screened funds

Church activism and coordinating groups

Tim Smith feels that there is an advisory, as well as a prescriptive
role: 'Church activists serve as an early warning system. If the

churches are concerned about a social issue, then it is possible that the matter could be an important factor for the corporation. The fact that the churches hold stock adds to their clout – by proposing shareholder resolutions, the church representatives have the power to make public specific concerns.'[11] ICCR publishes a regular newsletter called *The Corporate Examiner*, which examines corporate policies and practices with regard to labour, the environment, equal opportunities, genetic engineering, military production, etc. ICCR also coordinates the ethical campaigns of 250 Catholic orders and Protestant denominations with some $40bn of church investment funds. As one US investment manager said to me: '. . . when Tim Smith rings up the boardrooms of corporate America, they don't just listen, they jump to attention!' Other groups researching issues of corporate responsibility include the Investor Responsibility Research Center (IRRC) which produces a monthly newsletter on detailing activist proxy battles as well as covering corporate governance, environment and general social investment issues, and the Council for Economic Priorities also produces a similar publication.

After ICCR, the most influential group is the Social Investment Forum founded in 1987 by Joan Bavaria as the coordinating body for the whole movement in the US. The Forum holds quarterly meetings across the US to inform and advise investors about socially responsible investment and advocate its greater use. With over 1,000 members active in SRI, it is a kind of clearing house whose quarterly newsletter monitors the performance of ethical funds and covers developments in the field. The Forum also regularly holds conventions and meetings. A sign of the future was the first ever *international* conference on socially responsible investment, held in Montreal in June 1994. Hosted by the Canadian Social Investment Organization in conjunction with the American Social Investment Forum and UKSIF, this conference was called, appropriately enough, *Going Global*, and brought together over 200 specialists for two days of intensive discussions.

It is worth noting the Canadian role in social investment. The first fund, the Ethical Growth Fund, appeared in 1986. By the end of 1993 there were six responsible funds, with around C$ 200m invested in them. The Canadian Taskforce on the Churches and Corporate Responsibility (TCCR) was founded soon after ICCR in the US, while as mentioned above, the Canadian Social Investment Organization hosted the first ever international SRI conference in

Montreal. In 1988 Earthscan Canada launched the *Corporate Ethics Monitor*, a bimonthly monitor on the social and environmental performance of Canadian business. The *Monitor* analyses corporate practices in depth in such areas as community relations, charitable giving, progressive staff policies, labour relations, environmental record, etc., as well as a broad coverage of ethical investment in Canada.

Ethical Investment in the UK

In the UK church funds had been run on ethical lines since the formation of the Church Commissioners in 1948, but the concept of an ethical unit trust available to the general public was not mooted until the early 1970s. Here again, and at about the same time as his American colleagues, a member of the Methodist Church took the lead. Charles Jacob was a Methodist local (lay) preacher who in the 1960s became a partner in the top stockbroking firm of James Capel & Co. In the early 1970s, on returning to the City after an enforced three-year absence on health grounds, he changed direction to manage and centralize church funds for the Central Finance Board (CFB) of the Methodist Church as its first Investment Manager.

Unlike the Church Commissioners, who inherited their large investment funds in 1948 (see Chapter Ten for details), Charles Jacob initially had only a small fund to manage, but during his fifteen years in office his responsibilities multiplied nearly a hundredfold. This achievement of the CFB is one of the lesser known success stories of ethical investment in the UK. To finance his work he also took on board the management of certain unit trusts, charity, university and insurance portfolios. It was while working with the unit trust group that he first outlined his vision of producing an ethical vehicle offering a diversity of interest for the private investor.

In 1972–73 Charles Jacob, supported by Jeremy Edwards (now Managing Director of Henderson Administration) and Richard Rowntree of the Joseph Rowntree Social Services Trust, formulated a proposal for a new type of unit trust called 'Stewardship', an allusion to the rightful use of money as described in the Parable of the Talents (St Matthew, 25:14–29). While loosely modelled on the example of the ethical mutual funds in the US, the fund was constructed with a positive bias towards investment in companies whose products and services were of benefit to the community. While the fund avoided certain sectors (tobacco, breweries, gambling, armaments and South Africa), the constructive aims were paramount. As Charles Jacob said later: 'Such negative screening was never considered as a primary aim of the UK venture, which was envisaged right from the early days as a means of positive investment.'[12] Despite support from a large number of churches and charities, in November 1973 it was rejected by the Department of Trade: 'To our utter surprise and dismay it was turned down! It appeared that we were ahead of our time – the Inspectors were apparently concerned with a conflict of capital and conscience, and were not prepared to sanction the new concept . . . there was no mention of an ethical unit trust in this country for the next five years.'[13]

A further milestone within the Methodist Church was the establishment of an Ethics of Investment Committee in 1983 'to advise the Central Finance Board of ethical considerations relating to finance.'[14] Subsequently the Methodists joined with the Church of England and the Church Commissioners in the setting up of a Church Investors Advisory Group on ethical matters. This group was expanded over the years to cover all the main church denominations including the Quakers.

If the Methodist Church was one of the main contributors to the establishment of ethical investment in the UK, the Society of Friends (Quakers) was the other. Quakers played a significant role in the formation in 1973 by Charles Medawar of the Public Interest Research Centre and its offshoot Social Audit. Inspired by the work of Ralph Nader in the US, and closely linked with the Consumers' Association in the UK, Social Audit externally audited a number of large companies, often without the cooperation of the management, on social and consumer issues and their impact on areas such as employment and on the environment.

In 1979 the Young Friends Central Committee set up its working group on investments as a response to concern that the investment of Quaker central funds did not reflect the ethical beliefs of the Society. This produced a series of reports starting with *Responsible Investment – a Challenge for Quakers* (1980). Perhaps the most important result of all this work was the establishment of the Ethical Investment Research and Information Service (EIRIS) to provide a monitoring service for investments. This was largely funded by the

Society of Friends, the (Quaker) Rowntree Charitable Trusts, the Methodist Division of Social Responsibility, and Oxfam. Its first Executive Secretary, and later Director, was Peter Webster. He was a member of the Young Friends Central Committee as well as being a young Oxford graduate in mathematics who had also been active in social work. At the same time there was a major debate inside one of the UK's largest insurance companies on ethical matters. Friends Provident, as its name suggests, had been established on Quaker principles and by the end of the 1970s the management were undecided as to what extent these could still be implemented. Should Friends Provident stick to its ethical principles or should it become a normal insurance company like any other?

In 1980 Charles Jacob renewed his efforts to launch an ethical fund with the support of Nicholas Goodison, at that time Chairman of the Stock Exchange. Quakers and Methodists had worked together in 1973 and did so again now with support for these proposals from members of the Joseph Rowntree Charitable Trust. After considerable delays, approval in principle was finally granted by the DTI in late 1983. Tragically for Charles Jacob: '. . . by a strange quirk of fate, after so many years of waiting, by the time approval in principle was received from the DTI following consider- able delays, I was being faced with a vast expansion of both Church and company business and knew that I would no longer be able to give the time necessary for the depths of research necessary for the efficient management of an Ethical Unit Trust.'[16]

The problem was solved by two Rowntree trustees who knew of the ethical dilemmas facing Friends Provident, and were able quickly to persuade the latter that the establishment of an ethical unit trust would enable the company to split its investment into ethical and ordinary bands. And so it was that in May 1984 the Friends Provident Stewardship Trust was launched, the first ethical unit trust in the UK. Charles Jacob may not have run it, but his achievements are generally recognized as making him the 'father of ethical investment' in the UK, while he was to become one of the original members of the Committee of Reference of the new fund along with Charles Medawar and Trevor Jepson of the Joseph Rowntree Trust.

UK ETHICAL INVESTMENT – CRUCIAL DATES
and New Fund Launches (in italics)

1972
Charles Jacob becomes Investment Manager of Central Finance Board of the Methodist Church.
1973
Social Audit established
1972–73
Initial Inquiries to set up 'Stewardship' fund.
1979
Young Friends Investment Group set up to examine Quaker Investment Policy.
1983
Foundation of EIRIS
Methodist Ethics of Investment Committee founded
1984
Scargill vs Cowan court case
Friends Provident Stewardship Trust
1985
Social Audit Report on Investment in Tobacco Shares
Medical Investments Fund
Friends Provident North American Stewardship
Fidelity Famous Names Trust
1986
Buckmaster (nowCS) Fellowship Trust
1987
Abbey Ethical
N.M. Conscience
Target Global Opportunities Trust
Friends Provident Stewardship Income
1988
Christian Ethical Investment Group founded
Allchurches Amity Trust
Scot Equitable Ethical Trust
Acorn Ethical Trust
Merlin Jupiter Ecology Trust – first 'green fund'.
1989
Ecumenical Committee for Corporate Responsibility set up
INAISE established

Merlin International Green – first ethical investment trust
Henderson Green PEP
Homeowners Green Chip Trust
Eagle Star Environmental Trust
Sovereign Ethical Trust
TSB Environmental Investor Trust
Sovereign Ethical Trust
1990
Valdez Principles Promoted
PIRC launched Green Investor Code
Worldwide Fund for Nature ethical investment story
CIS Environ Trust
Clerical Medical Evergreen Trust
1991
UK Social Investment Forum launched
New Consumer launches Changing Corporate Values
Bishop of Oxford High Court case
NPI Global Care Trust
1992
Church Commissioners publish ethical investment policy
Co-op Bank's ethical loan policy
Abtrust Ethical Trust
Commercial Union Environmental Inv Trust
1993
Fiona Price Opportunity 2000 PEP
Friends Provident Ethical Investment Trust
Environment Investment Company
South Africa bans lifted
1994
Professional Investor green pages
Equitable Life Ethical trust
Sharp Ethical PEP

Three Campaigning Groups

As in the United States, a number of groups have arisen to help
push the subject forward – essentially to advocate and develop the
idea of ethical investment and greater corporate responsibility.
Taking them in calendar order of foundation, they are Christian

Ethical Investment Group (CEIG) 1988; Ecumenical Committee for Corporate Responsibility (ECCR) 1989, and UK Social Investment Forum (UKSIF) in 1991. EIRIS and PIRC have also both made major contributions to the field, but have each been covered in detail, in Chapters Two and Ten respectively.

The Church of England is a large investment manager in its own right. The centralized funds of the Church are run by the Church Commissioners, with the Central Board of Finance investing monies for the local dioceses, among others. As described in Chapter Ten, both have historically adopted ethical exclusion policies amounting to some 12% of the UK stock market. During the 1980s there was a growing feeling in the Church that the Church's investment managers should adopt a tougher line on South African investment. As Bill Whiffen, Secretary of CEIG later explained:

In 1986 the concern of the Churches around the world for the situation in South Africa led many to the view that the time for the progressive disengagement from the South African economy had come. The General Synod of the Church of England overwhelmingly passed a resolution on these lines. There was some sadness that the Commissioners did not respond to this change of mood by adopting much stricter criteria on the South African question. Instead they were only prepared to rule out companies which had more than a small part of their business in South Africa. To have complied with what was being asked . . . would, they said, have ruled out £80m of the Commissioners' investments and seriously distorted their portfolio.[17]

In 1988 these sentiments led Synod members to form the Christian Ethical Investment Group (CEIG) 'to promote a stronger ethical investment policy in the Church of England.' Although mainly an Anglican group, it welcomed members from other churches. CEIG's initial purpose was to persuade the Church Commissioners to sell holdings of companies with significant investments in South Africa. When that failed, Richard Harries, the Bishop of Oxford, Michael Bourke, now Bishop of Wolverhampton, and Canon Bill Whiffen filed a case for judicial review in the High Court. *The Bishop of Oxford et al vs the Church Commissioners* is discussed in Chapter Eleven. Suffice it to say that while the Bishop did not win his case, it was invaluable for the clarification of charity law with regard to ethical investment. CEIG played a major part in preparing and arranging funding for the Bishop of Oxford's case.

Whilst sticking to its original purpose, CEIG has also played a major role in developing mutual understanding of the Christian and financial world through a number of seminars and conferences often held in conjunction with EIRIS. In 1990 it held a seminar on : *Ethical investment – an idea whose time has come*, and in October 1991 on *Practical Imperatives for Churches*, with papers on ethical investment practice by the Methodist Church and the Church of Scotland. October 1992 saw *What has the Christian Faith to say to those in fund management?* with powerful speeches from Chris Holmes, of NPI, and Mark Hayes, of Shared Interest. In May 1994 CEIG on its own hosted a weekend conference, *Investing for the Future*, with over twenty leading experts not only in the field of ethical investment, but also law, banking and business generally, and cosponsored by the Co-operative Bank and the Ecclesiastical Insurance Group. The aim was to subject the debate on ethical investment, social justice and environmental issues to: 'some rigorous intellectual scrutiny, both in its ethical basis and in its practical application . . . the Christian tradition of theology and ethics has insights to contribute, but that it must also listen to those with experience of the investment world . . . the conference aims to advance thinking and practice in this area, and to generate ideas which will command respect.'[18] Most participants thought the conference succeeded in these aims.

At the end of 1992 CEIG produced a near-sixty-page report called *Our Best Interest*[19] to show how the Church might carry out an ethical investment policy in practice. Although the Friends Provident Stewardship fund emphasized both positive and negative criteria, many later funds seemed to lay more emphasis on negative exclusions. The report therefore argued the case for moving the emphasis of socially responsible investment away from what it saw as *a negative one of avoidance* to a *positive one* of what it called *constructive engagement*. This meant that investors should work with company managements to try to persuade them to improve their behaviour, rather than walking away by just selling their shares. (As the report stated, Jesus did not stand aside from tax collectors, but worked to convert them.) As described on page 21, a methodology of *ethical credit scoring* on a rating of one to ten was suggested. The report suggested four screening categories: the traditional one of *product acceptability*; the general *business ethics* of the company; how business affects the *social fabric* such as health and safety at work and equal opportunities, but also via Sunday trading and the abuse of monopoly power, and finally in terms of *environmental excellence*.

ECCR was founded in 1989, although it only really took off in 1992 when funding from the J. Rowntree Trust, Christian Aid and CAFOD enabled it to 'put the organisation on the map of church corporate responsibility action.' As its name suggests, it is modelled on the ICCR in the US, and Timothy Smith gave the keynote speech at the initial conference ECCR held in London in March 1992 to start its Race Equality in Employment Project (REEP). ECCR describes itself as 'a British focus for the study of corporate responsibility in both the churches and transnational corporations (TNCs) ; to produce educational material on the issues raised by TNCs, and to aid appropriate representations or campaigning by churches in the British Isles, especially where these churches are shareholders in British based TNCs.'[20] ECCR publishes a quarterly newsletter and has hosted a number of conferences on its main themes: corporate social responsibility with a particular emphasis on the responsibility of Western companies to the Third World and to the environment. Specific topics covered include: ethnic minority employment, health and safety at work, environmental protection, and the defence industries. Publications such as *Buried Talents* (1992), described the employment policies of some of Britain's top companies in regard to the employment of people from ethnic minorities.

The Greening of Industry? (1992) followed up the Rio summit to see how many of the UK's largest companies were following even the modest environmental requirements of the ICC Business Charter for Sustainable Development. ECCR found that sixty out of the top 100 companies had not signed even that. Letters were sent to the remaining sixty, of which thirty-one replied. Only seven of those had considered adopting the Charter. ECCR Coordinator Crispin White wrote: 'by the end of the report (readers) may be asking themselves whether a self-regulatory structure can ever be a satisfactory system to protect the environment . . . issues include the (low) status that environmental issues are given in companies . . . and the question of the (almost non-existent) training for the employees of the company.'[21] *On the Damascus Road* (1993) was a highly interesting study of the conversion and diversification of the defence industry in Hampshire following the so-called peace dividend. Hampshire is an area with a high concentration of suppliers of military equipment, especially close to the great army bases at Aldershot and the navy at Portsmouth, plus the Royal Aircraft Establishment at Farnborough.

At the end of 1993 ECCR produced a massive 400-page report on one British multinational ICI (and its spin-off pharmaceutical subsidiary, Zeneca). An abridged forty-page version, *Is the Best Good Enough?* was launched at a conference in April 1994 with speakers including the Bishop of Oxford, Rob Margetts, an Executive Director of ICI, and Keith Standring, National Secretary of the GMB union, as well as Mildred Neville, of CAFOD. That conference was a good example of increasing dialogue between the churches and industry. The same month also saw ECCR produce *Benchmarks*, thirty-seven points to measure and assess corporate responsibility, which is defined in relation to all the seven categories of stakeholders: local community, global environment, customers, employees, shareholders, suppliers and directors. 'The foundation principle that ECCR will want to work to is to hold a concept that corporate responsibility is to be applied in equal terms to all the STAKEHOLDERS.'[22] *Benchmarks* can be read with benefit by anyone interested in corporate responsibility and how to assess it.

The UK Social Investment Forum (UKSIF) was modelled on the US Social Investment Forum when it was established in 1991, with the object of bringing together the various strands of socially responsible investment in the UK and to act as a focus and voice for the industry. The Forum has three classes of membership: corporate, charity and individual. Its Board of Directors includes some of the best known names in ethical investment in the UK: Tessa Tennant (Chair), Peter Webster, Charles Jacob and Executive Director Pat Conaty of the Birmingham Settlement. UKSIF's aims are:
1 to inform, educate, and provide a forum for discussion and debate for our membership and the public at large about issues and developments in the SRI field.
2 to promote the understanding of socially responsible investment and to encourage the development of appropriate social investment practices and vehicles, both in terms of Stock Exchange investment and the wider Social Economy.
3 to identify, encourage and help develop working models which

demonstrate the effectiveness of SRI in protecting and preserving the environment, alleviating social hardship and stimulating sustainable economic development.

UKSIF started with a one-day conference in April 1991 on social investment and its future, and the conference stressed the need to combine 'ethical investment funds' with community-based development. After a steady start, UKSIF seemed to move up a gear in 1993 when Tessa Tennant and Pat Conaty took over the leading roles. There was a major review of the organization's purpose and strategy, while UKSIF's first ever newsletter appeared. In 1993/4 the Forum arranged seven meetings, including three major conferences in the first half of 1994. With CEIG in February it hosted *Faith in the City – The Social Use of Money* which was held in Birmingham. *Financing the Social Economy* in April was an all-day session chaired by Tony Gibson, of Neighbourhood Initiatives, with a number of other experts on community development including Pat Conaty; Angela Monaghan (on the US experience); Glen Saunders, of Mercury Provident and David Ralley, of ICOF. *Social Investment for Charities and the Third Sector Seminar* in May 1994 was another joint venture, this time with the Charities Aid Foundation. Speakers included Michael Brophy, Chief Executive of CAF, and Geoff Mulgan, of DEMOS (author of a major study on charity finance) as well as other speakers examining different ways in which the voluntary sector and social investment overlapped.

Even the UKSIF AGM at the end of June 1994 was no somnolent affair. As well as the necessary legal business, there were sessions on *Tomorrow's Company and Social Investment*, and *Women and Financial Services – Needs and Service Gaps*. Pat Conaty was justifiably pleased. 'I only work one day a week (for the Forum), but despite limited resources we've managed to arrange seven major events. That's what social investment is all about – people making things happen!'[23]

Details on how to contact CEIG, ECCR and UKSIF are in Appendix Four.

CHAPTER EIGHT

South Africa – A Case Study

Peace is not the absence of tension, but the presence of justice.
MARTIN LUTHER KING.[1]
Free at last, free at last, thank God, free at last. This is a joyous night for the human spirit.
NELSON MANDELA, ELECTION NIGHT, 3 MAY 1994.[2]

People sometimes ask, what is the point of ethical investment? If you sell your tobacco shares someone else will buy them. You may decide to withdraw your money from a bank with a dubious ethical record, but most people will not. The record of the twenty-year battle of financial sanctions against South Africa shows that there *is* a point, that sustained campaigns from ethical investors and bank boycotts can exert sufficient pressure to bring even a strong government to its knees despite possessing a large security apparatus and being blessed with abundant natural resources.

The US: Sullivan Principles and initial boycotts

Modern ethical investment arose in the United States around 1970, based on three themes: opposition to college endowment funds profiting from the hated Vietnam War; Ralph Nader's consumer rights activism and the issue of investment in South Africa. The Vietnam War now seems like ancient history, while even Ralph Nader's campaigns about the poor quality of General Motors cars feel like a vague memory. South Africa, however, is still a very real issue, and it is doubtful that if financial sanctions had not been exerted whether 1994 would have seen free democratic elections at last.

1970 was the year that South Africa was ejected from world bodies such as the United Nations, and in the same year the

Reverend Leon Sullivan, a keen supporter of civil rights for blacks, put forward proposals for minimum standards for US companies operating in South Africa. The Sullivan Principles were formally codified and launched in 1977:

1) Nonsegregation of all races in eating, comfort, locker room and work
2) Equal and fair employment practices for all employees
3) Equal pay for equal work
4) Training programmes for blacks and coloureds to prepare them for supervisory jobs
5) Steadily increase number of blacks in supervisory positions
6) Help employees outside work in such areas as housing, transportation, schooling, recreation and health.

The European Community passed a similar code of conduct, although many observers thought its definitions, particularly on minimum wages, were so weak as to be almost useless.

In the US South African investment was always a high-profile issue. A number of civil rights, labour and Church institutions arose in the 1970s to monitor company adherence to the Principles, of which the most well known is the Interfaith Center for Corporate Responsibility (ICCR) run by the Reverend Tim Smith. In 1982 Connecticut became the first legislature to establish social performance criteria for state investments and required all companies in which it invested to follow the Sullivan Principles. Trust funds run by the University of Wisconsin went further; following a period of consistent campus unrest and a legal opinion from the Wisconsin State Attorney General, university funds sold all their holdings of companies which did not pass the Sullivan test. New York State followed suit with its pension funds.

However, opinion was hardening in the 1980s as repression deepened in South Africa, particularly following the State of Emergency in 1985. Anti-apartheid groups campaigned for local government and labour pension funds to exclude all direct investment in the country and to sell the shares of all US companies that operated there. Many investment managers felt that this went too far but were willing to exclude US companies which operated strategic industries that supported the apartheid state, but kept non-strategic activities, particularly if they were industries such as food production that benefited the black majority. In 1983 the state of Massachusetts passed a measure prohibiting the investment of state funds in companies or banks doing business in South Africa. The US financial system took note of socially responsible investment in a big way when the two biggest pension funds in America, those of New York City and California, both issued social investment guidelines around the same time, both concerning South Africa.

The New York Pension funds had over $15bn in total assets, when in 1984 they set up the Division of Investment Responsibility. While the State legislature did not legally order its pension funds to sell their South African shareholdings, it required its trustees to be aware of such issues and in so doing, created an ethical investment policy for itself. As the Division stated:

> Critical elements include our right to vote proxies in ways that will help shape the broad social environment, our sponsorship and support of shareholder proposals and, ultimately, our decision to selectively divest both equities and fixed income securities supporting the regime in South Africa . . . US corporations doing business abroad are virtual extensions of the US itself and should embody its laws and ethical standards. It is quite proper to ask them this: if they abide by anti-discrimination and equal opportunity laws in the US, should they not then be required to resist the immorality of apartheid in South Africa?[3]

In 1986 the Californian state legislature passed a legislative amendment which required California's $50bn state pension funds to divest over $6bn from companies which had activities in South Africa. The argument was that the fiduciary duties of the trustees should be legally redefined to include social and environmental standards as well as the usual ones of finance. This was not universally popular. Basil Schwan, the chief investment officer of the main $34bn Calpers fund, complained that: 'they provided an economic argument for what's really a social issue.'[4] However, many other states followed suit. The amount of US pension fund money that was ethically screened regarding South Africa surged following the 1985 State of Emergency as the chart opposite shows:

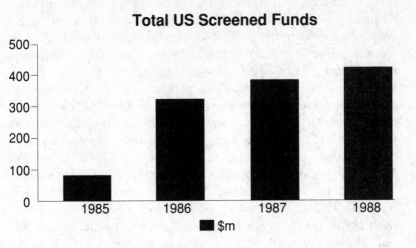

Total US Screened Funds

■ $m

It should be emphasized again that while these investment boycotts excluded direct investment in South African shares and loans, they also put huge pressure on US companies operating there to abide by the Sullivan Principles, and forced some of the largest and most powerful companies in the world such as IBM and Ford Motors to curtail their activities in the country. Ford is a particularly interesting example. Ford was the owner of a majority stake in the main South African car manufacturer, Samcor, but by the middle 1980s the company found that an increasing number of US investment funds were selling their holdings of Ford stock because of its South African involvement. There was also a growing movement for American labour and local authorities to boycott Ford products. The last straw for the company was the passage of the Anti-Apartheid Act in 1986, since it meant that Ford was prohibited from the necessary investment in Samcor to help it modernize its product line. William Kelly, a Ford official commented: 'When it appeared there would be major restrictions on how we do business, it began to seem that it was less tenable to stay . . . Our actions were not taken with the hope that we would get rid of the sanctions in the US. We wanted to disinvest under conditions that would preserve jobs and would make a contribution to black economic empowerment.'[4]

Ford's early attempts at restructuring Samcor were described by the trade unions as 'corporate camouflage', and it was obliged to sit down and negotiate directly with COSATU, the Congress of South African Trades Unions. The deal ultimately hammered out in November 1987 involved Ford giving the majority of its stake in Samcor (shares worth 24%) to an employee ownership trust, while its remaining 18% holding was sold to the giant mining conglomerate, Anglo-American. To reach agreement, Ford was also obliged to allow three trade union members to sit on the board of Samcor, and make charitable donations of some $10m in the Port Elizabeth area where the main plant was operated. Samcor also kept the critical right to keep using the Ford name for its cars. In the summer of 1987 Citicorp also sold its stake in its South African subsidiary to First National Bank of South Africa, the new name of Barclays National. This represented a concession to the continuous pressure from US investors for the bank to withdraw completely, but it also reflected the fact that its customers were disappearing. Citicorp SA was set up in 1958 primarily to service the subsidiaries of US multinational companies operating there. However, as more and more US companies disposed of their South African operations, Citicorp SA's sales and profits declined. Between 1985 and 1987, 135 US industrial companies totally pulled out of the country! Citicorp's withdrawal meant that there were no longer any US banks acting as a commercial bank within the country.

The Banks and the 1985 Debt Crisis

American pressure was not just on investment institutions to boycott the country, and on US companies to wind down their activities there. It hit at the heart of any financial system – the banks. Historically, South African banking has been dominated by British followed by American banks. The latter's presence consisted of the giant 'money centre' banks: Citibank; Chase Manhattan; Manufacturers Hanover, Security Pacific and Morgan Guaranty were the most prominent. In 1984, Citibank was threatened with the withdrawal by New York City Pension Fund of all its $20bn in deposits with the bank, if the latter did not cease making new loans to the apartheid regime. Not surprisingly, in February 1985 Citibank agreed to do so.

The last straw for the American banks was the declaration of the partial State of Emergency on 20 June 1985. In July 1985 the second largest US lender, Chase Manhattan, followed Citicorp's example and stated that it would not only not make new loans but that it would not renew old ones when they expired. Such 'roll-overs' of old loans being renewed are almost automatic in the banking world, and Chase's decision was a major blow to the Botha government. (Chase's Chairman, Jake Butcher, even described the country as an 'international pariah'.)[6] In fact, whereas most governments normally borrow in the form of long-term loans that last for ten years or more, virtually all of South Africa's debt was in the form of short-term bank loans which had to be renewed at least annually, and therefore the Chase decision caused an immediate financial crisis which resulted in South Africa announcing a default on its debts.

There is another point which should be made, and it is one which has not been generally recognized in the context of South Africa. In the 1980s financial deregulation made it easy for large companies and governments to borrow directly from the major capital markets and bypass the banks. In other words, rather than pay interest to the banks, who themselves borrowed the money from the money markets of New York, London and Tokyo, large companies could issue so-called 'commercial paper' themselves on the money markets and eliminate the banks' fees. Another huge source for loans which also bypassed the commercial banks and which tended to be used by governments was the so-called 'Eurobond' market. This simply meant that investment banks would issue loans for a country or company, and sell quietly to private investors in Europe who found it a tax-efficient way of receiving the interest.

While South Africa was able to raise some money in this way, it raised much less than it might have expected. The reason for this is that the world's largest investment banks are American, i.e. such companies as Goldman Sachs, Morgan Stanley and Merrill Lynch, who have the so-called 'placing power' each to sell hundreds of millions of pounds' worth of Eurobonds. Being warned by big US investors such as the Californian State pension funds not to deal with South Africa or risk losing all their highly profitable US business with them, they refused to deal with the apartheid régime. It is noticeable that they were not involved in Eurobond loans to South Africa from 1982:

MAIN EUROBOND UNDERWRITERS
TO SOUTH AFRICA 1982 TO 1984

	Bank	Country	Amount $m
1	Hill Samuel	UK	1397
2	Nedbank	SA	1158
3	UBS	Swiss	1111
4	SBC	Swiss	1038
5	Paribas	France	927
6	Suez	France	897
7	Bay Verein	Germany	861
8	Dresdner	Germany	847
9	CCF	France	847
10	Ost Lander	Austria	846

In August 1985 South Africa simply ran out of money and was forced to declare default on its loans, that is, it admitted that it could not afford to pay the interest on them or repay the capital when due. Whereas other Third World countries had done so from 1982 onwards, South Africa was unique in that it was in a fairly strong financial position. South Africa's foreign debt of $24bn was much less than the crippling debt burdens of over $100bn each carried by Brazil and Mexico, while its ability to pay was much higher. Economists normally measure a country's ability to pay its debts as its 'debt service ratio'; this is the proportion of its export earnings which are required to pay the interest on its foreign debt. Most Latin American countries had debt service ratios of over 40% when they admitted that they could no longer pay; South Africa's debt service ratio was only 9% in 1985, a level which is normally easily sustainable. The value of the currency collapsed – and despite the introduction of a system of foreign exchange controls, the value of the financial rand (the type used for investment) fell from $1.00 to $0.21 by the end of 1986.

What went wrong? Partly the large and increasing costs of running the apartheid system meant that this could no longer be funded at home but had to be supplemented by foreign borrowings. In 1980 spending on the security services took 18% of government spending, but by 1984 this had risen to 28% and was set to rise further after the declaration of the State of Emergency in the townships. Secondly, there was an ecological crisis; South

Falling value of rand 1980–1986

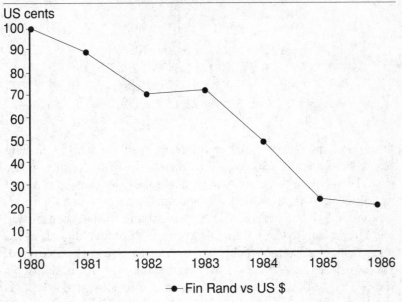

Value of Financial Rand

Fin Rand vs US $

Africa has traditionally been a large food exporter, but a series of droughts in 1982–85 meant that it had to import food for the first time. Given the importance of the Afrikaner farmer in the National-ist Party machine, this also put a further big burden on the state budget deficit in terms of farm support payments. Finally, the gold price declined steadily in the 1980s from a high of $850 an ounce in 1980 to around $320 an ounce in 1984. Gold traditionally accounts for around 50% of South Africa's export earnings and the weak gold price put further strain on the country. Nevertheless, it is hard to imagine that the basic strength of South Africa's resource base would not easily have enabled it to obtain finance to cover these problems if ethical investors worldwide had not been forcing com-panies to leave the country, and if Pretoria had not found itself excluded from the world's money markets on ethical grounds.

MAIN LENDERS TO
SOUTH AFRICAN GOVERNMENT 1985

	$bn	%
UK Banks	5.6	23.2%
US Banks	3.9	16.1%
Swiss Banks	2.0	8.3%
German Banks	1.4	5.6%
Other	11.2	46.8%
TOTAL	24.1	100%

One other interesting point is, while most of the world's leading banks were already winding down their links with Pretoria in the early 1980s, the Swiss banks were doing the opposite. Switzerland has three big banks which are among the largest in the world: Union Bank of Switzerland (UBS); Swiss Bank Corporation (SBC); and Credit Suisse (CS). They also run the Zürich gold pool, which along with the London gold market (run by Standard Chartered, Kleinwort Benson, Westpac, Midland Bank, and Rothschilds), is the biggest outlet for South Africa's main precious metal. UBS is the largest of the Swiss 'Big Three' and believed to be the most active player in the gold pool. UBS was also the bank most active in growing its loan portfolio in this period.

US political pressure finally paid off in 1986 when Congress passed the Comprehensive Anti-Apartheid Act (CAAA). This was actually vetoed by President Reagan, but the measure had received such public support that it was able to gain the two-thirds majority in both houses of Congress necessary to override the Presidential veto. The Act's aim was to: 'set forth a comprehensive and complete framework to guide the efforts of the United States in helping to bring an end to apartheid in South Africa and lead to the establishment of a nonracial, democratic form of government.'[7]

Among other measures it banned US banks from the making of new loans to South Africa, although political pressure had already achieved this a year earlier. The European Community set forth similar financial sanctions at the same time. The UK seemed to drag its feet until Mrs Thatcher came under huge pressure at the Commonwealth summit in Kuala Lumpur in October 1989, and the Foreign Office then issued voluntary 'guidelines' which in fact prohibited new loans to the country.

Barclays Bank and the UK Experience

The UK was slow to follow the US experience, despite the fact that for historical reasons it was the biggest foreign investor in the country. The Conservative Government that came to power in 1979 seemed (at best) disinterested in this as an issue, while the UK obviously lacked the force of the black activist lobby in the United States. Nevertheless, a number of groups, many of them church-based, pushed for change. In the early 1970s Christian Concern for Southern Africa (CCSA) was set up with a mainly Anglican and Methodist membership, and this produced reports on the South African subsidiaries of such major UK companies as ICI and GEC.

One of the leading lights of CCSA was the Methodist minister David Haslam who made a visit to South Africa in 1973 and on his return became convinced that one of the real problems was not just British companies operating in South Africa, but also the provision of bank credit by British banks to the South African Government. He founded a sister organization to CCSA called End Loans to South Africa (ELTSA). This put down the first ever shareholder resolution on ethical grounds when it put down a motion at the 1977 Annual General Meeting of the Midland Bank instructing the bank to end loans to South Africa. Although the resolution was not carried, it did evoke a response to David Haslam from the company: 'They said that they had not loaned any money since 1975, and would not be making any further loans in the future. We saw this, although the company would not admit it, as achieving our aims.'[8]

Of course eight years later the South African Government suspended interest and debt payments. David Haslam again: 'We felt particularly vindicated when South Africa stopped loan repayments in September 1985 – withholding $6.5bn owed to UK banks. We said to them "if you had listened to us ten years ago, you wouldn't be in this mess" – and our advice was free!'[9]

Another active group was the Anti-Apartheid Movement which had Bishop Trevor Huddleston as its President and whose classic 1956 book, *Naught for your Comfort* had brought home to many British Christians the true reality of life for the bulk of the South African population. These groups put huge pressure on the UK banks which were at the heart of the South African financial system: Barclays and Standard Chartered. The biggest commercial bank in South Africa was Barclays National (now called First National Bank of South Africa, see below), a subsidiary of Barclays UK, with Standard Chartered the second largest. Probably the most obvious symbol of the British campaign was the Barclays Bank 'Shadow Report'. This was deliberately designed to look at first sight like the report and accounts which Barclays produced every year. The 'Shadow Board' was set up in 1981 to monitor Barclays' activities in South Africa, and to produce an annual report publishing its findings. The Secretary was the Rev. David Haslam who had set up ELTSA eight years before. While Barclays denied supporting the apartheid regime, job advertisements inviting (white) managers to go to South Africa gave a different impression.

As well as publishing the reports, the Shadow Board helped to coordinate one of the biggest consumer boycotts ever held in Britain. As well as a significant number of individuals, trades unions, charities and a number of educational establishments including several Oxford colleges all withdrew their money from Barclays. Possibly the most significant in terms of size was the action of local authorities; for example, Rochdale Council took all its £200m deposit business away from Barclays in 1985. In August 1985 Barclays finally cracked when it announced that it would not be taking up its rights in a share issue by Barclays National in South Africa. The affect was to change the status of Barclays South Africa from a subsidiary to an 'associated company' in which Barclays owned merely 40%. This change of legal status meant that Barclays no longer had to consolidate Barclays National in its own accounts. In August 1987 Standard Chartered followed suit in an even more dramatic way; it sold its entire holding in Standard Chartered South Africa to a group of local investors such as the two big insurers, Liberty Life and Old Mutual. Standard Chartered Bank originated in South Africa, so this was a huge psychological blow to Pretoria. British banking retrenchment was completed in October 1987 when the Trustee Savings Bank (TSB) took over the merchant bank Hill Samuel and announced that it would sell the latter's large South African operation as soon as possible.

Customer boycotts and shareholder pressure

Anti-apartheid groups did not just target the banks. The biggest user of South African gold in the UK was the Ratners' jewellery chain, which controlled 31% of the UK jewellery market not only through Ratners' shops but also via such names as H. Samuel and Ernest Jones. Ratners was also a large jewellery retailer in the US. The company was very vulnerable to a customer boycott since the black community was a major customer in both countries. In the UK, black MP Bernie Grant headed a campaign which was given active support by the National Conference of Methodist Churches who actually provided pickets outside Ratners' shops. In July 1990 Ratners conceded, and agreed henceforth not to sell South African gold through its shops. A similar campaign had ruined sales of South Africa's gold coin, the Krugerrand, whose European sales dropped from 15m in 1970 to less than 0.5m in 1986 before the EC banned their sale.

The other main area targeted was oil. South Africa has no indigenous oil reserves and was therefore vulnerable to a boycott, while energy was of course of the greatest strategic importance. A voluntary UN oil embargo cost the regime an estimated $2.2bn a year. The giant Anglo-Dutch oil company Royal Dutch/Shell was believed to be a significant supplier of oil to Pretoria and was therefore the subject of a share action campaign like the one against Barclays. This campaign obtained the official support of the Methodist Conference and involved substantial shareholder support for motions opposing oil being supplied to South Africa at both the Shell and Royal Dutch AGMs for many years. US investors in the latter gained votes of over 2% of the company's total shares calling for an extraordinary general meeting to order Shell/Royal Dutch to follow the embargo.

Public action to persuade British investment professionals who run the bulk of UK financial assets to sell holdings in South Africa and to put pressure on British companies active there, was slower to occur. The first explicitly ethical unit did not emerge until 1984, while the big fund managers who run the country's huge pension funds were restrained by the 1984 Arthur Scargill judgment into believing that it was legally incorrect to consider ethical matters when making investment decisions. (As is shown in Chapter Eleven, this point of view is debatable.) The big pension funds were, however, under strong pressure from their trades union trustees, and therefore most excluded direct investment in South Africa on the grounds of ethics *and* financial risk, thus preventing any legal quibbles. (Indeed, after the Scargill case, the TUC produced a report arguing exactly that: *South Africa, a Bad Risk for Investment TUC, 1986.*) Pensions and Investment Research indicated in 1993 that a total of around £60bn of British investment funds excluded South African investments. While this looked impressive at first sight, this was only 8% of all funds and did not specify which criteria were being used. Most fund managers were probably only excluding *direct* investment in the country; and also doing so principally on the basis of risk, rather than on ethical grounds.

The fund managers really excluding British companies operating in South Africa consisted of ethical unit and investment trusts, who normally prohibited South African investment under a general category of 'oppressive regimes', plus the three fund management companies linked to the churches: the Church Commissioners, the Central Board of Finance of the Church of England (CBF), and the Central Board of Finance of the Methodist Church (CFB). (As described in Chapter Ten, the Church Commissioners run the central funds of the Church of England, while the CBF administers local diocesan funds, and also is a very large fund manager for charities in its own right The two Anglican bodies share a coordinated ethical investment philosophy. Some Anglicans felt that their two investment companies were not bearing sufficient attention to their Christian witness. The Christian Ethical Investment Group (CEIG) therefore gave strong backing to Richard Harries, the Bishop of Oxford, in his legal battle to compel the Church Commissioners to prioritize ethical issues when considering investments, with South Africa the keystone of his case:

> Over a number of years the General Synod of the Church of England called upon the Church Commissioners to disinvest from companies with a stake in the South African economy. The Church Commissioners responded by withdrawing their investments from companies that in their judgment had a major stake in South Africa, but refused to disinvest totally on the grounds that this would have restricted too much the number of companies from which they could receive a return. They have argued that to limit the market in which they could invest in this way would lead to unacceptably low financial returns.[10]

The Central Finance Board of the Methodist Church (CFB) was possibly the UK investment body which most addressed the question of UK companies operating in South Africa. From the early 1970s Methodist Conferences debated the subject at length and committed the Church to action in support of ending loans, trade flows and direct investment links with the apartheid system. As was mentioned earlier, David Haslam, a Methodist minister was a leading figure in setting up ELTSA and the Barclays' Shadow Report, and this work was continued by David Craine, another Methodist. In 1983 the Methodist Conference established an Ethics of Investment Committee with the following terms of reference:

a) To advise the Central Finance Board of the Methodist Church of ethical considerations relating to investment and

b) in particular to process information, including information from outside sources concerning companies with shareholdings in South Africa and to advise the CFB thereupon.

In February 1992 the South African Council of Churches (SACC) along with the South African Catholic Bishops' Conference (SABC) held a major conference at Broederstroom in South Africa to discuss ethical principles to help form an investment framework for the envisaged post-sanctions South Africa. The Methodist Division of Social Responsibility asked the CFB's Investment Manager Bill Seddon to represent them. He reported back:

> Given the dire economic need of the country as a whole and the Black population in particular, it would be a helpful gesture if UK church groups could move quickly to endorse such a call (for the ending of financial sanctions) and end its proscription of investments merely because of South African involvement. However, careful scrutiny of general ethical principles will be necessary to avoid supporting a status quo by economic means. Only in this way can the building up of significant exposure to the South African market within church investment portfolios be contemplated.
>
> (He also warned that:) The mining houses have an influence over the South African economy which would not be tolerated in many other countries... They are also seen as the prime beneficiaries of apartheid and supporters of government policies to bolster the system.[11]

Clearly, while the end of apartheid gave a moral imperative for ethical investors to help rebuild the country, this did not amount to a blank cheque. As Bill Seddon mentioned, the big mining houses made large profits out of the apartheid system. In many cases the black majority had little choice but to work in the goldmines. In 1900 over half the oil in the United States was produced by one company, Standard Oil, and the US Supreme Court then ordered its break-up into a number of pieces on anti-trust grounds. Given the dominance position of Anglo-American in the South African economy, some anti-trust action would seem inevitable in the long term. Following the end of apartheid, the big international investors looked again at South Africa. Sister Margaret Kelly, Secretary of the South African Catholic Bishops Conference, cautioned them in October 1993: 'We welcome the lifting of US economic sanctions, but warn against big business coming in and exploiting the people . . . The Bishops want to see the implementation of development programmes, but do not want to see the introduction of business whose sole aim is making profits.'[12]

The Community Growth Fund

In June 1992 a group of trades unions, led by the mineworkers, launched the first South African ethical fund as the unions wanted more control over where their pension funds were invested. The aim of the Community Growth Fund (CGF) was to: 'achieve sustainable long-term growth by investing in socially responsible companies.' By June 1993 assets had reached R 44.8m, and a year later jumped to R.129m (£20m using the 1994 financial rand rate of 6.5 to the pound) with the number of unitholders rising from 400 to 741 over the period. The value of the CGF fund rose 45.6% over the year, a performance putting it in the top three of South Africa's twenty-four general equity trusts. Professor Anthony Asher, Chairman of the Community Growth Management Company, reported: 'We have always believed it makes good sense to invest in progressive companies. The CGF is beginning to prove it. This year's results again illustrate that socially responsible investment is compatible with excellent investment returns.'[13] In August 1994 CGF was proud to announce its first overseas investor. This was the Calvert Group, one of the largest ethical fund managers in the US, which invested R3.6m.

Although investment management was handled by a fund management company called Syrets, investments were ethically screened by Unity Incorporation – a trade union controlled company chaired by veteran labour organizer Tommy Oliphant. Investments by CGF in a company's shares could only be made with the approval of the board of Unity Incorporation and after detailed investigation by the Labour Research Service. Of forty-six companies investigated in 1992–4, thirty-two were approved and fourteen rejected. CGF worked hard to persuade companies to alter behaviour. For example, engineering company Berzack Brothers was rejected in 1992 but approved two years later after CGF brought management and trade union MEWUSA together to construct a proper training and affirmative action programme. Tommy Oliphant stated: 'One of the legacies of the old South Africa is the weak disclosure permitted by the Companies Act. Companies which refuse to give Unity the information it needs will face automatic rejection.'[14] CGF plans for the future included the launch of a bond fund which would invest in the development of black communities through infrastructure projects like electricity or water supply.

To help assess companies for potential investment, CGF used seventeen investment criteria such as industrial relations and job creation, to get a social credit score out of 100 (points in brackets):

1 Jobs (14)   2 Industrial Relations (14) 3 Employment Conditions (13)
4 Training (7)   5 Equal Opportunities (7)   6 Health & Safety (6)
7 Product (5)   8 Affirmative Action (5)   9 Profit Retention (5)
10 Privatization (5)   11 Environment (4)   12 SA Location (4)
13 Disclosure (4)   14 Participation (4)   15 Political donations (2)
16 Social Spend (1)

There was also a general criteria of racial discrimination. Companies with a measurable policy to eliminate racial discrimination and to promote equality in the workplace received a positive assessment.[15]

The death throes of apartheid

The death throes of apartheid began in February 1990 when Nelson Mandela was released from twenty-eight years of captivity, and at the same time the State of Emergency was lifted, so removing a part of the apparatus of political oppression . Yet was this date fortuitous?

Looking at the financial record it seems unlikely. Summer 1990 was the date when the bulk ($13bn) of South Africa's foreign debt was due to be repaid. Rescheduling in 1987 had given it three years' grace, but the regime had no way of paying the debts that were falling due. It is generally estimated that a total of $12bn left the country in the five years from 1985. This so-called 'capital flight' was mostly due to foreign companies such as Ford and Citibank selling up and taking their money out of the country, although South African individuals also illegally sent money overseas. Despite having pushed the economy into recession in this period to generate a trade surplus, the 1985–90 total trade surplus only amounted to $10bn, so leaving a $2bn gap which had to come from the reserves of the South African Reserve Bank. By the beginning of 1990 these reserves were virtually exhausted.

Despite the fact that it was illegal to call for sanctions under the State of Emergency, the opposition knew that its inability to pay its short-term debts was the regime's Achilles heel.

'We ask you to block attempts by banks and international financiers to rescue Pretoria by agreeing to reschedule its foreign debts.' Oliver Tambo, ANC President, Stockholm June 1989.[16]

'As an immediate action, we need to restate our call to the bankers and governments not to reschedule South Africa's debt which falls due in 1990, nor to give apartheid any new loans or credits.' Rev Frank Chikane, General Secretary of the South African Council of Churches, Johannesburg June 1989.[17]

Normally a country in this situation would apply to the International Monetary Fund (IMF), the world's central bank, for a loan to tide it over. Even the British Government had to ask for an IMF loan in 1976. However, following a $1.1bn IMF loan to South Africa in 1982, the US Congress passed the Gramm Amendment forbidding the US Government to make loans to countries practising apartheid. Although technically the IMF is an independent body, in practice it goes along with its largest shareholder – the US Government. Hence South Africa could look for no help from this source.

At the same time, three years of negative growth left rural unemployment over 50%, with consequent social unrest, while it also reduced the government's ability to finance the vast security system required to maintain the apartheid state. Like the German generals in October 1918, the Afrikaner Establishment knew that the economic war was lost and the only alternatives were negotiated surrender or total collapse. The replacement of the hardline P. W. Botha as South African President in 1989 by the more conciliatory F. W. de Klerk is a clear sign, in retrospect, that they had accepted the inevitable.

The next three years saw slow but steady progress to free elections, and increasingly power slipped from the Afrikaner Establishment to the African National Congress (ANC). When the townships erupted in violence over the assassination of ANC activist Chris Hani in 1992, it was the broadcast plea for calm from Nelson Mandela which restored order. On 24 September 1993 apartheid finally expired following the establishment of the Transitional Executive Council to share power between the ANC and the Nationalist Government until the May 1994 democratic elections. On the same day the South African Council of Churches put out a statement: 'We therefore call on our international church partners and other groups who have stood in solidarity with us in opposing apartheid to cease all campaigns for the economic isolation of South Africa'[18]

Within a week of the SACC report the Methodist Church Division of Social Responsibility and the Overseas Division issued a statement called *Responsible Investment – the Fruit of Anti-Apartheid Action*. This called for an end to financial sanctions and consumer boycotts, and for investment to resume in South Africa to assist in the creation of a more just and equitable society. At the same time, Roy Foulds, of the Central Finance Board, recognizing the above statement, said that: 'It no longer seems appropriate for the (Investment) Committee to advise against the inclusion of any particular investment purely because of exposure to South Africa.'[19] At the same time five US responsible investment firms (Dreyfus, Working Assets, Parnassus, Domini Kinder and Calvert Group) announced that they would change their rules to permit limited investments in South Africa. The long battle was over.

Conclusion

Was it worth it? Did all these consumer boycotts and investment sanctions achieve anything?

'Financial sanctions have been a critical pressure point which has pushed the process of political transformation to where it is today.' ANC press release, August 1991.[20]

'Financial sanctions were the most demonstrably effective of all sanctions.'
Commonwealth Heads of Government, Harare October 1991.[21]

'The unmistakable conclusion is therefore that given the distorted shape of the apartheid political economy and its international linkages and within the context of especially the internal anti-apartheid struggle **financial sanctions have worked.**' David Craine, Southern Africa Briefing December 1991.[22]

The US investment professionals who played such an important role have no doubts:

> What SRI did in regard to South Africa should be considered a major victory . . . Corporate executives have a strong interest in the price of their company's stock options and were influenced in leaving South Africa because of the pressures by public employee and university funds. I know. They told me so. Robert Schwartz June 1993.[23]
>
> Divestment hearings began in the early 1980s with a handful of social investment professionals willing to provide the expert testimony that allowed legislators to make the argument, against most of Wall Street, that divestment was not just morally justified but also possible financially. I know, because I was there. And Bishop Tutu has repeatedly appeared before crowds of social investors to encourage our activism and to tell us that we are, in fact, having an impact. Joan Bavaria, June 1993.[24]

Responsible Investment – the Fruit of Anti-Apartheid Action (October 1993) probably deserves the last word:

> The creation of the Transitional Executive Council (TEC) structures and the setting of 27th April 1994 as the date for elections, are clear marks of the long-awaited victory for the democratic process. These political advances have been won by a courageous and tenacious struggle of those within and without South Africa who have kept faith in the vision of a fully participatory, nonracial state. *No other issue in our time has involved such a broad global consensus of people and organisations, and the effect of their combined concerted action against apartheid has been immense . . . The ethical responsibility of investors and investment policies is now an accepted principle in the commercial world, largely pioneered by antiapartheid action.*[25]

CHAPTER NINE

Ethics in Banking

'. . . today most businesses are rediscovering ethical and community values. There has been a distance between business and local activists which needed to be bridged . . . Economists say that in the long run ethical businesses prosper. Few of Britain's biggest and best businesses today would not claim to be part of their communities. It is not a fashion – it is the long-term recipe for success.'[1]

TERRY THOMAS, MANAGING DIRECTOR, THE CO-OPERATIVE BANK.

The Co-operative Bank – ethical banking in the High Street

The reputation of most British banks is low, possibly at an all-time low. The student group LAMB (Lloyds and Midland Boycott) urges students to boycott the big four banks on the grounds of their environmental policies and debt repayment schedule from the Third World.[2] Small businesses complain that the banks urged them to borrow money during the economic boom of the late 1980s and then pulled the plug when the economy turned down. A study by the American credit rating agency Standard & Poors found that NatWest and Barclays increased tariffs for small businesses by 24% and 21% respectively in 1992. It concluded: *'The ability of the banks to increase tariffs in a recession is a powerful demonstration of the strength they enjoy as a result of their dominant market share. While raising charges drew criticism, the lack of competition meant that business customers had little choice but to pay the higher charges.'*[3]

Overdrafts seemed to become immediately repayable once the business struggled, and when they were called in, sometimes despite good long-term order books, the small businessman lost his business, his livelihood and often his house into the bargain. It is also well known that when the government cut interest rates after the pound left the Exchange Rate Mechanism in September 1992, the banks kept theirs up and pocketed the difference. Staff morale is not too good either as long-standing managers are made redundant while the big banks' city operations pay their staff millions of pounds in bonuses. Compared to this poor reputation, the fact that Terry Thomas of the Co-operative Bank (TCB) can use words like 'ethical and community values', and not be derided, says a lot for the TCB's ethical policy and his identification with it. While a small savings bank can prosper attracting 'niche customers' to ethical products, the Co-operative Bank is a major clearing bank. It is one of only ten settlement banks recognized as the heart of the UK banking system by the Bank of England and as such competes headlong with the likes of Barclays, Midland, etc. Its successful adoption of ethical principles must make even them pause for thought.

The Co-operative Bank was formed in 1872 to provide banking services to the cooperative movement. It is 100% owned by the Co-operative Wholesale Society (CWS), which along with the Co-operative Retail Society (CRS) dominates the co-operative movement in the UK. The CWS is also the owner of the Co-operative Insurance Society (CIS), although apart from a common parent there seems no formal contact between the bank and the insurance company. In 1972 the TCB was incorporated as a private company in order to obtain the clearing bank status achieved in 1975 which the Bank of England would not have granted to a co-operative. In May 1992 the bank surprised the banking world by publicly announcing an ethical stance prohibiting involvement with tobacco companies or high polluters. It also stated its opposition to blood sports, factory farming and the testing of cosmetics on animals in the following terms:

Our Ethical Policy

THE BANK'S POSITION IS THAT:

1) **It will not invest** in or supply financial services to any regime or organization which oppresses the human spirit, takes away the rights of individuals or manufactures any instrument of torture.

2) **It will not finance** or in any way facilitate the manufacture or sale of weapons to any country which has an oppressive regime.

3) It will not invest in any business involved in animal experimentation for cosmetic purposes.

4) It will not support any person or company using exploitative factory farming methods

5) It will not engage in business with any farm or other organization engaged in the production of animal fur.

6) It will not support any organization involved in blood sports, which it defines as sports which involve the training of animals or birds to catch and destroy, or to fight and kill, other animals or birds.

7) It will not provide financial services to tobacco product manufacturers.

8) It will try to ensure its financial services are not exploited for the purposes of money laundering, drug trafficking or tax evasion by the continued application and development of its successful internal monitoring procedures.

9) It will encourage business customers to take a pro-active stance on the environmental impact of their own activities.

10) It will actively seek out individuals, commercial enterprises and non-commercial organizations which have a complementary ethical stance.

11) It will not speculate against the pound using either its own money or that of its customers.

12) It will continue to strengthen its Customer Charter of new standards of banking practice.

The bank's ethical stance was backed by a £1m advertising campaign. The Chemical Industries Association and the Cosmetics Association complained to the Advertising Standards Authority about one of the advertisements regarding environmental damage: '*Our customers know that there are some things we will never invest in.*' The Authority rejected the complaint. The ethical campaign was also recognized as outstanding by experts; the bank won the British Environment and Media Award 1992, and the Campaign Press Award for Financial and Corporate Advertising 1993. This was clearly identified with Terry Thomas who became Managing Director in 1988.

Marketing Week described him thus: 'In Manchester Terry Thomas is known as "God". This more a reflection of his basic integrity than the frightening omnipotence normally associated with deities . . . candour is typical of Thomas, about whom few, if any, have a bad word.'[4]

Or as he himself put it: 'Being regarded as an ethical banker, or less generously a fool-hardy banker, is a significant burden to carry through one's career . . . what sort of society have we developed where a promise or even an aspiration to behave in an ethical manner is regarded as brave or as putting yourself and your organization at risk?'[5]

Thomas is no 'holier-than-thou theorist', but a practical businessman who has used an relatively unglamorous part of the British banking scene to launch a variety of interesting and successful products. TCB pioneered interest-bearing current accounts, was the leader in offering free current account facilities in 1974 and in 1991 it launched a 'free for life' Gold Card, which by the end of 1993 made the Co-operative Bank the biggest gold card operator in the UK. In 1992 the bank also made a big move into 'armchair banking' with less use of the branches and most transactions handled via the telephone. Finally, TCB is the only major clearing bank which is committed to independent financial advice, and the bank is building up its network of such advisers (CBFAs). As described in Chapter Four, good independent financial advice must be the best option, and this move should be welcomed. TCB gained a lot of public credibility when it first announced in September 1992 that it would not speculate against the pound. (This was the time when the pound's value collapsed following its dramatic exit from the Exchange Rate Mechanism and foreign exchange dealers made fortunes betting against it. One speculator, George Soros, made a profit of £1000m!)

Yet it is for its ethical policy that the Co-operative Bank is, rightly, known. On becoming Managing Director in 1988, Terry Thomas obtained the Board's support for a mission statement in two halves. Firstly, that the bank has to be successful, innovative and profitable, but secondly that it should achieve these goals in a socially responsible and environmentally acceptable way. This fits in with the traditions of social service of the bank, but also with Thomas's own beliefs: 'I found the Eighties very difficult. The whole fashion for individualism and denying society existed was totally alien to my way of thinking.'[6] Hence the bank's ethical stance developed naturally from its Mission Statement '*to be non-partisan in all social, political, racial and religious matters . . . to act as a caring employer, and to be a responsible member of society by promoting an environment where the needs of local communities can be met now and in the future.*[7]

Terry Thomas said that this ethical campaign appealed in particular to the most potentially profitable bank customer: one of social class ABC1, and in the age group 25–40, who had previously not tended to bank with the Co-op. In business jargon the bank got a much better 'mix' of client who spent more on higher margin (i.e. more profitable) products. The launch of the ethical stance was preceded by a three-year research study of actual and potential customers' views on ethical issues in banking. 'Once completed, we were delighted to find that the values held by some 20% of the adult population had not materially changed in 150 years. A minority of the better educated, younger managerial or professional, with slightly more women than men, did care about ethical issues, was aware and concerned with what was happening to our society and to our environment.'[8]

From TCB's point of view this ethical approach proved a great success in financial terms. After several years of stagnation the bank's deposits grew 10% in 1992 (year to Jan 1993) to £2.6bn. Over half of TCB's new customers said that the ethical stance was the reason why they had opened an account with the bank. The growth of deposits helped the bank make a profit of £9.8m after several years of losses including a loss of £6.0m in 1992, while the bank's policy of rejecting unethical business cost it only six out of 250,000 corporate accounts. The improved profitability gained, at least in part, by the ethical stance can be seen by the Table below:

CO-OPERATIVE BANK
– FOUR YEAR PROFITS RECORD

Year	1990	1991	1992	1993
Total loans £m	2,597	2,408	2,636	2,739
Pretax profit £m	–14.9	–6.0	9.8	17.8

However, in April 1993 a media storm broke out when the press discovered that the CIS Environ Trust, a 'green' unit trust, was invested in the parent of the Huntingdon Research Centre, one of Europe's biggest animal-testing laboratories. Although the centre no longer tested cosmetics on animals, it did spray beagles and monkeys with insecticides. It seems unfair to blame the Co-operative

Bank for the actions of the CIS, a sister company over which TCB had little control. In September 1993 the bank's fund management arm, CIM Fund Managers, launched the first ethical unit trust aimed specifically at the charity and pension fund market. Note that they are a totally separate company from the CIS. TCB also has a tradition of 'engagement', rather than exit, i.e. it tries to persuade customers to improve their behaviour. As one Co-operative executive said to me: '. . . look, one of the banking customers when we announced the ethical stance was a battery poultry farmer. If we had just told him to take his account elsewhere, he'd have just carried on as before. We told him we valued his custom, but that he had a year to improve his business. He is no longer involved in poultry farming, he is still a Co-op Bank customer, and he is actually more profitable than he was before!'[9]

The Co-operative Bank was one of the pioneers of affinity cards in the UK, where a charity receives a donation in return for every account opened. In July 1993 it announced that the affinity card that it had launched five years previously for the RSPB had raised £1m for the charity, the highest amount for a credit card (Visa) that supports only one charity. The RSPB card has 50,000 account holders and is free for life as long as it is used at least ten times a year. TCB pays £5 to the RSPB for every new account opened, and donates 25p for every £100 spent with the card.

TCB's social responsibilities have a broader aspect outside banking entirely. It played a major part in the campaign to bring the Olympics to Manchester, where its head office is based, and in 1992 the Co-operative Bank gave £200,000 to fund a professorship of Corporate Responsibility at Manchester Business School, the first significant chair in this subject in the UK. In the summer of 1993 it announced a three-year sponsorship worth £170,000 a year to Christian Aid. In return Christian Aid will print the Cooperative Bank logo on the 17m envelopes that it sends out each year. Terry Thomas is happy with that: 'Personally my main interest is in the practicalities of banking – in getting things done! I'm most interested in people issues'[10] and that the bank has managed to hold onto the values inherited from Robert Owen and other pioneers of the co-operative movement. 'I would like to think that I tried to make those values relevant and commercially viable today to be my epitaph. You could just say that I'm a born-again zealot.'[11]

In conclusion, the Co-operative Bank deserves all the credit it gets for bringing ethics to the High Street. The economics textbooks tell you that commercial banking is all about efficiency and profit margins and that customers will fight to get an extra basis point of interest (in banking terminology, a basis point is one hundredth of a per cent). It is encouraging that the Co-operative Bank is proving them wrong. The fact that TCB's ethical policy is bringing in valuable up-market customers means that the big high street banks will have to take note.

Two Ethical Building Societies

The origins of the building society movement go back to the end of the eighteenth century. The first known building society appeared in 1775 in Birmingham, and the first Building Society Act was passed in 1834. Originally they were groups of people who clubbed together to help each other buy houses and were terminated when this had been achieved. Late in the century 'permanent' societies were established, to enable a continuous stream of people to buy their own homes, but the nature of building societies did not change; legally they remained 'mutual societies', that is owned by their members. Building societies grew rapidly in the 1950s, '60s and '70s with the rise in home ownership, but the structure of the movement did not change. They were tightly regulated by the government, but given certain privileges in return. Essentially they were only allowed to lend money which they had raised from their members, unlike the commercial banks who were able to borrow from the money markets. Building societies were also only allowed to lend via mortgages – the sale of personal loans or insurance was forbidden; but in return they had an effective monopoly on mortgage lending in the UK, and they were allowed to coordinate their interest rates, i.e. they were a permitted cartel. This meant that when the housing market was booming, the building societies would impose rationing of mortgages which helped dampen down the surge of buying. They were also able to require conservative lending, i.e. they were unlikely to lend much more than twice an individual's salary nor advance much more than 75% of a property's estimated value.

All this changed with the Thatcher Government's policy of deregulation. The building society cartel was broken up; banks were able to offer mortgages and the building societies to sell new products such as endowment mortgages. Lending criteria were relaxed up to four times main income, although in retrospect it appears clear that this fuelled the housing boom of 1987–90, and the subsequent unprecedented collapse in house prices. Certainly the problem of 'negative equity', where people's mortgages are greater than the value of their houses, did not occur in the old days of the cartel. As big banks and building societies move into each others' territory it becomes more and more difficult to tell them apart. It was hardly surprising that in 1989 one of the largest building societies, Abbey National, turned itself into a fully fledged bank, nor when in May 1994 Lloyds Bank announced that it would try and take over the Cheltenham and Gloucester, another large building society. Is there any role for the traditional, small building society conscious of its mutual roots? The success of the Catholic Building Society and the Ecology Building Society suggests that if such societies stick to their traditional roots and thus differentiate themselves from the quasi-banks that the big societies have become, they can indeed thrive.

1. The Catholic Building Society (CBS) was founded in 1961 to *'serve the housing needs of the Catholic community in England and Wales'*, although it should be noted that applicants' religion is not recorded. What really distinguishes CBS, apart from its saving roots in the Catholic community, is two things – its determination to be a traditional building society and a commitment to the poor. Note that its policy is to *'serve housing needs'*, and that in practice this means making far more loans to poorer applicants than ordinary building societies would countenance, while there is also a deliberate policy of also making more loans available to women, as the Society's Lady Chairman Mrs Nona Byrne said in a speech in September 1993:

'Housing problems increase rather than reduce, caused by marital breakdown, more older people living alone, and more unemployment. The Society continues its policy of making home loans on lower cost property within the means of those with lower than average incomes. Equal priority has always been given to women, who each year receive over 30% of our home loans, far higher than the average of other societies.'[12]

This was shown in 1989, when the CBS compared its lending policies with others:

CBS LOAN PORTFOLIO

	CBS	All Societies
Loans to first time buyers 1989		
Proportion of all home loans	56%	50%
Average purchase price	£23,547	£41,272
Buyers income below £9,000	43%	17%
Women buyers	21%	(8% est.)

In 1993 43% of all the CBS's home loans were made to women. Managing Director Francis Higgins spelled out the CBS's social policy and how it deliberately tried to help families in financial trouble. He also emphasized how in 1993 it had assisted women left with a broken marriage and children to support: 'All were at risk of becoming homeless, because their existing lenders would not continue their home loans, or would not grant new loans on alternative housing. We have refinanced those loans on affordable terms . . . In addition we have been able to assist several families to transfer from council housing to home ownership, thus freeing scarce public housing for younger families to rent.'[13]

The society's total assets have grown steadily over the years, up from £17m in 1989 to £22.6m in 1993. These loans are funded by over 4,000 private investors, and while the origins are in the Catholic community, including over £1m saved by Catholic charities, CBS is reaching a wider audience. As the Lady Chairman puts it: 'In recent years many Anglican and Methodists, to whom our ethos as a traditional society appeals, have joined us.'[14] In September 1993 the CBS completed the enlargement of its premises, following which the Directors reported in March 1994 that the extra space would enable: '. . . *the Directors . . . to resume actively planning future developments, based on . . . a survey designed to explore the extension of existing services to a wider geographic membership . . . We shall review* (the effects of increased competition) *on our objectives of financing home ownership for the less well-off sectors . . .*'[15]

As the Catholic Building Society gets better known, its determination to remain a traditional building society, with a focus on meeting people's housing needs rather than using those needs to make a quick profit, is likely to be a powerful force behind the society's expansion. And so it should.

2. The Ecology Building Society is another society which has rejected the commercialization which has taken over the sector. It was

founded only in 1981 with £5000, but by 1989 it had 2,500 private investors and £5m in assets. It lends mainly to small-scale community projects or to companies with a proven ecological record. General Manager Bob Lowman stated that: 'We would not go all out to get bigger just for the sake of it. The Society is determined to keep to its ecological philosophy.'[16] In practice this can mean inner city terraced houses or back-to-backs, as well as more obviously attractive rural properties. By the end of 1993, despite sticking to its principles, demand by green customers to lend to it, as well as for its services, had pushed total assets over £10m with over 4,000 members. Bob Lowman again: 'One of our major areas of lending is to renovate semiderelict properties. Conventional lenders look at a property valuation and the ability of the borrower to repay. We have a third factor to consider; whether the mortgage will meet one of our ecological criteria.'[17]

The bank with no money

Mercury Provident's origins lie in the Anthroposophical movement, a group founded by the Austrian thinker Rudolf Steiner but now known principally for its work in education, both with ordinary children and the handicapped (children with special needs), and also for organic farming. Mercury Provident itself was founded in 1974 as an Industrial and Provident Society, a sort of savings club, to help raise longer-term finance for the Steiner movement's various institutions such as Camphill schools for the mentally handicapped as well as organic farming and Weleda – a manufacturer of natural medicines and toiletries.

From 1980 Mercury increased their work outside the Anthroposophical movement. They were lucky enough to do so before the 1980 Banking Act – while Mercury had to raise loan stock in order to become a bank, the rules were substantially looser then than they are now. The name 'Mercury' was chosen because the bank was seen as a messenger transferring money from resource-rich investors to resource-needy borrowers. The philosophy of the bank has always been that 'people should be able to use their money consciously', and one of its key features has always been that it tries to bring borrowers and lenders together in such a way that each is aware of the other's aims, purposes and needs. 'A bank should be a lens between borrower and lender, a transparent broker, not a powerhouse of finance nor a repository of wealth devoted to the interests of its shareholders.'[18]

There are three very distinctive things about Mercury:

1) **Target accounts**: these provide a facility for individual depositors to direct money to specific Mercury loan projects or lending sectors.
2) **Ethical interest rates**: these allow interest rates to be set with reference to the needs of both borrowers and depositors.
3) **Social Collateral**: where communities lack money capital, Mercury uses the concept of borrowing communities where projects are supported by personal guarantees of no more than £1,000 per person from twenty to fifty people. Security on property is not the preferred choice as it runs counter to Mercury's philosophy that banking should be more social in its mode of operation.

In 1994, Mercury's target accounts offered depositors the opportunity to choose an interest rate between 0% and 2.5%, but in return for the low rate, investors were able to specify or 'target' the project of their choice. Investors could also buy nonvoting ordinary shares in Mercury itself – these have a discretionary dividend of 3%, 5% or 7%. The use of social collateral is Mercury's biggest innovation – for example, in December 1985 when they launched a financing package for the Centre for Employment Initiatives, a not-for-profit consultancy which raised £40,000 based on guarantees and loans from 500 people.

In 1986 Mercury became a public company with share capital of £225,000 and deposits of £1.47m, and by 1990 deposits exceeded £4m. By 1991 500 loans had passed through the company's books, but despite the unusual loan criteria, only two loans had gone bad, a remarkable record. By the end of 1992 Mercury had 1,700 customers and deposits of £7.7m, while its borrowers were social ventures, community projects and environmental trusts as well as its base of schools and homes for the disabled and organic farms. In 1978 the company set up the first ethical pension scheme. Currently it has twenty-seven employers contributing to it and assets of over £3m. Fifty per cent of the assets are used by Mercury for 'social projects', the rest is invested in normal stock market investments ethically screened by Duncan Lawrie.

Glen Saunders is one of the key Executive Directors, and at first sight looks like a normal banker, although his words are hardly traditional:

> We started in a very unusual way – we had very little money, and we tried to find projects we liked before raising the money to lend to them. We became known as 'the bank with no money'! We call ourselves a social bank, and that means that we use traditional banking techniques and practices in our loan evaluation procedures, such as cash flow and working capital needs, etc. We are a social bank because our aims and procedures are subject to social objectives; not only do we lend to ethical businesses and projects, but we lend in an aware way. Transparency is very important to us, so we show what all the projects are and invite investors to target their money at a particular project. What social banking *is not about is cheap loans*, or throw-away money, what you might call 'soft loans', where people don't really expect to pay them back. What it is about is *understanding the social entrepreneur*, and using special techniques to help him/her.
>
> If you like, it is a conventional banking approach applied to natural assets, i.e. people and the environment. I also think it important to stress that as the welfare state is retreating in most countries, social and environmental initiatives such as ourselves become more and more important. It is vital that the voluntary/charity/social sector understands this and is prepared to be more entrepreneurial, more creative. We feel we have done this with our mutual guarantee system, which mobilizes social support for a project, say a trust to build low-cost, environmentally friendly housing in the East End of London, and that social support, this community spirit, is a natural asset. These projects work well because the community becomes involved in the project, it's not some distant council or bank doing this, and because of this community pride, the project will not be allowed to fail financially. None of the mutual guarantees has ever failed to be paid back; most of the projects have done well, but where they haven't, individuals have paid in more than the amount of the guarantee they were obliged to, in order to help keep the project going.[19]

Future developments include investments in renewable energy generation and Third World involvement. For several years Mercury

Provident has had close links with a Dutch bank called Triodos with very similar objectives to itself. As 1994 ended talks on a possible merger of the two banks were under way. The increased knowledge of social banking in Europe which this will bring, plus the continuing development of Mercury's products, should make the future for the bank an exciting one.

Credit Unions – a lifeline for the poor

'The trouble with banks is that they only want to lend you money when you don't need to borrow it.' Marx – Groucho.

In February 1994 the House of Commons Social Security Advisory Committee produced a report called *Outside the Banking System*[19] which showed that even in 1994, 20% of the British population still did not have a bank account. Of this group, 40% were pensioners and a further 40% had incomes of less than £150 a week, mostly single parents or people who were unemployed. The report was not sure whether this was entirely due to people being excluded from banking facilities. Most people who have worked with low-income families could have told the learned committee the answer.

Official interest rates in the middle of 1994 were 5.25%. A high-income family could borrow on a mortgage for 6.5% and get an unsecured overdraft for 8%. A poor family would find it very difficult to get bank credit; if it did, the best it would achieve would be a 'personal loan' with interest charges of around 20%, while unpaid credit card bills accumulated at around 23%. An easy answer would be to buy goods from a store on credit, but here the interest could easily be over 30% APR (APR is a measure of the rate of interest adjusting for the rate of payment.) For a family forced to go outside these measures the rate of interest could be practically anything; APRs from moneylenders have been recorded at levels of £10 per week for a £50 loan, which is an APR of over 1000%.

The only answer for such people is a *credit union*, which is simply a community of people who form a self-help savings and loan cooperative. The first credit union was formed in Germany by Friedrich Raiffeisen in 1849 to help local people escape from debt and poverty. The movement grew rapidly in Canada and the United

States, and there are now some 14,000 American credit unions with a membership of sixty million people. In Africa there are 1,200 credit unions and some 5,000 in Asia. Even in Ireland over a quarter of the adult population (700,000 people) belongs to one, but for some reason they have been slow to take off in the UK. At the end of 1993 there were 270 credit unions belonging to the Association of Credit Unions (Abcul) with some 90,000 members and some £30m in savings. Abcul is the larger of the two British national federations of credit unions, the other being the National Federation of Credit Unions (NFCU).

How do they work in practice? The answer is quite simple, a group of people get together and decide that they want to form one. Advice on this is provided by either of the associations mentioned above. Normally it is recommended that a *study group of at least 15 to 20 people* run a savings club for at least six months under rules from Abcul or NFCU before applying for registration as a credit union with the Registrar of Friendly Societies, which is legally required before a credit union can be set up. The key points of credit unions are the following:

1) Common bond
2) Cooperatively and democratically run
3) run on a voluntary basis
4) encourage regular savings
5) provide cheap loans.

Before a union can get legal approval it has to satisfy the Registrar that there is a 'common bond' of membership in one of three ways: that potential members live in the same local area, that they belong to the same parish church or other body or that they all work for the same company. These bonds of community, association or occupation ensure that there is a sufficient pool of people (200 is the normal minimum) to be viable. Regular social contact makes members aware of each other's circumstances, so big loans to, for example, an unreliable alcoholic do not happen, while ordinary members are unlikely to default and have to face their neighbours with having done so. As a result of this informal credit risk assessment and social loan guarantees, default rates for credit unions are extremely low, normally under 1% as they are for Mercury Provident. The first British credit union was based on a Catholic parish in Wimbledon, but in general they tend to be secular. The largest British union is the London Taxi Drivers with over £1m saved.

Secondly they are a cooperative, where each member has one vote regarding the election of the officers, irrespective of the size of the savings or loans each member has. All officers are elected annually and are unpaid. It is a common experience of credit unions that someone with no previous financial experience, such as a miner or welder, gradually accumulates book-keeping experience and training and becomes the leading light of the union. There is a strong social side to credit unions, a strong sense of a local community working together to help each other. After finishing the official day's business, it is often carried on socially in the pub or working man's club.

For most people the most obvious and attractive feature of credit unions is that they make cheap loans, which they do, but this only happens as part of a disciplined structure of saving. The maximum rate of interest a credit union can charge is 1% a month, which is an APR of 12.68%, while members' savings attract interest from 5% up to 8%. A credit union is not a bank, it can only lend money which its members have already saved, and must have reserves of at least 10% of total loans (about double what the big banks have). Hence all members are encouraged to have regular savings schemes via a passbook, although the sum could be as small as £1 a week. For the poor used to living in debt, introducing the habit of saving is important. The most anyone can save with a credit union is £5,000 and the most that they can borrow is £5,000 above their savings, i.e. the greatest possible loan is £10,000. Normally there is a minimum savings period of three to six months before a member can borrow money. No more than 5% of total loans may be made to one individual.

The churches have been active in promoting them. The Church of England's Board for Social Responsibility sponsored a project, *Linking Up*, on credit unions, while its Church Urban Fund has allocated over £30,000 in ecumenical grants to aid their foundation. The *Tablet* made the following interesting point:

For a Christian perhaps one of the main attractions is that the movement offers the better-off a way of showing solidarity with the poor. The better-off Christian will be able to save more than the poorer saver, and in that way will be increasing more rapidly the pool of money available to make loans to all members ... Forming a credit union is one of the most useful social

activities open to a Christian. Many people are oppressed by
debt . . . credit unions, by helping their members put aside quite
small sums and by making comparatively small unsecured loans
for items such as school uniforms, can make credit accessible in a
responsible way to people whom the mainstream financial institutions will not even look at.[21]

The Charities Aid Foundation – a charity merchant bank?

'The Charities Aid Foundation could be described as a charity or a
financial institution. In fact it is both . . . By combining the two,
CAF has been able to pioneer a revolution in giving.' Michael
Brophy.[22]

Chapter Thirteen, The Social Economy, looks at the rapid changes
currently occurring in the charity sector. One of the main sources of
information on these changes is the Charities Aid Foundation
(CAF), itself a charity, whose annual survey, *Charity Trends*, is an
authoritative record of these developments. This has now been
taken a stage further with the publication of: *Dimensions of the
Voluntary Sector*. Yet at the same time CAF appears to be turning
itself into a specialist bank for the charity sector. Michael Brophy,
CAF's Executive Director, has been described as: 'one of the sector's most energetic and innovative entrepreneurs.[23]

Most people in the voluntary sector would probably agree with
that, although it is probably also fair to say that not everyone in the
voluntary sector is comfortable with CAF's commercial edge. The
growth has been organic but taken CAF a long way away from its
roots. For example, in order to have authoritative statistics on the
changes in the charity field, CAF set up a large Research and
Statistics unit. Much of this information enables it to give expert
advice to both charities and donors ranging from a charity search
facility on one side, to the *Directory of Grant Making Trusts*, and
CAFcert, a management consultancy on the other. Michael Brophy
explains: 'We needed to have the data to make giving effective. It
was part of the professionalism. We're a sort of merchant bank
offering an investigating service to advise donors on the range of
charitable interests and needs.'[24]

In fact, CAF has steadily grown from the 'back office', i.e. administration, to offering 'front office' services, that is, investment management. In 1975 CAF started CAF Nominees to offer a custodian/tax/dividend service to charities, a service which the obligatory closure of the Official Custodian under the 1992 Charities Act should make popular. CAF is also the leader in the 'Gift Aid' market, and in the year to April 1993 CAF received £68m in charitable donations, of which £12m was under Gift Aid. Appeals Administration is another key service, covering covenant administration, membership management, credit card transactions, etc. A logical step, with large sums of money flowing in and out, was to set up a charitable banking service to enable charities quickly and easily to earn interest on clients' money, so CAFcash, an interest-bearing deposit account was established with Bank of England approval in 1986. By April 1993 it had £101m invested. It was hardly surprising that in July 1993 the CAF Newsletter announced: 'CAF has relaunched its services for charities under a single banner. CAF Charity Money Management bands together CAF's covenant and appeals administration and its investment funds, to show how it can meet every money management need of charities. Charity Money Management as a "one stop shop" is likely to appeal to charities who want direct links from collected funds to investments.'[25]

While cash management is probably the most important function for any charity, a large number have medium-term funds which they invest in common investment funds (cifs are essentially a form of unit trust specifically for charities) to gain some mixture of income and capital growth. In 1991 CAF established two cifs, the investment management carried out by the leading stockbroking firm of Cazenove and Co. By April 1994 the CAF Balanced Growth Fund, invested mainly in UK equities, was worth some £69.2m, while the CAF Income Fund, invested mainly in government securities and other fixed interest securities, had reached £38.2m in size. One apparent gap in CAF's product range is any kind of ethical cif as the two funds managed by Cazenove are run on normal lines. Michael Brophy is optimistic about the long-term potential in investment management: 'We have some advantages – we know the charity sector, and we are not in it for the money. We should be able to offer schemes every bit as competitive as anyone else.'[26]

Reviewing this chapter, two themes have consistently emerged. The first is *ethical integrity*; how ethical banks state their aims quite clearly and emphasize transparency and disclosure in assessing how successful they are in reaching them. Secondly, the *rapid convergence* which is happening in the financial sector as elsewhere. A rising number of banks are adopting ethical principles and are prospering, while many larger charities are increasingly using commercial techniques with increasing overlap to the financial sector.

CHAPTER TEN

The Institutional Investors

Pension funds are becoming perhaps the most vigilant and influential custodians of long-term corporate strategy . . . as any chief executive officer will tell you, nothing concentrates the mind so much as an inquiry from a major institutional investor about his or her company's practices.

ROBERT REICH, US LABOR SECRETARY.[1]

Pension funds should engage in the process of change by exercising their influence as owners in relation to the companies in which they invest.

PIRC.[2]

Few people probably realize the dominant role of the big investment institutions in the financial life of the country. In particular, the rapid growth in funded pension funds from the second half of the 1970s onwards transformed the mix of share ownership.

Percentage ownership of UK Equities

	1963	1975	1981	1992
Individuals	58.7%	37.5%	28.2%	21.3%
Charities	2.7%	2.3%	2.2%	1.9%
Industrial	4.8%	4.1%	5.1%	2.9%
Overseas Investors	4.4%	5.6%	3.6%	12.1%
Government	1.6%	3.6%	3.0%	0.8%
Insurance Companies	10.6%	15.9%	20.5%	16.5%
Pension Funds	7.0%	16.8%	26.7%	34.7%
Investment Trusts	9.0%	10.1%	7.1%	4.1%
Unit Trusts	1.2%	4.1%	3.6%	5.8%
Percentage Institutional	27.8%	46.9%	57.9%	61.1%
Value	£27.0bn	£45.0bn	£92.0bn	£620.6bn

Sources: 1963, Diamond Commission; 1975, Department of Industry; 1981, 1992 Stock Exchange.

Despite Mrs Thatcher's policy aim of wider share ownership, the proportion of UK company shares held by individuals continues to decline. While more individuals did own shares at the end of the 1980s than at the end of the 1970s, their relative influence was dwarfed as the proportion of UK equities owned by the big invest-ment institutions marched remorselessly upwards. 'Institutional' in the above table refers only to British investment institutions. If overseas investors are included, the majority of which are US pen-sion funds, then almost three quarters of quoted British industry is controlled by investment institutions!

Most investment professionals use purely financial criteria in their work. There are, however, institutional investment managers who do apply ethical or social principles in their work: fund managers employed by the churches and charities. The churches in total have some £4bn of funds managed ethically to some degree, while there is probably around £6bn of charity funds subject to some investment constraints. Local authority and private sector pension funds using PIRC's socially responsible investment services, although not necessarily forcing their investment managers to use positive and negative ethical criteria, amount to £34bn. This total £44bn is, of course, of a different order of magnitude compared to the £800m of ethical unit trusts often described as constituting the whole universe of 'ethical investment'.

Of course, unlike ethical investment unit trusts which can select their own criteria, institutional fund managers are bound by a 'fiduciary duty' to get the best return on the funds entrusted to them. The UK is unique in having churches with their own in-house institutional fund managers running clergy pension trusts and char-ity money which are not directly open to the individual investor as are unit trusts. The largest of these is the Church Commissioners.

The Church Commissioners and their role in the Church

The Church Commissioners have received a lot of publicity in recent years, if mostly of an unwelcome kind relating to poorly performing property investments, yet their role is generally still not well understood. Few people outside the Church understand how vital their work is to that of the Church of England. In 1993 the

Church of England had 16,300 churches in use across the country, while there were some 11,100 active clergy and a similar number of pensioners with a running cost of £630m in total. The largest contributor was parish donations of £372m, but this only produced 59% of the sum required. The next biggest contribution was the £146m coming from the investment income of the Church Commissioners.

CHURCH COMMISSIONERS: FINANCIAL SUPPORT FOR THE CHURCH

	1991 £m	1992 £m	1993 £m
Clergy Pensions	58.3	63.9	69.4
Stipend Contributions	65.5	59.8	58.8
Clergy Housing	12.5	8.9	6.0
Cathedrals etc.	11.8	12.4	12.2
TOTAL SUPPORT	148.1	145.0	146.4
Pension as % of total	39.3%	44.0%	47.4%
CC Stipend %	45.0%	41.0%	37.0%

(The CC stipend contribution is the above contribution as a percentage of the *total* clergy wage bill.)

It can be seen from the above table that pensions as a proportion of the total expenditure rose steadily in the early 1990s, while the contributions to stipends declined. The Commissioners are unusual in that legally they are a charity, but pension payments have taken an increasing proportion of the Commissioners' income at the expense of allocations to the most needy dioceses. (Technically, they are exempt from the Charity Commission, but subject to general trust law, as was demonstrated in the Bishop of Oxford case.) Like many charities, they are allowed to distribute only the *income*, but it could be argued that this is too restrictive as pension funds pay out both income and capital gains – what is called *total return*.

In the summer of 1992 a lot of publicity was given to the fact that the value of the Commissioners' assets had fallen by £800m between 1989 and 1992, reducing the value of the income producing assets to £2.2bn. The problem was that the Commissioners had borrowed money to fund property developments, inevitably a fairly risky procedure. The Commissioners had used borrowings before in the successful development of the Metro Centre in Gateshead, the largest shopping centre in Europe worth more than £200m. However, the late 1980s saw interest rates soar and property values sink and several property companies went into receivership. The *Investors Chronicle* stated: For a conservative institution, the Commissioners have pursued a high-risk strategy in allocating so much of their resources to property.[3] 'We have learned some bitter lessons', was Dr Carey's comment.[4] Yet while this strategy, with the benefit of hindsight, was clearly mistaken, there were good reasons for it.

The problem for the Church of England in the early 1990s was that donations were flat, in line with the general trend in the charity field, while both stipends and clergy pensions were rising faster than the rate of inflation. A commitment had been made to the General Synod in 1980 regarding upgrading clergy pensions and without additional resources being made available for them. Over the twenty years to the end of 1992 full-service pensions rose by 63% above the rate of inflation. (Even so, the minimum full-service pension was the hardly princely sum of £7833 p.a.)

The Lambeth Group which examined the property lending saga found three main problems:

1) The Commissioners had increased an already large exposure to property, and compounded the problem by borrowing to finance speculative property investments.
2) Their Assets Committee failed to receive regular and accurate reports from executive management.
3) The Commissioners took on commitments to finance clergy benefits in excess of their financial capacity.

It seems that the Commissioners were driven to take a calculated risk on property development by the unrealistic demands put upon them of steadily rising pensions coupled with the restriction of only distributing income. As Dr Carey put it to the General Synod in November 1993: '. . . we have been living beyond our means for many years'.[5] The *FT* agreed : '. . . the collapse brought belated recognition that the Church had become overdependent on the Commissioners.'[6] The situation was probably compounded by the complex structure and history of the Commissioners which is discussed next.

The Church Commissioners – history and structure

The Commissioners owe their origin to two separate bodies which were merged in 1948: the Governors of Queen Anne's Bounty and the Ecclesiastical Commissioners. Queen Anne's Bounty (QAB) dates back to 1704 when the Queen handed back to the Church certain assets deriving from taxes on the clergy called '*first fruits and tenths*', which had been originally paid to the Pope and then appropriated by Henry VIII at the Reformation. QAB was decreed to be for '*the augmentation of the maintenance of the poor clergy*', and in practice meant two things. Firstly, to raise the stipends (salary) of poor clergy by endowing funds to make permanent grants to them – 'benefices'. Secondly, to help manage and improve the quality of parsonages.

The Ecclesiastical Commissioners (EC) were founded in 1836 on the heels of the parliamentary Great Reform Act of 1832 as a reforming body within the Church. One of their tasks was to look at the relative wealth and duties of the dioceses. Another was to take over the administration of the estates of the cathedrals and in return pay the stipends of the bishops, deans and canons. A third was to support the creation of new parishes which were springing up in the wake of the Industrial Revolution. The main assets of the EC derived from the former estates of the bishops – the Bishop of London in particular owned valuable property. A major event contributing to the current responsibilities of the Church Commissioners occurred in 1954, when in return for a capital sum of £8.5m, they assumed responsibility for the payment of clergy's pensions from the Pensions Board. The Commissioners have taken on more and more responsibilities since the 1950s, adding to the complexities of their task. Ultimately, the Commissioners' duty is described as '*to manage the investments entrusted to us to maximize our financial support for the ministry of the Church of England, particularly in areas of need and opportunity.*'

Other Church of England bodies are the Central Board of Finance (CBF) and the Pensions Board. The CBF was set up in 1920 as the financial executive of the Synod, which involves management of Synod's funds and various other duties including the management of the Central Church Funds for the dioceses, plus external investment management services – of which more later. The Pensions Board is the administrator of the pension scheme as well as having a wider responsibility for the care of retired clergy. It also runs eight residential homes and one nursing home with the latter having a trust fund of £60m. From time to time it has been suggested that these arrangements should be simplified – in 1994 the Archbishops' Commission on the Organization of the Church of England was established to look at some of these issues.

The Church Commissioners – ethical investment in practice

The investment of funds is delegated to the Assets Committee, a statutory body under the 1947 Act creating the modern Commissioners. It consists of the First Church Estates Commissioner who is Chairman, a clergyman Commissioner, and three to five lay Commissioners who are *'well qualified to assist in the management of the Commissioners' assets'*. The Assets Committee historically has had exclusive power to act in all matters regarding the management of assets. It monitors the estates, the investments and the commercial property departments in regard to both investment strategy and ethical issues, and supervises their actual management.

As was explained in the Bishop of Oxford case, the Commissioners try and be 'good landlords', i.e. they apply ethical principles to all their investments. A sign of the way they coordinate their ethical investment policies with the CBF was given in May 1994. It was announced that all three Church of England investment bodies, the Church Commissioners, the Central Board of Finance and the Pensions Board, had lifted their ban on investment in South Africa following the first ever democratic elections there. A rare insight into the Commissioners' investment policies was given in May 1994, by Antony Hardy, Securities Investment Manager:

> Currently the Church Commissioners has around £1.2bn invested in stocks and shares (i.e.£800m equities, £400m bonds). Our twin sister bodies the Central Board of Finance has some £800m in securities (including a big cash fund), and the Pensions Board about £100m, i.e. over £2bn of securities are managed under the Commissioners' ethical guidelines. Although the CBF has its own independent investment management operation, it operates under the CC ethical guidelines, and uses the ethical research papers

produced by the Commissioners' staff for their own use, e.g. on subjects like South Africa.

The investment policy of the Commissioners is determined by the Assets Committee, and if a decision has to be made on ethical policy it can be determined there. The Church Commissioners have long-standing ethical guidelines banning investment in certain areas : arms, alcohol, tobacco, gambling and newspapers. (The latter is more of a political exclusion, as it is felt that most newspapers support a political party and therefore investment in one might indirectly indicate support for the party that paper backed.) In modern business life few companies are based on a single product, but most are rather conglomerates, so it takes research to assess how significant an area like defence might be. The prime responsibility of the Commissioners is of course to the beneficiaries, and we are restricted in that we are legally able only to distribute investment income. A clear and distinct financial return is the first priority.

The issue of armaments is a good example of how complex and difficult ethical investment issues are in practice. Should you exclude a textile company which in practice produces uniforms, and sells over 50% of its product to the Ministry of Defence? On the other hand, GEC sells less than 25% of its turnover to the MoD, but that still amounts to £500m of defence sales, a huge amount. GEC also has a significant number of parishioners working for it. The Church Commissioners' approach has been for the Assets Committee to debate the issue, if necessary discretely requesting further information from the company, before finally reaching a decision on whether the holding in that company should be sold.

Conglomerates raise important issues of corporate governance. Almost inevitably, they must have made aggressive takeovers to have become so big. In a situation where one company is seeking to take over another, the Church Commissioners would have private meetings on a one-to-one basis with the management of each. They would look at the different ethical/social standards of target and predator, and be very wary if it looked like a case of asset stripping. On the other hand, not all takeovers are bad. Sometimes there is a case for stripping the dead wood away at the top of a company – there may be good second-tier management which can be released to run it.

Multinationals are another difficult area. For example, the South African subsidiary of a British company might have a good record on employee rights and high wages, employment of black people, and other forms of positive discrimination, yet should it be sold because it operated there? Another example might be social responsibility questions; many UK companies are transferring production to countries where labour costs are significantly lower – should this be supported?

Sunday trading was an issue which the Commissioners found to be a very difficult one. Of course, not only was this a simple ethical issue, companies were breaking the law. Other matters which are regularly discussed are questions of corporate governance and executive salary issues. Lastly, it is worth noting that the Church Commissioners only have a small staff to consider these issues. On the other hand, the Commissioners receive great cooperation from companies in which they invest and visit, much greater than they would have been likely to get otherwise given their often relatively small holding in companies.[7]

There are a few final points worth making regarding the Commissioners. Firstly, that their ethical investment stance has not been at the expense of investment performance in their securities portfolio – for the ten years to end 1992 they had a compound return of 16.8% compared to an industry average of 15.5%. Secondly, that they did make representations to a number of companies regarding Sunday trading in 1992, and in the same year 'disinvested a proportion of our holdings in this sector'; as in the case of South Africa, ethics and financial caution may have worked in the same direction.

Finally, as argued elsewhere in this book, ethical investment is not just about excluding a *product*, it is about the ethical integrity involved in the *process* of decision-making which requires openness and disclosure. In my opinion the Commissioners succeeded in their declared aim in response to the Lambeth Report: '*We tried to respond fully and openly to criticism and to ensure that people had the facts about past events and about our plans for the future.*'[8]

The Central Board of Finance

The Central Board of Finance (CBF) is sometimes confused with the Church Commissioners, but is a totally separate body. As mentioned above, the CBF itself was established in 1920 as the financial arm of the General Synod, and in 1958 the Church Funds Investment Measure enabled it to set up its own Investment Office. The CBF operates under the same ethical guidelines as the Commissioners, and at the most senior level contacts between the two bodies are not infrequent. The CBF Investment Office provides investment management services to Church of England parishes, dioceses and other charitable trusts.

In 1987 the CBF was absorbed into Church, Charity and Local Authority Fund Managers Limited (CCLA), a company 60% owned by the CBF Investment Fund, 25% by the Charities Official Investment Fund and 15% by the Local Authorities' Mutual Investment Trust (LAMIT). CCLA is one of the largest fund managers for charities. The Charities Official Investment Fund (COIF) was established in 1960 as the first common investment fund in the UK. Common investment funds, normally known as cifs, are a type of unit trust specifically for charities. They have two advantages: they are free of UK taxation both on income and on capital gains, and they also count as narrow-range investments under the 1961 Trustee Investments Act, which enables charities to bypass the investment restrictions of that act. COIF has become one of the largest cifs with around £500m invested in its three funds: Investment, Fixed Interest and Deposit. LAMIT provides similar services to COIF, but to local authorities.

In total at the end of 1993 CCLA had investment funds under management of £1.8bn, of which only the £873m invested in the CBF was operated under the same ethical guidelines as those used by the Church Commissioners. The CBF Report and Accounts sets out the ethical investment philosophy:

In managing the CBF we endeavour to operate a clear but sensible ethical policy within the limits of legal constraints. We have regard to both negative and positive ethical considerations in selecting and retaining investments and we regularly review them. Our present criteria exclude investment in companies if their business is in armaments, gambling, tobacco, breweries or newspapers. However, given the complexity of many major company groups, some of our investments may have some interests in these areas . . . At present the restrictions collectively exclude from investment about 12% of the UK equity market and from time to time investment performance is affected by this.[9]

The CBF has found that ethical guidelines have had an adverse impact on performance: '. . . *its ethical restrictions have had some negative effect in the last five years* . . .' and it therefore takes a cautious line regarding ethical investment. According to Richard Coulson, client services manager: '. . . it is possible to operate satisfactorily within ethical guidelines provided the exclusion is modest. We would be concerned about the effect on investment performance if more than 15% of the available UK equity market was excluded.'[10]

The Central Finance Board of the Methodist Church

The youngest of the church-based fund management companies is the investment unit of the Central Finance Board of the Methodist Church. The Central Finance Board (CFB) was established by Act of Parliament in 1960 as the investment arm of the Methodist Church, although funds under management were fairly small until the early 1970s, when built up by Charles Jacob MBE. The latter is often described as the 'father of ethical investment' in the UK for his pioneering work which resulted in the launch of the first ethical unit trust (see Chapter Seven for more details). However, his earlier work in creating an ethical investment unit for the Methodist Church is often overlooked. Charles Jacob retired in 1987, but total funds under management continued to see vigorous growth and exceeded £500m in 1994, as the table below shows:

Year to end Feb	1992	1993	1994
CFB Investment Funds £m	390	454	527

Of all the church investment bodies, the CFB most clearly asserts its Christian values as the 1993 Report and Accounts illustrate: '*They* (CFB staff) *represent the Church's face in the world of finance. Christian stewardship of money must, I believe, take place in the overall context of the Gospel.*' Roy Foulds, CFB Secretary.[11]

'The rights and wrongs of investment in South Africa have been the springboard for the development of thinking on the whole field of the ethics of investment . . . we have been involved in this movement to maintain portfolios which are consistent with the moral stance and teachings of the Christian faith ... However, more important than all else among our ethical duties is to stand as a Christian witness in this most worldly of arenas.' Bill Seddon, Investment Manager[12]

Created by statute, the CFB is limited to looking after the affairs of Methodist churches and charities. All investments apart from cash deposits must be made through a corporate trustee of the Church, with all the CFB funds having charitable status. The day-to-day investment functions are carried out by an investment unit, monitored on a monthly basis by an Investment Committee. Ultimate responsibility resides in the Central Finance Board itself which consists of members directly elected by the annual Methodist Conference, representatives of the Districts and three *ex officio* members. As reported in Chapter Six, despite a relatively severe ethical policy excluding 25% of the FTSE 100 Index, the ten-year investment performance was an impressive 18.1% average annual increase, 1.5% above that of the FT All Share.

The CFB is unique in church bodies in having a distinct ethical investment advisory committee. Bill Seddon describes it thus: '... to turn to the way we conduct our ethical wrestling bout. In 1983 the Methodist Conference, which is the governing body of the Church, established the Ethics of Investment Advisory Committee ... its purpose is to advise the Central Finance Board of ethical considerations relating to finance. The Committee also submits an annual report to the Methodist Conference. Legal responsibility for making any decision to dispose of shares rests with the Board but the Division of Social Responsibility is empowered to make any divestment public.'[13]

As argued many times in this book, the *process* of decision making in ethical investment is at least as important as the *products* excluded, which normally get all the attention. The CFB is clearly aware of this – Bill Seddon again: 'Consideration is given to the ethical standards of the stockbrokers, moneybrokers and banks with which we deal, as well as the companies in which we invest ... the investment unit is charged with taking the day-to-day investment decisions within an ethical framework. To facilitate the process, it is felt crucial that the unit employ committed Christians who want to be responsible for managing a portfolio that truly reflects the ethical judgment of the Methodist Church.' [14]

Other church groups

Another church fund which should be noted is the £200m invested in the Church of Scotland Trust, with similar ethical guidelines to the Church Commissioners.

Compared to Anglicans and Methodists, the Catholic Church in the UK has had a fairly low profile with regard to ethical investment. It is worth noting, however, that the Catholic Archdiocese of Birmingham in 1980 analysed its investment portfolio with regard to fifteen UK companies operating in South Africa. It sent out a questionnaire to them on six areas: wages; black advancement; industrial relations; migrant labour; desegregation and fringe benefits. Holdings of three companies which failed to meet the required standards were sold. [15]

Representatives of the main English church bodies meet occasionally in the Church Investors Group to discuss matters of mutual concern. In their different ways, all the main church investment bodies are tackling the problem posed by the Rev Timothy Smith, the doyen of American church-based ethical investors. '. . . as investors there is a faith-filled message to have us look at these funds which have been entrusted to us and be faithful stewards of those funds, and to not find ourselves in a kind of an outward schizophrenia, with our social values and gospel values in one pocket, and our financial values in another, and never the twain shall meet.'[16]

Charities

The charity sector is one of the most rapidly growing areas of investment management. Every year Investors Chronicle magazine publishes a league table of the top charity fund managers and the expansion in the sector can be seen in the table opposite.

Investment funds of charities were estimated to be £25bn by the end of 1993, but this excludes religious and educational bodies, and an accurate figure is probably nearer £40bn. In the past, several charities have felt embarrassed by publication of lists of investment holdings generally viewed as contrary to their expressed aims. The classic example is the 1985 publication by Social Audit of holdings in tobacco shares by a number of medical and cancer charities – who then sold them. The law accepts that an inappropriate investment

TOP TEN CHARITY FUND MANAGERS
FUNDS UNDER MANAGEMENT

	1991 £m	1993 £m	1993 Rank
1 CCLA	1174	1824	2
2 Cazenove	953	2021	1
3 Flemings	793	1382	5
4 Barings	778	1336	6
5 MAM-(Warburgs)	709	1399	4
6 Schroders	558	1640	3
7 Foreign & Colonial	353	762	7
8 J. Capel	342	342	16
9 Lazards	336	454	11
10 Morgan Grenfell	316	550	10
Assets of top ten.	6312	12514	

policy can damage a charity, and therefore ethical limits in accordance with the aims of a charity are recognized by law – see Chapter Eleven. That said, it is surprising how few charities appear to have thought out fully their investment policy. Hard statistics on this are lacking, but a rough estimate of charities with explicit ethical investment policies might be £6bn.

A good example of a charity with a well-structured ethical investment policy is the £800m Joseph Rowntree Trust, which is hardly surprising as it was one of the founders of the ethical investment movement in the UK. The following investment policy is imposed on their investment managers, Henderson Financial Management.

JOSEPH ROWNTREE CHARITABLE TRUST
ETHICAL INVESTMENT CRITERIA
(As at 27April 1994)

TRUSTEES ARE CLEAR THAT <u>THEY DO NOT WISH TO HOLD</u> SHARES IN COMPANY GROUPS WHICH

– have any of the following **military** involvements: if they have been involved in the sale or production of the following – nuclear weapons systems; strategic or non-civilian goods or services for

nuclear weapons systems; weapons systems; strategic goods or services for military users, including those used in weapons systems;
OR have been involved in construction or management of, or provision of strategic services for, military or nuclear bases;
– are classified as major **arms traders** by Campaign Against the
Arms Trade;
– are among the 'big Four' British **banks** (Barclays; Lloyds; Midland; NatWest).

TRUSTEES ARE LIKELY TO OBJECT TO HOLDING SHARES IN COMPANY GROUPS WHICH

– derive more than 10% of their reported annual turnover from the
production or sale of **alcoholic drinks**; OR are among the top ten
brewers of **beer** or distillers of **spirits** in the UK;
– manufacture **cosmetics, soaps or toiletries** unless they are
animal-test-free;
– derive more than £10m of their annual turnover from gambling;
– publish, print or wholesale magazines that the Campaign against
Pornography & Censorship says contain material that falls within its
proposed legal definition of **pornography**, or newspapers that have
a 'page 3' type photograph of a topless woman;
– derive more than 10% of their reported annual turnover from the
sale of **tobacco or tobacco products**, or derive any turnover from
the production of tobacco or tobacco products;
– have been found to be in partial compliance with, or total or
substantial violation of, the International Code of Marketing
Breast-Milk substitutes in the Third World;
– have reported making **political donations** exceeding £150,000
in total in the last five financial years.

TRUSTEES WOULD WISH THE MANAGERS <u>TO CHECK WITH THE TRUST BEFORE ACQUIRING</u> SHARES IN COMPANY GROUPS WHICH

– have had three or more public complaints upheld against them by
the Advertising Standards Authority in the last two years;
– manufacture **pharmaceuticals, medicines, or vitamins** unless
they are animal-test-free.
– derive any turnover from the sale of **animal fur products**;
– are classified as **Banks or Merchant Banks** by the Stock Exchange;

– derive more than 3% of their reported annual turnover from **gambling**;
– have been involved in the sale or production of **non-civilian goods or services for weapons systems**;
– have been involved in the **export of goods or services for military users** or which have exhibited at defence equipment exhibitions;
– have received any turnover from the uranium fuel cycle, handle radioactive waste, or supply equipment or service – other than safety and security equipment – **for nuclear plant or facilities**;
– supply ozone depleting chemicals (ODCs) or engage in industrial or food or energy conservation activities, which often use ODCs, unless their products are ODC-free;
– in relation to **water pollution,** have exceeded: at least one parameter for a Red List substance on a discharge consent during the last year covered; or a discharge consent on the same parameter three or more times at any one sampling point; or their discharge consents more than 35 times; or have been convicted during the period covered and fined any sum on at least one occasion, following a prosecution by the National Rivers Authority or a River Purification Board;
– have been convicted during the period covered following a prosecution by Her Majesty's Inspectorate of **Pollution** in England & Wales or Her Majesty's Industrial Pollution Inspectorate in Scotland;
– have received approval from MAFF or HSE to market **pesticide products** in the UK which have active ingredients on the Red List;
– the same part (subsidiary, associated or parent company) of which has been convicted more than once during the period 1/4/91–31/3/93 following a prosecution by the **Health & Safety** Executive;
– have reported making political donations exceeding £10,000 in an annual report in any one of the last five financial years;
– distribute **films or videos** that have been cut to obtain an 18 certificate;
– have paid a minimum wage to **South Africans** below the local Minimum Living Level(6)+ 50% in the last year analysed; or do not give enough information to allow an accurate assessment of minimum wages paid in South Africa; or have a workforce there which is less than 75% black African; or do not give enough

information to assess the proportion of their South African workforce that is black African;
– retail joinery or timber through DIY outlets, retail wooden
furniture; or manufacture or wholesale joinery or use timber or
joinery in the construction of buildings or boats or manufacture or
other wooden goods; or import, merchant, or process timber, unless
tropical-hardwood tree-free; or engage in mining or other activities in tropical regions unless tropical forests are not cleared; or
extract tropical timber.

TRUSTEES ARE ESPECIALLY INTERESTED IN INVEST-
ING IN COMPANIES WHICH HAVE POSITIVE ACHIEVE-
MENTS IN TERMS OF THEIR PRODUCTS OR SERVICES;
AND EMPLOYEE, CONSUMER & COMMUNITY RELA-
TIONS.
(The Trust ethical policy document then goes on to specify how it
uses EIRIS to assess various positive factors, and then concludes) –

In all the negative categories except the first, such positive aspects of
a company's record might, in view of Trustees, outweigh the negative aspects.

I have quoted the J. Rowntree Trust ethical investment criteria
virtually in full because it seems to me to be a well-thought-out
example which could be used as a model by other charities. Firstly, it
is a *practical example* which has been used by the Trust for a number
of years. Secondly, because it not only spells out the ethical categories required, but shows how *they are measured*. As such, it has clear
ethical integrity, and for example, to the objection that 'pornography
is purely subjective', it can point to an expert campaigning group,
the Campaign Against Pornography & Censorship. Likewise for
baby milk or the arms trade.

Pension funds and shareholder activism

'US institutions, which now manage more than half the country's
equities ... are ignoring their social responsibilities through com-
puter-driven investing. By focusing, for example, on short-term
performance criteria, US institutions sold some big airlines in the

1980s to unsuitable buyers, not caring what happened to the employees or the millions who depended on their services.' Louis Lowenstein, Rifkind Professor of finance and law at Columbia University.[17]

The beginning of this chapter showed some figures illustrating how pension funds were the largest single owner of UK shares . At the end of 1993 they were the largest type of institutional investor with assets of over £500bn, overshadowing the £400bn invested in life insurance companies and dwarfing the £95bn in unit trusts and £40bn in investment trusts. One group of pension funds who have led the way on such subjects as corporate governance and environmental liability, realizing that this is in their best long-term financial interests, are the local authorities. Currently there are ninety-eight such pension funds in the UK with total investment assets of around £45bn. The largest is Strathclyde and Tameside at just under £3bn, while the smallest is Orkney at £15m.

Such schemes are regulated by the Department of the Environment under the Local Government Superannuation Scheme (LGSS). Legally, these are statutory bodies in which the benefits are guaranteed, and not being trusts, are governed by specific investment rules. What this means in practice is that since the pension benefits are guaranteed, the local council taxpayers would have to top up any shortfall if the investments failed to produce sufficient assets to pay the pension liability. As a part of local government, LGSS funds also have a duty to maintain the standards expected of them – for example, in the case of South Africa it was argued that the duty of local councils regarding race relations empowered them to avoid investment in that country.

Likewise, many local authority pension funds have backed the PIRC Environmental Code (see Chapter Five) as consistent with their role as a representative of community interests on environmental matters and their position as monitor and regulator on a range of environmental issues.

Local authorities have increasingly publicized their work in these areas. However, the most prominent single unit discussing a range of corporate responsibility and social investment issues for pension funds is Pensions and Investment Research (PIRC), which as a group has made an outstanding contribution to the development of socially responsible investment in the UK . Alan McDougall, Joint

MD, was the administrator of the National Union of Mineworkers pension scheme in the early 1980s, and hence lived through the Scargill court case. He then went on to the GLC where he developed 'the London Financial Strategy', and went to be the first Chair of the UK Social Investment Forum. Anne Simpson, Joint MD, previously worked for the Transnationals Information Centre on banking and finance; as well as being a Research Associate at Birbeck College, she wrote the 1991 book *The Greening of Global Investment*. Stuart Bell, Research Director, was active in the financial boycott of South Africa as well as writing on a number of corporate responsibility issues.

PIRC grew out of an investment advisory unit for the Standing Conference on Local Authority Pension Fund Investment (Sclapfi), which was set up in 1982 to coordinate the investment activities of local authorities and became a separate company in 1986. Alan McDougall described its aim thus: 'We had an imperative to make socially responsible investment financially acceptable . . . it was our view that there was nothing socially responsible about losing money. If we were dealing with money, it had to be commercial.'[18] Currently PIRC advises local authority pension funds with £18bn of investments, as well as private sector funds of £16bn. (In order to do so PIRC plc had to register under the Financial Services Act). It describes its goal as '*to enable its pension funds' clients to develop prudent long-term investment strategies which both meet the wider economic best interests of beneficiaries and which recognize pension funds' wider responsibilities.*'[19] PIRC coordinates shareholder action campaigns on behalf of its members and provides proxy voting advice to its clients. It undertakes research projects including its own database, which, for example, is the only source currently monitoring companies' compliance with the Cadbury Code of Best Practice on corporate governance. *PIRC Intelligence* is a monthly bulletin covering corporate responsibility and ethical investment issues.

PIRC's arguments that looking beyond the purely short-term financial interests of the fund is in the interests both of society and of a pension scheme itself are cogently set out in *Socially Responsible Investment : A Strategy for Local Authority Pension Funds* – the following being some extracts:

1 With immense financial power comes responsibility. Not only do pension funds have duties to their members, they also have wider responsibilities which stem from their role in the economy.

2 *Pension funds' investment strategies, voting policies as shareholders and relations with companies can have a profound impact upon wider society and in turn, on the investment returns they receive. Local authority pension funds are in a leading position of influence. Their wide range of responsibilities for the environment, economic development and social welfare puts them in a unique position in the investment community.*

3 *Pension funds are long-term investors. Over the long term there is a great deal of mutual interest between shareholders, corporations, employees, the wider community and the environment... Wealth creation, sustainable development, equality of opportunity and corporate accountability are some of the goals which are shared in common. Socially responsible investors use their position of influence as owners to initiate positive change in corporations to the mutual benefit of a company's stakeholders.*

Is PIRC right in saying that there is a long-term mutual benefit between pension schemes and society? Critics like the National Association of Pension Funds (NAPF) have argued that a pension fund has only one objective, to maximize the benefits of its members; but that misses the point. As Elizabeth Holtzmann said in Chapter Five, no one disputes this – that is the clear fiduciary duty of pension scheme trustees. The real point is if this is best served by a short-term trading approach, where the shares of a company which does not fit are sold, or whether pension trust managers should work to improve the performance of poorly performing companies, and if necessary force them to do so. Most pension funds have long-term liabilities, over twenty-five years in some cases, so they ought to take a long-term investment strategy. The active dealing approach also incurs costs which reduce the return from investments.

Does the active management strategy work? The evidence suggests not. The WM company analysed the performance of a large number of pension schemes for the five years to the end of 1991. It found that the self-invested funds (which tend to have low turnover) grew by 10.2% a year on average, whereas the large active external managers could only manage a return of 9.7% and the smaller active managers only achieved 9.2% a year. In May 1994 Nestlé Rowntree stated that it was dropping the three external managers of its £1.3bn pension scheme. Despite the fact that they were Mercury Asset Management (Warburgs), Phillips and Drew and Barings, three of the leading names in pension fund management, they had underperformed the in-house team over the previous six years.[20]

People sometimes wonder why shareholder activism is comparatively rare in the UK, whereas it is commonplace in the US. There are two main reasons. Firstly, in the US, voting at AGMs takes the form of one vote per one share held – the so-called 'poll' system. In the UK, unless a poll is demanded, there is one vote per shareholder, and matters are normally decided by a show of hands. *PIRC Intelligence* argues: '. . . *we consider that the dual voting system should be reviewed in favour of voting by proxy on all occasions. We consider that this would be fairer since it would accord one vote per share, thus giving shareholders a say which corresponded to their investment stake in a company.*'[21] At a time when there are calls for 'shareholder democracy', it is hard to argue.

The other main reason is that technically it is much easier to force a company's AGM to consider a resolution in the US than in the UK. In the UK the support of 5% of the shares, or of 100 different shareholders, is required to put forward a resolution, whereas an individual shareholder can do so in America. In the US the cost of such a resolution is borne by the company, whereas in Britain shareholders have to pay for circulating the material. According to Stuart Bell: 'The rights for shareholders to be involved in agenda setting by proposing resolutions are much too restrictive. The problem at the moment is that the agenda is set entirely by directors. If it is not relevant to shareholders the AGM becomes a dull exercise in public relations by the company.'[22] In September 1993 Hanson Trust proposed changes to its Articles which would have eliminated the right of shareholders to nominate a director unless backed by 10% of the votes, while it would have also required shareholders to have at least 5% of the votes to amend resolutions. Following a PIRC-led campaign, Hanson dropped these proposals.

Corporate governance, or ownership is not control!

'Pension funds can do better for their participants by behaving like owners and maintaining a long-term perspective in investments. I

urge pension plans toward an active, committed style of investing.'
Olena Berg, US Pensions and Welfare Assistant Secretary.[23]

'. . . the law of trusts inveterately and unchangingly does not permit
a trustee to profit personally from dealings with the trust estate. Yet
a corporate manager or director, in a similar position as a fiduciary,
has no such strictures. It is almost tautological that recent MBOs
have served first and foremost, the personal pocket-book interests of
management.' Bob Monks, Lens Inc.[24]

Corporate governance is a huge subject in its own right on which
whole books have been written. In essence, in the nineteenth century a business was run on a small scale, and usually by its owner. As
the twentieth century developed, companies became larger and
floated their shares on the stock market, where they were bought by
a large number of individual shareholders. In the 1960s the economist J. K. Galbraith in books such as *The New Industrial State* argued
persuasively that this process had resulted in a divorce between
ownership and *control*. He suggested that shareholdings had become
so widely dispersed that the senior managements of large companies
could ignore them and in effect ran companies for their own benefit,
and not, as the textbooks argued, for the benefit of shareholders. In
1976 Peter Drucker wrote *The Unseen Revolution*, in which he
argued that the gap had been bridged by the creation of workers'
pension funds, which then owned 25% of corporate America, and
by the end of the century will own over 50% of it.

However, as I mentioned in connection with ESOPs, ownership
does not automatically mean control, unless there is a way of exercising it. Since the late 1980s this point has been forcefully made
in the US by the largest institutional investor, the $100bn
Californian State Pension Fund normally known as Calpers, that
institutions *must* vote their shares. Dale Hanson, chief executive of
Calpers, put it this way: 'Our entire investment philosophy is based
on the premise that we are long-term investors. Our average holding
period is between eight and ten years . . . Calpers has no motives
other than to improve corporate performance so that investment
value is increased . . . we seek a return to corporations being ac-
countable to their shareholders. If accountability exists, we are
confident that corporate performance will follow.'[25]

An analysis of Calpers' shareholder activism by the consulting firm Wilshire Associates found that an active shareholder policy paid strong financial dividends. From 1987 to 1992 Calpers targeted forty-two US companies for shareholder action. This group had significantly underperformed the US benchmark, the S&P 500 Index, in the previous five years. Wilshire found that after Calpers had contacted them, in the subsequent five years they outperformed the S&P 500 by 41%. The study also found that shareholder activism had the most financial benefit when it focused on corporate strategy in a dialogue with management. In 1988 the US Department of Labor extended the concept of fiduciary duty to proxy voting, i.e. institutional investors were now *obliged* to use their votes. The UK Cadbury Code followed suit in 1992 by concluding that institutions should make positive use of their voting rights.

Another key date in modern corporate governance was April 1989, when Bob Monks informed the board of Honeywell Inc that proposals to limit shareholder powers were unacceptable. Honeywell was a large US computer and defence company whose poor profits performance had been reflected in a stagnant share price. Monks formed a shareholder action group, including Calpers, to oppose the board's proposals, and a fierce proxy battle began about this. In May it was announced that the board's proposals had been defeated, and in July 1989 Honeywell announced a major restructuring. Over a three-month period the value of Honeywell shares rose 22% to $89. Monks said later: 'We do not claim to be responsible for all of the gain . . . perhaps Honeywell management would have announced a restructuring even without external pressure. But we believe that our demonstration of shareholder concern – and power – played a substantial part in the gains realised.'[25]

The 1989 Honeywell proxy battle was historic for a number of reasons. It was the first time that institutional shareholders joined forces with private investors for a proxy initiative which defeated a corporation's anti-takeover proposals. It was also the first time that a revolt of institutional shareholders demonstrated a substantial improvement in share value. Since 1989 Bob Monks has formed his own company, Lens Inc, to force change on a number of poorly performing companies. Probably the most famous was a two-year battle in 1990–92 with the giant US retail chain Sears Roebuck, where Monks even stood as an independent director. He was not elected, but the company was eventually forced into a major restructuring plan which involved selling off its financial operations to concentrate on retailing, while over the period the share price almost doubled from \$24.75 to \$44.75.

Corporate governance does not just extend to improving corporate strategy, or even increasing a company's awareness of potential liabilities such as in the environmental field. In the UK there has been a feeling in recent years that while many long-serving employees were being made redundant, the directors of many companies were rewarding themselves unfairly with excessive pay, share options and long-service contracts. PIRC had aired these issues for several years before the City commissioned the Cadbury Committee to examine them. PIRC advised their clients to vote against such option schemes. Anne Simpson stated that: 'share options are a poor motivator as executives can only gain but not lose money, while they do not encourage share ownership as executives tend to cash in their gains at once.'[27]

At a time of global recession, the £25bn Postel Pension Fund led a campaign against the habit of directors granting themselves rolling three-year contracts, so that even if they were incompetent, it could cost hundreds of thousands of pounds to get rid of them. People also wondered why, when many employees received little or no pay rises, executives should be getting large pay rises. In the year to October 1993 the remuneration of the highest paid directors of the 653 FTSE nonfinancial companies rose by 10.5%; underlying inflation was two per cent, and the profits of these companies fell by 3.5%.

The Cadbury Committee recommended that corporate governance should be policed by nonexecutive directors, but the signs are not hopeful. A survey by accountants Binder Hamlyn in July 1994 found that nonexecutives were ineffective in enforcing high standards of corporate governance, principally because the nonexecutives themselves were not of high enough calibre. The survey added: *'Since many nonexecutives admit that they spend too little time on their directorships and have insufficient underlying knowledge of the business, it is not surprising that they find a dominant chairman or chief executive a significant inhibiting factor.'*[28] The US has a tradition of dominant chief executives, but there is a growing acceptance of the role of a *lead director*, an outside director who can mobilize the outside directors if things go wrong. The GM company has crystallized the concept of a lead director in its new, highly acclaimed board guidelines on corporate issues.

Relationship investing

'Institutional investors are trapped in a system that undermines the long-term earning power of the American companies on which they must depend for the bulk of their portfolio investments.' Michael Porter, Professor of Harvard Business School.[29]

Michael Porter's books *Competitive Advantage* and *The Comparative Advantage of Nations*[30] have been best sellers, making him one of the most influential economists of his generation. In the late 1980s he was appointed to the Council on Competitiveness, an agency of the Federal Government. His 1992 report for the Council stated that the average US institution held the shares of a company for less than two years (ten years ago the average US pension fund used to hold shares for over seven years). Since institutional investors focused on short–term quarterly earnings, company managers were forced to do likewise, sacrificing long–term investment in areas like research and development and staff training which are essential to a company's long-term competitive advantage. There is also the question of whether this short-term, trading-orientated style of investment management is efficient. Earlier I suggested that the acid test of performance statistics suggest not. Jonathan Charkham is a former adviser to the Bank of England (now an adviser to PIRC) and author of a recent book on corporate governance: '. . . the benefits of diversification diminish sharply after one has bought about fifteen to twenty different stocks . . . I must say I find it curious that some funds diversify as much as they do, and I can't see any real advantage in it because it means having to keep an eye on a much wider range of shares and it means any resource has to be spread more thinly.'[31]

Porter's answer to these questions was 'relationship investing', where large investors stop seeing company shares as pieces of paper to be bought for a quick trading profit, but rather that institutions should rediscover the advantages and responsibilities of ownership. They should have board seats and have access to inside information, in return for which they would, of course, be restricted in their ability to sell shares. This idea has been quickly taken up in the US. *Business Week* magazine describes relationship investing as: '. . . whenever there is an established, committed link between a company and shareholders . . . it begins with shareholders taking a real interest in the company – asking questions of the board, and not trading the stock like pork bellies – and goes all the way to taking a big stake, a board seat.'[32]

Howard Davies, Director General of the CBI in the UK, believes that '. . . there is some evidence that relationship investing is successful', and that it is a subject '. . . which we would do well to consider seriously.'[33] Alan McDougall has no doubts: 'The underperformance of a company can be related to its governance structure. Relationship investment is more cost-effective and more efficient both for the fund and the company itself. It cuts out all the administration and lobbying involved with having lots of shareholders. It acts as a credible monitor, and the company will always know with whom they have to deal.'[34]

CHAPTER ELEVEN

Ethical Investment and the Law

The legal framework

Anyone investing their own money can do with it as they like as long as they satisfy the requirements of the criminal law and the Inland Revenue. The vast bulk of wealth in Britain, however, is owned not by individuals but by institutions which manage it to pay pensions or insurance policies. Once money is managed by someone on behalf of other people, a whole complex of law becomes involved, and anyone interested in ethical investment for pension funds, charities or unit trusts needs to have some understanding of this. Certainly any one *recommending* ethical investment to a charity or pension fund or even considering doing so, as a trade union trustee for example, *must have a basic legal awareness*.

Anyone writing about the law faces a difficult dilemma. Law is a complex and subtle subject which has developed its own rich jargon over the centuries, and, some people would say, even its own way of thought. An example at random from 'Beginners Page', a regular article in *Pensions World* magazine which tries to explain legal concepts to non lawyers: 'A trust is an obligation binding on a person (called a trustee) to deal with property over which that person has control, for the benefit of persons (known as beneficiaries), who may include the trustee ... The trust obligation is known in law as an equitable obligation and is historically governed by equity rather than common law.'[1]

Many non-lawyers may already find their eyes glazing over. The dilemma is this: to be accurate, legal advice needs to be precise and therefore expressed in legal terms, but such jargon is more or less unintelligible to a member of the public. Some people might well argue that in that case it should be left to the solicitors and judges who understand it. In my view that is quite wrong. Firstly, the law regarding ethical investment is often mentioned by nonlegal experts in the City and in the financial press in such a way as to suggest that they are not really aware of the law's rulings on this subject. For example, it is frequently stated by investment managers that their only legal duty, and that of the trustees who employ them, is to maximize the financial return on the funds under their control. In fact, this is dubious advice for the pension funds which make up the bulk of the country's investment assets; for the growing charity sector it is incorrect.

Secondly, professional legal expertise is not cheap – an hour with a partner in a top London firm of solicitors can cost over £250! A knowledge of the basic legal setting helps the client enable the legal adviser to establish what the legal problem actually is more quickly and accurately than otherwise would be the case, thus saving expensive legal time. To give a practical example, a charity trustee, worried about the extent to which his trust's funds could be used in a campaigning role, would help a solicitor to use his professional skills to the best advantage by providing copies of the governing constitution and of correspondence with the Charity Commissioners when the charity was set up and minutes of how the trustees had discussed this in practice. A basic legal understanding also gives the non-expert greater control over the process of taking legal advice by the simple fact of understanding more of the jargon!

Anyone considering any kind of action which might have possible legal consequences should, of course, take professional legal advice. It is ironic that the major court case which is always quoted regarding pension funds and ethical investment was fought on one side with the legal advice being disregarded. This was the famous legal battle brought by Arthur Scargill in 1984 to force the trustees of the mineworkers' pension fund not to invest overseas or in alternative sources of energy which were a rival to coal. In legal circles it is generally now known as the Megarry case, the name of the Vice Chancellor who presided over it in the High Court, although at the time it was described as Cowan vs Scargill. Arthur Scargill dismissed his legal advisers and presented his case himself to the court. Even at the time this looked like an own goal, or as Sir Robert Megarry put it later: 'Where the argument is predominantly on law, as it was in this case, few would contend that even a fluent and well advised layman is on a parity with an experienced leader. That is one important fact in assessing Cowan versus Scargill. One cannot say what would have emerged had the defendant's case been presented by a Chancery silk, particularly in the bound and rebound of ideas between Bench and Bar.'[2]

The Vice Chancellor here seemed to say quite explicitly that if Mr Scargill's case had been represented in court by a senior barrister, the outcome, and hence the whole perception of pension fund law regarding social investment in the UK, might have been quite different! The vital importance of taking professional legal advice was therefore demonstrated by the Megarry case. The 1986 Martin case established that trustees must use their discretion and not simply *rubber stamp* the advice of their professional financial advisers. In the field of charities the Charity Commission is making great efforts to improve the professional awareness of charity trustees, which includes the law.

Hence it is hoped that this chapter will help non-lawyers understand the legal framework in which anyone managing or being the trustee of other people's funds is operating. It aims to improve the legal understanding of investment law by those involved in positions of financial responsibility or in financial management, and thereby to enable trustees and others with such financial responsibility to make the best use of the legal resources open to them. Hopefully, it will enable them to save legal time by asking more accurate questions and to have a better understanding of the answers given.

Trust law

Like many things in British life, the law on pension funds and charities is hallowed with the dust of antiquity. Trust law dates back to the Middle Ages and was originally devised for family settlements. The classic case was that of the knight going off to fight in the Crusades, and not trusting the competence of his wife in financial affairs, entrusting the job of managing his estates to someone else, the person entrusted being a *trustee*. In reality, the most common case was probably that of young children (minors) who inherited an estate and were clearly unable to run it. The key concept behind trust law is that the person owning or having the right to some property, *the beneficiary*, is not competent to run it through youth, mental illness, or whatever, and that someone else has to run it for his/her benefit.

Hence the key distinction is between the trustee – the person who has *control* of an asset and the beneficiary who *owns* or who has the right to it. A trustee has what is called a *fiduciary duty*, which means that he/she must act reasonably and honestly at all times for the benefit of the beneficiary when he or she is dealing with the latter's property. The trustee must not use it for his or her own benefit and must act in the beneficiaries' interest even if this *conflicts with his/her own wishes*. In a celebrated case in 1886 Lord Halsbury pronounced: '. . . the goodness of a trustee's motives cannot justify the propriety of an investment.'[3] It can be seen from this how the mineworkers' pension fund trustees could be legally obliged to invest in alternative energy sources despite their wish not to do so. An interesting point, and one which will be discussed in more detail later, is *what does benefit mean in this context?* It does not necessarily mean financial benefit, nor when it does mean that, need it be to the exclusion of everything else.

Another point worth establishing is the concept of equity; in law as in general usage it means fairness, but it also has a special sense where 'equity' is a branch of law. All the layman needs to know is that trusts are governed by equity rather than the common law, which means the court is less bound by precedent and more by the facts of the case, or as pensions solicitor Anna Kelly puts it: 'What this means in practice is that the court has a great deal of freedom to interfere with trusts, and to develop and apply flexible rules. Equity concerns itself more with fairness than with strict formalities . . . One major advantage of equity is that it is flexible, but on the other hand sometimes it has the disadvantage of being unpredictable. The courts are able to exercise a considerable degree of supervision over trusts.'[4]

Like other branches of law, equity is not static. Trust law principles are defined and clarified, and sometimes modified, by the judgment of the court (i.e. the judge) in a particular case. The overriding principle however is *that the interests of the beneficiaries must be paramount.* There is one important caveat here which is not always given the prominence it deserves – the trust itself through its trust deed may limit the freedom of the trustees in what in law is called an 'express provision'. The classic example is of a cancer charity whose trust deed forbids investment in tobacco shares. As Ian Gault of Herbert Smith describes it: 'If we consider first the express provisions of a trust, the important point to note is that the express terms of a trust will usually displace any implied powers and duties under general trust law. Thus, it is perfectly possible for the trust deed of a trust to limit the range of permitted investments to those which are considered ethical. Alternatively, the trustees may be given specific power to adopt ethical criteria in their investment policy. *If the governing documents are drafted so as to permit or encourage the adoption of ethical criteria, this puts the position beyond doubt.*[5]

Although pension funds dominate other trusts in terms of size, in terms of age they are mere newcomers. Funded pension schemes were only introduced at the beginning of this century and only grew to their present massive size when they were encouraged by the 1975 Social Security Act. The majority of law on the subject therefore derives from individual trusts – the sort of widow-and-orphan case which so intrigued Dickens and the other Victorian novelists – or from cases involving the charity sector. In either case the law has always, rightly, demanded a high level of caution from trustees to take no risks with their beneficiaries' money. As Lord Halsbury put it in 1886: 'As a general rule the law requires of a trustee no higher degree of diligence in his office than a man of ordinary prudence would exercise in the management of his own private affairs. Yet he is not allowed the same discretion in investing the monies of the trust as if he were . . . dealing with his own estate . . . it is the duty of a trustee to confine himself to the class of investments which are permitted by the trust, and likewise to avoid all investments of that class which are attended with hazard.'[6]

Of course in the Victorian period married women had limited legal rights, with divorce practically unknown. It was also a period when stock markets were unregulated and unscrupulous share promoters were able to raise money for projects with little hope of success. Hence it can be seen how the trust law of the Victorian period was a response to the needs of the time. Whether it was really sensible to regulate modern pension funds in such a way was a key question which was addressed by the 1993 Goode Committee on pension trust law. This is a huge subject deserving of a book on its own, but suffice it to say that while Professor Goode thought that the current arrangements were satisfactory, others argued that a comprehensive Pension Fund Reform Act was required.

In Goode's 1000-page report there was a clear statement of the right of pension funds to consider ethical investment:

*As trustees they are perfectly entitled to have a policy on ethical invest-
ment and to pursue that policy, so long as they treat the interests of the
beneficiaries as paramount and the investment policy is consistent with
the standards of care and prudence required by law. This means that
trustees are free to avoid certain kinds of prudent investment which they
consider the scheme members would regard as objectionable, so long as
they make equally advantageous investments elsewhere ... What
trustees are not entitled to do is to subordinate the interests of the
beneficiaries to ethical or social demands and thereby deprive the beneficiaries of investment income or opportunities they would otherwise have
enjoyed.*[7]

This statement from the Goode Report reflected how the concept of
trust law regarding ethical investment had developed over the previous ten years in three famous court cases.

From Arthur Scargill to the Bishop of Oxford

Trust law had not had to consider the concept of ethical investment
before 1984, but in the following seven years three landmark cases
established the basic legal framework. The first was the Megarry
(Scargill) case, followed by two concerning the desire of beneficiaries to force trustees to exclude investments in South Africa. In
1986 Lord Murray examined the desire by a newly elected Edinburgh council to force the sale of all council investments in South
Africa. In 1991 the High Court under Vice Chancellor Sir Donald
Nicholls had the unusual spectacle of a Church of England Bishop,
(Richard Harries, the Bishop of Oxford), using legal means to try
and force the Church Commissioners, who administered the central
Church of England funds, to adopt a more Christian investment
policy.

As mentioned earlier, the Megarry case centred on the desire of
the National Union of Mineworkers (NUM) to force the
mineworkers' pension scheme to prohibit the fund from investing in
alternative energy sources which were a competitor to coal. The
pension scheme was unusual in that it required the approval of both
employer and union trustees before it could implement its investment plan, which was regularly updated. At the 1983 NUM annual
conference a motion was passed calling for the pension fund to stop

investing overseas, and also to end the purchase, and eventually ownership, of oil shares. This was then presented to the next meeting of trustees. The way it was put forward is probably not irrelevant to the later case. Alan McDougall, a pensions administrator for the NUM at that time, later wrote: 'What followed was an unmitigated disaster. Arthur Scargill took it upon himself to present the policy at the next trustees' meeting – but without adequate prior research, financial analysis, or external advice as to how it was to be implemented in practice. It was presented as a political gesture – not as a considered investment strategy.'[8]

The case, therefore, hinged on the question whether pension funds could or should take account of ethical or social factors in deciding investment policy. Judge Sir Robert Megarry came down firmly on the side that they could not. In his view, in law a pension fund was a trust like any other, and hence the trustees were subject to an overriding duty to act in the best interests of the beneficiaries of the trust. For a pension fund, *best interest* was normally understood as the best financial return on its investments subject to a degree of prudence, since the sole purpose of a pension scheme was financial – to fund pension benefits. He therefore ruled that the union trustees could not enforce their policy. He gave four principles underlying his decision:

a) The duty to act in the best interests of the beneficiaries.

b) The duty of trustees to ignore their own beliefs in order to comply with a).

c) The duty to act prudently, which includes taking professional advice, and also requires consideration of diversification of investments.

d) In very rare instances, even for a trust such as a pension fund concerned only with financial benefits, the word 'benefit' might accept less than the best financial returns.

In his judgement Vice Chancellor Megarry really reiterated traditional principles of trust law, and what was novel was their application to pension schemes. The primacy of beneficiaries' interests in (a) and the duty of trustees to ignore their own beliefs in (b) were similar to Lord Halsbury's judgments one hundred years before. As Sir Robert put it: 'Trustees may have strongly held social or political views. They may be opposed to any investment in South Africa, or other countries, or they may object to any form of investment in companies concerned with alcohol, tobacco, armaments ... Yet under a trust, if investments of this type were to be more beneficial to the beneficiary than other investments, the trustees must not refrain from making investments by reason of the views they hold.'[9]

The requirement to act prudently and take professional advice in (c) was also in line with precedent. The duty to consider diversification was more modern and derived from the thinking behind the 1961 Trustee Investments Act. The publication of that Act marked government recognition that in a period of inflation the traditional cautious investment of trust funds in absolutely safe government bonds might not be in the best interest of the beneficiaries. Only investment professionals could sensibly assess this risk.

The diversification argument is an important one for ethical investment since it can be used to rule out ethical constraints on investment on the basis that this impedes diversification. This should not be a problem for most ethical funds. The 1961 Act was concerned that trustees should look at investment in company shares and property as well as the traditional 'narrow range' of buying government bonds. If a fund considered that, for example, it did not want to hold any British companies with significant activities in South Africa, and this meant that it was unable to buy shares accounting for around 10% of the UK stock market, this would be unlikely to be a problem under the diversification rules if financial experts advised that this would be unlikely to hurt the fund's investment performance. If it wanted to avoid companies which in total excluded 50% of the UK stock market, then financial advisers would almost certainly have to assess this as a negative, which would be a problem.

Sir Robert Megarry's fourth principle (d) was significant, since even he conceded that even for a financial trust 'benefit' may not only mean the maximization of financial returns. He gave the example of a pension fund where all the beneficiaries have strict views on moral matters and condemn the arms trade, tobacco, etc.: 'The beneficiaries might well consider that it was far better to receive less than to receive more money from what they consider to be evil and tainted sources. "Benefit" is a word with a very wide meaning and there are circumstances in which arrangements which work to the financial disadvantage of a beneficiary may yet be for his benefit . . . But I would emphasize that such cases are likely to be very rare.'[10]

The Megarry judgment has generally been viewed as ruling out ethical investment for most pension schemes. However, there are some points to note which suggest that a future case might reach a more liberal conclusion. In a later essay on the case, the Vice Chancellor pointed out, as mentioned earlier, that Mr Scargill's decision to dispense with legal advice had not advanced his case, and that employing a senior barrister might have resulted in a different decision. He also suggested that if the mineworkers had presented their case differently to the trustees in terms of preference rather than absolute veto, the result of the case could have been different:

> What was at issue was a matter not of preferences or policies but of exclusion. The wide powers of the trustees were to be subjected, by fiat of the trustees, to a total prohibition on certain types of investment, come what may. The defendants' requirement was absolute . . . . A policy of preference, rather than prohibition, is by no means a like case. If other things are equal, it may well be contended that an investment in A Ltd instead of B Ltd, made because the great majority of the beneficiaries oppose investment in B Ltd and so gratifying the majority, will neither harm nor benefit the minority, and so will in general be for the benefit of the beneficiaries at large. Such a contention seems to have considerable force.[11]

As well as Mr Scargill and the use of expressed preference rather than absolute veto, the Vice Chancellor gave a third reason why pension schemes might be able to consider ethical issues in future, since, like other trusts, they were able to draft their trust deed to include ethical objectives:

> Finally, not enough attention has been directed to questions of drafting and amendment. If it is desired to impose a prohibition on overseas investment or oil, the scheme may be drafted so as to produce this result; and a scheme with an obnoxiously wide investment clause may be amended under the power of amendment that every properly drafted pension scheme contains. If in exercising their powers of investment, the trustees are required to

give effect to the views of the majority of the beneficiaries, the scheme can say so.[12]

This line of thinking was shared by others at this time. According to a book on pension fund investment published in 1990:

> ... when confrontation is not sought (unlike Cowan versus Scargill), there is still much scope for trustees quietly to take into account the moral, social and political views of beneficiaries and of themselves, since it will in practice be difficult to prove that at the time a particular investment was made, it was not equally as financially meritorious as certain other possible investments. The inevitable uncertainty in the stock market makes it difficult to assess which particular investment or type of investment would be best in terms of capital growth, income and risk: a reasonable amount of leeway must be afforded to trustees.[13]

There is one other consideration which should be taken into account in the Megarry case, which took a much more restrictive view of ethical investment than had been expected by legal experts. Judges are human too, and the Vice Chancellor, one of the most senior judges in the country, was probably not amused to be lectured at in his own courtroom by a trade union leader. The court case also took place against the background of the 1984–85 national miners' strike. Some people undoubtedly regarded the mineworkers' legal battle as political propaganda for that strike, rather than a rational attempt to take broader social considerations of their members' interests into account.

The political fall-out from the miners' strike may have overshadowed the next important case in 1986 when the newly elected Labour council in Edinburgh ordered its trust funds to sell shares of UK companies with significant South African exposure. This was decided by Lord Murray in the Scottish Court of Session, the case also being known as Martin vs City of Edinburgh after the Conservative councillor who challenged this policy. Lord Murray ruled against the council on the grounds that the trustees had not taken into account whether this new policy was in the best interests of the beneficiaries. They had also not discussed this with professional investment advisers. He made one advance on the Megarry judgment by emphasizing that although trustees must take professional advice, the ultimate responsibility is theirs and they cannot therefore be made to 'rubber stamp' the financial advice given:

> If the law requires that . . . the duties of trustees in seeking to secure the best interests of the beneficiaries are merely to rubber stamp the professional advice of financial advisers, I find myself unable to agree . . . I cannot conceive that trustees have an un-qualified duty . . . simply to invest trust funds in the most profit-able investment available. To accept that without qualification would, in my view, involve substituting the discretion of financial advisers for trustees.[14]

The Murray judgment therefore established two significant points. Trustees should take professional financial advice into account; if Edinburgh council had discussed their policy in advance with investment experts, and if the latter had agreed that such a policy would not harm the beneficiaries' interests (in practice avoiding South Africa would have been to their distinct benefit), then the decision might well have been different. Secondly, that although trustees had to take expert advice, they were not bound by it as the ultimate responsibility was theirs.

The Church Commissioners in the dock

The Bishop of Oxford case was more subtle than the Murray one since the Church Commissioners were technically a charity even though one of their main functions was the payment of clergy pensions. In fact, the Church Commissioners were established in 1948 by statute (Act of Parliament) to administer the central funds of the Church of England, although these in turn dated back to a gift of lands made by Queen Anne to the Church in 1704 (Queen Anne's Bounty) 'for the augmentation of the poor clergy'.

In 1990 the Church Commissioners' funds amounted to about £3bn, of which land accounted for £1.7bn, and stock exchange investments some £780m. The income on this money was used for three main purposes: to pay about half of all clergy stipends (salaries), to cover their housing costs and to pay virtually all their pensions. In 1986 the subject of the Church Commissioners' investment policy in South Africa was raised at the General Synod, the 'parliament' of the Church of England, together with a motion calling for them to sell all shares with a South African exposure. The Church Commissioners rejected this motion, while they described as 'wholly mistaken' the associated contention that their purpose was 'for the advancement of Christianity by and through the Church of England'.

In 1988 the Christian Ethical Investment Group (CEIG) was founded by a number of bishops and other clergy 'to promote a stronger ethical investment policy in the Church of England'. CEIG repeatedly tried to negotiate with the Commissioners regarding their ethical investment policy, but to no avail. Since their establishment in 1948 the Church Commissioners had adopted an ethical investment policy which excluded investments in defence industries, gambling, alcohol, tobacco and newspapers. The Church Commissioners did not invest directly in South Africa, nor did they invest in companies with a significant amount of their business there. Together these ethical exclusions meant that the Commissioners could not invest in 13% of the British stock market.

In 1991 the Bishop of Oxford and two other clergymen went to the High Court under Vice Chancellor Nicholls technically seeking legal establishment of two declarations which would have forced the Church Commissioners to include ethical considerations in their investment policy. In reality, the case was fought to determine whether they should disinvest in British companies with any kind of presence in South Africa, which would have increased the ethically excluded proportion of the stock market from 13% to 37%. In Judge Nicholls's words:

> Their concern is that the Commissioners give insufficient weight to what are now called 'ethical' considerations . . . The Commissioners attach overriding importance to financial considerations, and that is a misapprehension of the approach they ought properly to adopt when making investment decisions. The Commissioners ought to have in mind that the underlying purpose for which they hold their assets is the promotion of the Christian faith through the Church of England. The Commissioners should not exercise their investment functions in a manner which would be incompatible with that purpose even if that involves a risk of incurring significant financial detriment.[15]

Vice Chancellor Nicholls went on to repeat the principle that it was axiomatic that the main duty of trustees was to further the purpose of the trust of which they were trustees. He made an important distinction between what he called 'functional property' and 'investment property.' Functional property would be property used for the purposes of the charity or trust. He gave the examples of the National Trust owning country houses or the Salvation Army running hostels for the destitute. Here investment criteria need not apply. Nicholls did not say so, but the obvious example for the Church of England was property owned to house the clergy, 'the glebe'. By contrast, investment property was designed to generate a financial return. (Of course, as described in the previous chapter, it was a programme of property investment on purely financial grounds which did great damage to the investment assets of the Commissioners.) According to the judge:

> . . . the purposes of the trust will be best served by the trustees seeking to obtain therefrom the maximum return, whether by way of income or capital growth, which is consistent with commercial prudence. That is the starting point for all charity trustees when considering the exercise of their investment powers . . . In most cases the best interests of the charity require that the trustees' choice of investments should be made solely on the basis of well-established investment criteria, having taken expert advice where appropriate, having due regard to such matters as the need to diversify, the need to balance income against capital growth and the need to balance risk against return.[16]

Vice Chancellor Nicholls therefore rejected the Bishop of Oxford's case, holding that the Church Commissioners were right in their current ethical investment policy. He seemed to say that even for an obviously Christian body, ethics were a matter of opinion. The Commissioners' current ethical guidelines were acceptable, not because they followed from Christian principles, but because they made little difference to the financial returns! He considered that the Bishop's proposed restrictions would have the practical effect of reducing diversification and were therefore unacceptable on those grounds. As Sir Donald Nicholls described the exclusion of gambling, arms, tobacco or alcohol:

There are members who believe these business activities are morally wrong, and that they are in conflict with Christian teaching and its moral values. But . . . it (is) obvious that many committed members of the Church of England take the contrary view. To say that not all members of the Church of England eschew gambling, alcohol or tobacco would be an understatement . . . These are moral questions on which no single view can be shown to be 'right' and the others 'wrong'. As I understand the position, the Commissioners have felt able to exclude these items from their investments despite the conflicting views on the morality of holding these items as investments, because there has remained open to the Commissioners an adequate width of alternative investments.[17]

If one may criticize a High Court judge, Sir Donald Nicholls's reasoning seemed confused here. The question was surely not to try to define Christian morality, a huge and impossible task (for example, the Catholic Church would clearly have added contraceptives to the excluded list), but to ascertain the best interest of the beneficiaries of an explicitly Christian charity. Since these beneficiaries had voted in the General Synod to adopt a more restrictive ethical policy, their wishes were clear. If, on the other hand, ethical criteria were as subjective as the Judge suggested, then since any ethical policy automatically reduces diversification, he should have instructed the Commissioners to drop their ethical criteria and invest in the whole of the stock market! As leading charity lawyer Andrew Philips said later, discussing the Commissioners' case:

The reasons for the bringing of the case were twofold. Firstly to challenge the assertion by and on behalf of the Church Commissioners that benefiting the clergy and their dependants was not a means to their charitable ends of advancing Christianity, but the end itself. The second assertion, flowing from it, was that 'the financial interests (of the clergy and their dependants) are always paramount' . . . The Commissioners are only allowed to take Christian factors into account 'provided those financial interests are not adversely affected'. In common parlance, this adds up to . . . the potentially hypocritical position where the Commissioners can only take Christian considerations into account insofar as that carries no significant risk . . . the Judge intervened to tell the Church Commissioners' Counsel that he 'balked' at the absoluteness of that position.[18]

Sir Donald's 'balk' led him to make some very interesting observations on charity law. He listed some instances where ethical criteria should be taken into account. He did stress, however, that he thought that (a) and (b) below would be fairly rare:

a) when the objects of the charity are such that investments of a particular type would conflict with the aims of the charity. Much-cited examples are those of cancer research companies and tobacco shares, trustees of temperance shares and breweries and distillery shares, and trustees of charities of the Society of Friends and shares in companies engaged in production of armaments. If, as would be likely in those examples, trustees were satisfied that investing in a company engaged in a particular type of business would conflict with the very object their charity is seeking to achieve, they should not so invest.

b) when trustees' holdings of particular investments might hamper a charity's work either by making potential recipients of aid unwilling to be helped because of the source of the charity's money, or by alienating some of those who support the charity financially . . . The greater the risk of financial detriment, the more certain the trustees should be of countervailing disadvantages to the charity before they incur that risk.

c) Another circumstance where trustees would be entitled, or even required, to take into account nonfinancial criteria would be where the trust deed so provides.

d) This is not to say that trustees who own land may not act as responsible landlords, or those who own shares may not act as responsible shareholders. They may. The law is not so cynical as to require trustees to behave in a fashion which would bring them or their charity into disrepute.

e) Trustees may, if they wish, accommodate the views of those who consider that on moral grounds a particular investment would be in conflict with the objects of the charity, so long as the trustees are satisfied that course would not involve a risk of significant financial detriment.[19]

The Nicholls case clearly identified that pension funds and charities, although both legally 'trusts', have very different aims and objectives. A pension scheme is a body to collect the forced or voluntary savings of individuals in order to produce a fund of assets which will pay the pensions to those individuals when they retire (and in some cases, sickness or death benefits). Its sole purpose would seem a financial one, although the beneficiaries have the right to add other guidelines if they see fit.

On the other hand, a charity is a body to carry out an officially recognized charitable purpose, run by voluntary trustees, often with the aid of a large number of unpaid workers. Clearly, both trustees and voluntary workers must have a belief in the aims of the charity. There is a risk that they would not provide this free labour if offended by the investment policy of the charity. At the same time, many charities rely on donations from the public for their funding, again emphasizing the importance of the public's support of the charity's aims and the public's perception that it is carrying it out. It would seem clear that the reputation, and possibly the financial backing, of cancer charities suffered in 1985 when Social Audit revealed their holdings in tobacco company shares. Hence, the main objective of a charity cannot be financial, and it must take account of other factors.

That said, while the general principles of the Nicholls case were a useful clarification of charity law, the specific judgment in the case of the Church Commissioners appeared dubious. Clergymen are not ordinary employees, but men who have decided to follow a vocation where monetary reward is of secondary importance. If they, therefore, require the trustees of a trust of which they are beneficiaries to follow the Christian principles which persuaded them to become clergymen in the first place, even at some financial cost, it would seem wrong to deny them.

Charities investment powers

The first Poor Law in English history was promulgated by Queen Elizabeth I in 1601, and the preamble to that Act defined what it called heads of charity. The four heads of charity are still used today as the basis of definition in English law of what a charity is. They are:

1 the relief of poverty
2 the advancement of education
3 the advancement of religion
4 other purposes beneficial to the community.

It is worth remembering that before it can come into existence a charity has to justify its existence under one of these headings. It then needs to formulate them, *its objects* in a constitution, and describe how it intends to achieve them, *its powers*. Only when its constitution and purpose has been approved by the Charity Commissioners (or Parliament in some rare cases), can it legally call itself *a charity*. It is then given a specific number as a registered charity and can claim the associated tax advantages of being a charity, such as rate relief. For the ethical investor, the point is the established legal framework of charities, with very tight guidelines as to what they should do, and close regulation by a body with real teeth, the Charity Commissioners. It has rarely happened, but the Commissioners can, if they feel it is necessary, dismiss the trustees of a charity and take over the running of it themselves.

As mentioned earlier, from Victorian times trustees were required to use great prudence in the investment of charitable funds, which normally meant their investment in totally safe government bonds (gilts). However, the late 1950s saw increasing inflation and the government recognized that inflation was destroying the real value of these supposedly safe assets by passing the 1961 Trustee Investments Act (TIA). This was seen at the time as a great liberalizing measure, since, as well as requiring trustees to consider diversification, it made a legal distinction between what were called 'narrow range' and 'wider range' investments. Narrow range investments were essentially gilts, and had to account for at least 50% of a charitable fund's investment portfolio, while wider range investments included 'blue chip' company shares and a special form of unit trust for charities called a Common Investment Fund (CIF).

The TIA also only allowed company shares to be bought which had 'trustee status', which was defined as having paid a dividend in each of the previous five years. The privatization and new issue programme of the 1980s meant that there were several of the financially strongest companies in the UK which failed this test, such as Abbey National and Welcome, and which could not therefore be bought by funds bound by the TIA. It should be added that any charity wishing to get around the provisions of the TIA could do so by inserting a clause in their governing constitution specifying the trust's investment powers, although such a change would need the approval of the Charity Commissioners.

Over the last thirty years, investments in UK equities have done much better than investments in UK gilts, so the 1961 Act is often derided as too restrictive. However, in the context of its time it was far-seeing. In the 1930s, many companies went bankrupt and their shares became worthless, so secure gilts did much better than equities as a whole in that period. After the war, most investors such as the big insurance companies feared another Great Depression and invested most of their assets in gilts with only a minority in equities. It was only the success of George Ross-Goobey's mainly equity portfolio in the 1950s with the Imperial Tobacco Pension Trust which led investment managers to switch from gilts to equities. By the mid-1990s the average pension fund had around 85% of its money in equities compared to only 5% in gilts.

Charities should not be too worried about breach of trust in regard to diversification as long as they take professional financial advice, as the 1992 case of Miss Nestlé vs National Westminster Bank showed. As *Solicitors Journal* reported it:

> ... the appeal concerned the investment policies pursued by the defendant bank and its predecessor, the National Provident Bank, from 1922 when the trust was established on the death of Miss Nestlé's grandfather to 1986 when she became absolutely entitled to the fund. She had received £269,203, but contended that had the fund been properly managed her interest would have been worth more than £1m. Part of the fund had been invested in equities and part in fixed interest shares but, because the bank had failed to inform itself of the true scope of its investment powers, it had invested only in bank and insurance shares rather than a wider spread of equities. The bank had failed to conduct a regular and periodic review of the investments.

The Court of Appeal agreed that Miss Nestlé's claim had properly been dismissed. Lord Justice Dillon explained that the onus was on her to prove that she had suffered loss because the equities were not diversified. She had not done so. The bank had little to be proud of in its handling of the fund, but no breach of trust had been proved which had caused loss to Miss Nestlé. Lord

Justice Leggat added that by the undemanding standard of prudence the bank had not been shown to have committed any breach of trust resulting in loss.[20]

The above would seem to reiterate that the law does not require a trustee to obtain the maximum possible return on his/her funds. Given the uncertainties of investment this can only be known in retrospect. A trustee should ensure that the funds are run prudently and take professional financial advice to get a good return.

In the mid-1980s the government became worried about possible malpractice in the charity sector, and in 1987 the Home Office commissioned the Woodfield Report *An Efficiency Scrutiny of the Supervision of Charities*. Following Woodfield, in 1989 the government published a White Paper on the subject, *Charities: a Framework for the Future*, which announced its intention of producing: '. . . *a stronger and more modern framework of supervision, which will equip the Charity Commission for a more active role, narrow the scope for abuse, encourage trustees to shoulder their responsibilities, and ensure continuing public confidence in the sector.*' This became law in the Charities Act 1992. The government then passed the Charities Consolidation Act 1993, which combined the 1992 Act with earlier legislation such as the 1960 Act. While the White Paper considered that the current system of trust status and supervision by the Charity Commissioners worked well, it was concerned about the loose regulation and general administration of many charities and the possible scope that this might leave for malpractice or even fraud. It therefore introduced a number of new measures to tighten up general practice. The main points being:

a) a strengthening of the Charity Commissioners' investigative powers.
b) introduced a new obligatory regime of trust accounting.
c) tightened up the rules disqualifying someone from trusteeship.
d) introduced new rules for the regulation of fund raising.

The 1993 Charities Act had two clauses affecting the way charities could invest their money. The Act announced the abolition in five years' time of the Official Custodian, which had traditionally managed the investments of smaller charities, so from then on they would have to manage their affairs themselves or hand their investments over to a professional investment manager. The second gave the Home Secretary the power to vary the investment rules of the 1961 Trustee Investment Act, but, to general surprise, by the end of 1994 he had not done so.

The Charity Commissioners clearly play an active role in guiding charities in what they can and cannot do. It is interesting that in 1987, five years before the Nicholls case, they accepted that financial return should not be the sole criterion for a charity:

> While the normal duty of charity trustees in exercising their investment powers is to provide the greatest financial benefits for present and future beneficiaries, financial return is not in all cases the sole consideration. The trustees should not invest in companies pursuing activities which are directly contrary to the purpose or the trusts of their charity, and they should have the discretion to decline to invest in companies which are inimical to its purposes. It would, for example, be entirely appropriate for the trustees of cancer relief charities to decline to invest in tobacco companies, for the trustees of charities of the Society of Friends to decline to invest in the arms industry and for the trustees of temperance charities to decline to invest in breweries.[21]

In 1993 the Charity Commissioners had to redraft their guidance notes in the light of the new Charity Acts. CC 3, *Responsibilities of Charity Trustees*, now said:

> Trustees have the general duty of protecting all the charity's property. They are accountable for the solvency and continuing effectiveness of the charity and the preservation of its endowments . . . The trustees must decide what form of investment will be most suitable for the needs of their charity and obtain skilled advice for this purpose. They should bear in mind the long-term future of the charity as well as the short-term, and try to counteract the effects of inflation on their capital and income.[22]

It is highly significant that they did not say anywhere that trustees must maximize their financial returns.

In the light of the above, and the Nicholls' decision, it is disappointing that financial advisers continue to advise charities that they must maximize their income. Every year the *Investors Chronicle* produces a major and useful survey of the charity field. The section which came out in November 1993 had three pages on ethical investment, the first time that this subject had been covered in the *IC* charity review. It stated baldly: 'A more basic reason why charities tend to invest in areas that might appear to conflict with their values is the clear obligation, under charity law, to maximize the value of their funds. This position has not essentially been altered by the legal ruling on the Church Commissioners. It could even be said to have been reinforced.'[23]

Quite wrong! It then went on to give the real reason why charities did not invest ethically – their investment managers did not recommend it: 'Not surprisingly, the most common reason given by respondents to the EIRIS survey for not adopting an ethical investment policy was that their fund manager had advised against it.'[24]

It is worth noting that outside the Church investment bodies, no leading charity investment manager is known for having any expertise in socially responsible investment.

This lack of understanding of ethical investment was revealed by a fund manager, quoted in the same article: 'With diversity in commerce, finance and industry, where any firm may have interests in defence, tobacco, South Africa, gambling or nuclear power, it is very hard to find a truly ethical investment. Ethical investors have been forced to accept unacceptable percentages, with the result that they are forced into a conflict between principles, trustee responsibilities and available investments.'[25]

In December 1993 the *Financial Times* produced a similar survey. Again, one of the leading charitable investment managers gave the same misleading advice: 'The legal position is quite clear. The trustee's primary responsibility is to maximize the return to the fund.'

CHAPTER TWELVE

A New Model for the Company?

The feeling is getting round that there are other things to notice about a company, things just as important as profits. The time is say five years from now. The place is some company's general meeting. The Chairman rises to his feet, listen to what he, or it could be she, has to say: 'Fellow shareholders, fellow stakeholders, fellow customers, fellow employees, suppliers, and fellow members of the human race.'[1]

In the 1980s and early 1990s economic growth seemed to slow and to be associated with steadily rising levels of unemployment, social tension and crime, and environmental pollution. Some analysts wondered whether this was, in part, due to changing circumstances which made the traditional model of the company no longer appropriate. By an ironic coincidence, at the same time as right-wing think-tanks were advocating ever greater use of the free market as the solution to all economic, social and environmental problems, industrialists and management strategists increasingly wondered whether something was not wrong with the very heart of the capitalist system, that is, the very nature of the company itself. In other words, was there a natural ecology of business? Had modern business exploited and abused its social capital and was it now reaping the cost in terms of poor returns and ever rising expenses of crime prevention and internal security?

The responsible company

While Adam Smith is often quoted as the advocate of free-market competition, his strictures against the limited liability company are often forgotten. Even before the dawn of the first Industrial Revolution, Smith realized that such a company necessarily entailed the permanent division of labour, and one hundred years before Marx, the creation of a 'lumpen proletariat'. 'The man whose whole life is spent performing a few simple operations . . . generally becomes as stupid and ignorant as it is possible for a human being to become. The torpor of his mind renders him incapable . . . of forming any just judgment concerning many even of the ordinary duties of private life.'[2]

It is worth coming back to the question of the limited liability company and its role in society. Created at the end of the seventeenth century, it was banned in the 1720s in the aftermath of the South Sea Bubble when it was thought that such a permanent corporation was an incentive to speculation. Writing fifty years later, Smith's view was that the benefits of economic specialization or 'efficiency', derived from the individual's pride in his own business, and the knowledge that this business would be likely to prosper with him the only beneficiary if it produced quality goods. If the business did not make goods of sufficient quality, it would fail, and the big loser would be the owner. He contrasted this adversely with a joint-stock company with absentee owners and salaried employees with much less interest in what they produced: 'The directors of joint-stock companies, being the managers rather of other people's money than of their own, it cannot be well expected that they should watch over it with the same anxious vigilance with which the partners in a private copartnery frequently watch over their own.'[3]

Limited liability was revived in the 1850s as the collapse of a number of dubious railway flotations brought innocent investors to bankruptcy and was made generally available in the Consolidated Companies Act of 1862. Unlimited liability seems a sensible structure for the man who runs his own business, legally called a sole-trader. If he takes all the risk, he gets all the benefit, and what is more important, he is in control of the business and can judge which risks to accept and which to decline. The 1862 Act marked the explicit recognition by the law that the dominance of the small-scale family-owned business of the first Industrial Revolution was over, and that the increasing scale of production required external, passive investors who had to be given protection in some way.

Like many things in British life, the legal concept of limited liability grew up little by little, without great consideration being given to the possible implications. In 1897 Salomon vs Salomon established the principle that a corporation was something different from its members. This was confirmed in 1947 in a famous court case, whereby in 1943 the government had nationalized the aircraft manufacturer Short Brothers, paying the depressed wartime share price. Even though the auditors demonstrated that the net assets of the business were worth substantially more than the offer, the courts held that the shareholders were not entitled to asset value because they did not own the company and it had not been liquidated. Lord Justice Evershed remarked that: '. . . shareholders are not in the eye of the law part-owners of the undertaking. The undertaking is something different from the totality of its shareholdings.'[4]

Two hundred years after Adam Smith, the British industrialist George Goyder revived the whole question of the role of limited liability in a series of books such as *The Responsible Company* in 1961, and *The Just Enterprise* of 1985. Goyder observed that modern British industry was dominated by a few, large companies whose scale of operation was vastly greater than the cottage industry of the period of the first Limited Liability Acts. Yet the law had not altered to take account of this change. George Goyder thought that there was a major flaw in company law – it failed to state what the purpose of a company actually was. 'It gives to the directors, as agents of the shareholders, de facto control of the company's policy and to the other interests, such as the workers' – no corresponding rights. Unlike previous forms of work organization, of which the fifteenth-century guilds and the chartered corporations which followed them are typical, a limited liability company is not constitutionally concerned with quality or value, or with the public interest.'[5]

All other legally privileged bodies such as charities have to justify their rights to such privileges, but the limited company does not, despite having enormous power. Goyder does not mention it, but the only previous company system based on power without responsibility in British society were the monopolies granted to favourites by the Tudors and Stuarts and abolished by Parliament as unjust in the seventeeth century.

Some industrialists like the unrestricted power of modern company directors. Sir Owen Green, the Chief Executive of BTR wrote a letter to the *Financial Times* attacking the Cadbury proposals on corporate governance. 'The concept of ownership, as distinct from membership, of a limited liability company is novel, untested and inappropriate. The expression "owner" does not appear in the Companies Act, and the normal obligations of a true owner are, except in respect of unpaid share capital, nonexistent. Perhaps the description has been introduced to stir a perceived apathy illustrated by the voting habits of members of companies.'[6] George Goyder concluded however, that the only way forward was for company law to be changed to reflect all the people affected by the operation of business, for whom he coined the word 'stakeholders'. These included shareholders, but also employees, customers, suppliers and society in general. He called for law creating a company which: '. . . seeks to act as a responsible member of the community of which it is a member and one that can be called to account where there is gross failure to act justly. It means legislating for the responsible company.'[7]

The horizontal, empowered manager

The global recession of 1991–93 was the most severe since the Great Depression of the 1930s. If it had not been for fast growth seen in the Asian 'tiger' economies, the world economy would have actually declined in 1993 for the first time since the War. It was also remarkable for something else again. For the first time since the 1930s business executives and professionals like solicitors and accountants found their dreams of lifetime employment shattered, and they joined the rising tide of unemployment. Remarkably, this process showed no sign of stopping even after the end of the recession. The American General Electric company (no relation to Britain's GEC) was in the forefront of this approach, cutting the number of layers between the factory worker and Chairman Jack Welch from nine to four, and reducing its head office staff from 2,100 people to 800. BT reduced its number of staff by 95,000 in the five years to 1993, with the number of levels in the company falling from twelve to six, and 6,000 middle managers made redundant in 1992. Why were such large companies as British Gas and British Telecom, or Sainsbury and British Petroleum, continuing to reduce their managerial staff to levels that would have seemed unthinkable ten years ago?

The answer lay partly in the management theory of 'business re-engineering' which swept across the globe in the last few years. Invented by management consultants James Champny and Michael Hammer, the core concept was that managers needed to focus on the company's 'operating model', i.e. be able to identify exactly what the company's real competitive edge over its competitors actually was. It was argued that when directors analysed their sales, they found out that the real reason their customers bought their products was very different from what they had thought. A further development was the concept of the 'horizontal organization', the idea that with modern information systems the old hierarchical model of the company, with separate divisions such as marketing or finance all reporting upwards to top management, had become archaic and actually impeded a company's ability to respond to changes in the marketplace. Hence sales, marketing and finance teams were all to work together at the lowest possible level. In such cases the vast head offices of most large companies had become an unnecessary overhead to be removed or 'delayered'.

The Economist in April 1993 ran an article entitled 'The Fall of Big Business.' It noted the big problems at some of the world's largest companies such as General Motors, IBM and Philips, and the struggles of others such as Matsushita and Daimler-Benz, and predicted 'The humbling of big firms has only just begun. Economic recovery will offer some respite, but not much. In a broad range of industries, powerful forces are moving against big companies. New technology has spread around the world, trade barriers have come down, financial markets have been deregulated, and consumer tastes have converged.'[8] *The Economist* suggested that these trends would harm big business rather than aid these global giants as had earlier been thought.

These themes were further developed by Peter Drucker – the doyen of business strategists, who argued that large integrated corporations were increasingly dinosaurs who would be forced to contract out most of their functions to independent consultants employed as and when needed, or face the risk of extinction. The big company simply could not do everything well, and increasingly was being forced to contract out such weaknesses to specialists who were the most efficient in a particular area. Drucker noted that many big companies such as General Motors and IBM were on their third or fourth round of cost-cutting, delayering and re-engineering, but that after a brief period of improvement, their results start to slide again:

A company beset by malaise and steady deterioration suffers from something far more serious than inefficiencies. Its 'business

theory' has become obsolete. Every business, in fact every organization, operates on a set of assumptions regarding the outside
(customers, markets, distributive channels, competition) and a set
concerning the inside (core competences, technology, products,
processes) . . . The diagnosis is fairly simple. Whenever a business keeps on going downhill despite massive spending and
heroic efforts by its people, the most likely cause is the obsolesce-
nce of its business theory.[9]

Drucker emphasized that most of the great corporations which
dominate world trade today such as the large oil, steel and food
companies came into existence in the period 1890–1914 and have
not changed much since then despite two World Wars, global
depression in the 1930s and rapid technological change since 1945.
Whereas for most of the post-war period the proportion of people
employed by large companies steadily increased, this was reversed in
the 1980s, so that the proportion of the US workforce employed by
the Fortune 500 (the 500 largest companies in America) fell from
30% to 13%! 'Corporations once built to last like pyramids are now
more like tents. Tomorrow they're gone or in turmoil. And this is
true not only of companies in the headlines like Sears or GM or
IBM. Technology is changing very quickly, as are markets and
structures. You can't design your life around a temporary organization.'[10]

What Drucker called 'post capitalist society', others might prefer
to call the third Industrial Revolution, since its institutional framework remains an economy based on private property and competing
firms. His point was that the first Industrial Revolution from 1780
supplied industrial power to previously craft industries; however, the
typical scale of business remained small, typified by the family-
owned workshop. The second Industrial Revolution began one
hundred years later with the application of knowledge to the process
of work itself; large companies began to flourish on the back of
increasing economies of scale and there was increasing need for a
class of professional managers to run such companies. Drucker
notes that the height of this system was the period 1945–90, when
large multinationals such as Exxon and IBM appeared to dominate
the globe. For such companies, the competitive edge they enjoyed
enabled them to have a vast 'command and control' system of
middle management to run the business.

Now, however, such a system of middle management merely absorbs, distorts, and impedes the flow of the only key variable – information. 'The current emphasis on re-engineering essentially means changing an organization from the flow of things to the flow of information.' Drucker argued that this meant the end of the authoritative managerial culture of the last one hundred years and its tranformation into one of equals working together towards a common goal. 'To build achieving organizations, you must replace power with responsibility ... The new organizations need to go beyond senior/junior polarities to a blend with sponsor and mentor relations. In the traditional organization – the organization of the last 100 years – the skeleton, or internal structure, was a combination of rank and power. *In the emerging organization, it has to be mutual understanding and responsibility.*'[11]

Yet even if empowering or giving individual managers much more responsibility is the way of the future, how can this be done? In particular, how can this be achieved in a world lacking the common values which were prevalent in the 1950s? Society is much more aggressively individualistic now; if you remove the command and control mechanisms from large companies, how do you ensure that individual managers do not use their increased power to benefit themselves rather than the company as a whole? This is a particular problem in the service sector, the largest and most rapidly growing part of a developed economy, where salesmen and local managers are often paid large bonuses for short-term good performance. Meeting such sales targets may later emerge not to have been good for either the client or the company's reputation, as many British insurance companies can attest. One answer is to take the formerly dry, academic subject of business ethics and see if this can be turned into an effective management tool.

Business ethics in a secular society

In an 1988 article called 'Morality in Management', the British company director George Bull tried to find a way out of the insistence on expediency in modern management practice, that the end justifies the means. He concluded that the greatest influence on modern boardroom practice was Machiavelli's old book, *The Prince*, quoting: 'In the actions of all men, and especially of princes, where there is no court of appeal, one judges by the result.'[12] Over the following years the field of business ethics has arisen to provide a different answer to that question. Indeed, an academic looking for a new field to move into could do a lot worse than switch into business ethics, one of the few booming areas of academic life.

Yet to what point? As the British Airways' 'dirty tricks' campaign, and the scandalous misselling of personal pensions demonstrated, this academic success story did not seem to have had much impact on the moral behaviour of businessmen in practice. A number of large companies that were audited to be in good shape, such as the two conglomerates Polly Peck and British & Commonwealth, suddenly collapsed. In 1993 the hotel chain Queens Moat Houses saw its £1bn stock-market value apparently vanish overnight, while Robert Maxwell's depredations escaped the attention of government regulators. The problems in Lloyd's Insurance market has caused many investors or 'Names' to see a lifetime's wealth melted away for risks they claim that they did not understand. Even in the City, with its focus on short-term financial returns, large investment institutions have protested about 'corporate governance' and the excessively high salaries many directors have been awarding themselves.

In a major article published in the *Harvard Business Review* in May 1993, 'What's the Matter with Business Ethics?' Andrew Stark, an Assistant Professor in Toronto University's Faculty of Management, dared to venture that the Emperor's new clothes were truly nonexistent: that business ethics provided little concrete guidance to managers in the moral problems that they repeatedly face; that the subject itself lacked a sense of direction and was myopically obsessed with its own concerns. He concluded that: 'Far too many business ethicists have occupied a rarified moral high ground, removed from the real concerns and real-world problems of the vast majority of managers. They have been too preoccupied with absolutist notions of what it means to be ethical . . . with dense and abstract theorizing.'[13] However, he saw rays of hope, quoting another ethicist that: '. . . the really creative part of business ethics is discovering ways to do what is morally right and socially responsible without ruining your career and company.'[14] In future it must demonstrate that business ethics can offer a practical way out of the mess modern business seems to have got itself into, where the mass of decent business executives feel forced by the 'system' to do things that they know may be damaging to the community.

Stark identified as showing the best way forward the work of Laura Nash, whose 1993 book *Good Intentions Aside* was clearly based on extensive personal experience. The title gave the clue to the book. 'My subject is the . . . behaviour of the inherently decent, average manager . . . after consulting with thousands of such managers at all levels of the corporation, I have concluded that they have the normal range of ethical instincts and a desire to see that these instincts are not compromised at work. At the same time, their good intentions do not necessarily provide automatic immunity from wrong-doing.'[15] In other words, the typical Anglo-Saxon approach that corporate ethics is a matter best left to the individual had become outmoded. Her stated aim was to find out why the normal moral values of private life no longer seemed to function once the manager entered his office. Managers were torn between: 'the fear that living up to ethical obligations will impose an immediate cost on the bottom line (profits), and the fear that employees who adopt unethical standards will pose a financial liability down the road.'[16]

If Adam Smith warned against the limited liability company, how much more would he question today's huge multinationals, where even senior managers feel themselves cogs in a vast machine, or as Nash put it: 'Every manager regularly faces decisions that are problematic from a moral standpoint, and over which he or she does not have total control: decisions where people will inevitably get hurt; . . . where the commitments of the organization and a manager's performance goals are at odds with the individual needs of certain employees or customers.'[17]

Her solution to these dilemmas was to look at case studies where such huge corporations as Johnson & Johnson or Nynex had successfully reorientated individual self-interest to longer-term goals of value creation and service to others. She suggested a 'Coventantal Ethic', resonant to American ears of the Pilgrim Fathers. Under this ethic the role of business is defined as the creation of value to a democratically controlled marketplace. It is a system where business gets a fair return for fair value, with profit becoming the *result* of business rather than its *aim*, and where business relationships are seen more in terms of relationships than tangible products. This has political consequences; many countries in Eastern Europe and the Third World are experimenting with capitalism for the first time. Historically, such a transition process has been associated with exploitation and corruption not conducive to liberal democracy, and

Nash therefore argued that if capitalism is to be seen as a voluntary social contract between the public and business, there must be some mutual covenant between them. 'Democratic capitalism, resting on a system of voluntary exchange and political commitments to individual freedom and discretion, is at heart a system dependent on the creation of trust.'[18]

Nash showed how large companies, such as the healthcare company Johnson & Johnson with its *Credo* programme, re-established a positive commitment or 'covenant' to a common vision. While a number of large companies have achieved this, it is not easy to carry out. Workers at all levels can see through a superficial boardroom commitment if the directors speak of common values but do not explicitly lead by example. Directors can set the agenda, but they almost have to eat, live and breathe it. She found that her 'Covenantal Ethics' only worked to become an integral part of a company's culture if it got a total commitment from a person, rather than merely being an intellectual cost-benefit exercise. On the positive side, companies like J & J, Penney, Hewlett-Packard, IBM and many others found that having a distinct set of corporate values helped to create a high level of company morale, and reassured the public when things go wrong, i.e. it was good for profits as well. (Peters and Waterman found that a high level of corporate identification was a good indicator of business success in their best-selling management guide, *In Search of Excellence*.)

Business ethics in the real world

John Drummond is a very experienced senior business executive who set up his own ethics consultancy called Integrity Works based in Kensington, West London. He can be described as the UK's leading teacher of business ethics to the corporate sector, having recently done so to some of the largest companies in Britain. In 1993 along with Andrew Wilson of Ashridge Management College, Drummond published the first systematic and detailed survey of business ethics in British industry, called *The Importance of Being Ethical – Business Ethics and the Non-Executive Director*. In December 1992 the Report of the Cadbury Committee had sent shock-waves through the boardrooms of the UK, with its explicit criticisms of the way some companies were being run. It advocated a code of good practice to improve corporate governance, stressing the need for non-executive directors to ensure this, including business ethics: 'Non-executive directors should bring an independent judgment to bear on issues of strategy, performance, resources – including key appointments – *and standards of conduct*.'[19] (my emphasis).

Shortly after Cadbury, Drummond and Wilson sent survey questions to non-executive directors of Britain's 500 largest companies, of which 118 gave usable replies. All of them felt that business ethics was a very important issue, and 56% of the companies had discussed business ethics at board level in the previous six months. The main conclusions of the report were that for most companies it was the chief executive who determined what the business ethics of the company should be, if any. Although 43% had ethics codes, only 8% carried out an ethics audit, while 61% put their faith in old-fashioned disciplinary measures.

Recently Drummond has helped British Airways and National Westminster Bank devise codes of ethics. NatWest's Code of Conduct is an impressive ten-page guide, called *It's Good Business*, which was circulated to all the bank's 90,000 staff worldwide. I visited John Drummond to discuss what business ethics felt like in practice. As you might expect from someone who has been responsible for communications for IBM (UK), Honeywell and TSB, he combines clear articulation with a high level of energy and enthusiasm:

The thing is, most people *do want to be ethical*, but they are unsure to what extent they can do this in the corporate field. A code of practice is just a start, but it's a necessary beginning because people do need to know what the core corporate values are. However, even junior staff are no fools, they know well enough that a code of practice is just a piece of paper, and that if their manager puts pressure on them to make a sale against a customer's interest because it's needed to meet the quarterly profits target, then the whole exercise becomes a waste of time. That's why having devised a code of practice, the directors have to be seen to lead by example, and you then have to make sure that these 'integrity values' are communicated across the whole organization. A company's code of business ethics needs to be thought through carefully, with consultation with its employees, and not just worked out by the chief executive on the back of an envelope.

If you take the view, as I do, that a company's reputation is its most valuable asset, (I call it a 'meta brand'), then companies need to be aware where they could be vulnerable to problems in such areas before the problems and associated bad publicity emerge. Companies need to create a clear code of practice, they need to implement internal controls systems to make sure that it works, and they need persistence to convince middle managers that it's for real. I think that the real challenge in this area for most British business is to implement objective measurement of how core values are being adhered to, an 'ethical audit' if you like. But note that the aim is not the negative one of punishing poor performers, but the positive one of building corporate values based on integrity and reliability.[20]

Drummond believes passionately that good ethics are good business. Given the information age we live in, poor ethics will be noticed and sales will suffer. 'As never before, the media and others are now sensitive to ethical breaches. It is increasingly unlikely that ethical transgressions will go unnoticed. Remember the nostrum: "News is what someone somewhere doesn't want to see in print, anything else is advertising."[21] He points out that customers are increasingly confronted with an almost infinite number of choices of what to buy, particularly in financial services where many of the products are highly complex and difficult for the ordinary man to understand. In such a situation, a company's reputation is its strongest selling point. 'Look at the success of the Co-operative Bank in carving out a niche for itself as an "ethical bank", and compare that with the large insurance company recently fined and forced to suspend its entire salesforce for poor advice; other things being equal, who would you buy a pensions product from?'[22]

In 1994 John Drummond published a new book with Bill Bain called *Managing Business Ethics*. In an introductory chapter Drummond stated that business ethics was in the same position as quality control ten years before, something that most companies used to do on an ad hoc basis, with some kind of check at the end of the production line the main enforcement technique. Now companies realized that in a globally competitive marketplace, that approach was totally inadequate, and they used 'total quality management' with quality built-in at all stages of the product from design to delivery, as an integral management tool. If Drummond is right, business integrity will become a vital and integral part of modern corporate life, just as quality control has done. As he points out, 're-engineering' by most large companies means individual managers have far more power than before, but: '. . . to decentralize and devolve company operations without a set of clearly understood and enforced corporate values is to court disaster. In a rapidly changing business environment it is suggested that effective performance and maximum profitability can best be secured by empowering individuals . . . while at the same time insisting that the company's ethics are not negotiable.'[23]

The evidence supports John Drummond's belief that good ethics equals good profits. The British management writer Tom Lloyd argued in his book, *The Nice Company*, that companies perceived to be 'nice' attract and keep better staff, and that this also helps them retain customers, a far more profitable enterprise than winning new ones, with substantial evidence to back this up. A recent study, *Corporate Reputation: Managing the New Strategic Asset*, of America's largest companies (the *Fortune* 500), found that the rate of attrition even of the largest companies was much greater than generally expected: 'It is sobering to remember just how fragile organizations are. A look back at *Fortune* magazine's roll call of the top 500 American corporations shows that two thirds listed in 1956 have disappeared. Only 29 of the 100 biggest US firms are still there one working life later.'[24]

The authors found that the survivors were companies with a strong moral core, which protected their reputation and core values, rather than paying attention to the cultivation of an image.

Towards company social audits

If companies do carry out internal 'ethical audits', it would seem only a matter of time before this overlaps with the demands of ethical fund managers for more social information on a potential company investment. This could be 'hard' financial and quantitative reporting on such issues as health and safety at work, employment of minorities etc., or it could be 'soft' in the sense of a statement of a company's integrity values such as J & J's *Credo*, or involvement with local communities. Of course, this is already happening in the field of environmental audits, where 'green experts' like Merlin and

Ecofin are in a position to give companies positive feedback on the usefulness, or lack of it, of such audits. I feel strongly that the marketplace is just beginning to wake up to the comparative advantage that the best ecology investors have over other more traditional fund managers in this area.

It therefore seems inevitable that by the end of the century many companies will have a 'social audit'. The pioneering work of Traidcraft in this respect is described in the next chapter. Of course, 'backwoodsmen' will cry out that the last thing business needs is the burden of more reporting, facing as it undoubtedly does the challenge of global competition. Yet in a fast-moving and knowledge-based society it is essential constantly to assess what a company is doing. The British motorbicycle industry was confident that the tried and tested ways of doing things were the best and is now as extinct as the dinosaurs. Business in the twenty-first century will need social audits to tell itself how it is achieving its integrity goals, it will need them for customers who are increasingly sophisticated and it will need them for investors who need to know potential liabilities and advantages. Lastly, it will need them for governments which are increasingly laying off some welfare burdens onto the corporate and charity sectors, and which therefore need some measure of their effectiveness.

Many businessmen know that in their bones business has to work with society, and cannot operate in a vacuum outside it. In September 1993 several of Britain's leading executives wrote to the *Financial Times* under the corporate banner of the charity Business in the Community. These included Neil Shaw, Chairman of Tate & Lyle, Eric Nicoli, Chief Executive of United Biscuits, Sir Anthony Cleaver, Chairman of IBM (UK), Sir Allen Shepherd, Chairman of Grand Metropolitan, and Peter Davis, Chairman of Reed Elsevier.

Business in the Community has always agreed that the primary role of business is to create sustainable wealth by meeting customers' needs . . . (but) business can help to build the social environment it needs for long-term wealth creation . . . There is clear evidence that customers increasingly expect businesses to play their part in tackling social issues; in 1992 *Mori* research found that 73% of adults are more inclined to buy products from companies that support the community and society . . . A survey by *MSS* of the UK's top 1,000 companies found that 75% believe that employee involvement in the community improves morale, 71% that it builds teams, and 65% that it offers training opportunities. Employees are even more enthusiastic – 84% told *Mori* that a company that supports society and the community is probably a good company to work for.[25]

Charles Handy is one of the most stimulating and influential of Britain's thinkers on management. A visiting Professor at the London Business School and former executive of Shell, Handy, like Peter Drucker, has not confined himself to management theory, but looked to broader issues such as the future of work itself.

In his latest book, *The Empty Raincoat* published in early 1994, he came to similar conclusions: '. . . it will be increasingly difficult for shareholders to know what they are buying into, or to what sort of risks they are exposed. It will be all the more difficult because the real assets of the business, the intellectual assets, will still be largely unquantifiable, *unless accountancy groups come up with new measures*. In the best business today the market value of the business is three or four times the tangible assets, and in a good manufacturing company, labour costs should not be more than 10% of the product price. **That leaves a lot of unmeasured space.**' (my emphasis).[26]

The RSA Inquiry

It is not surprising that Charles Handy, as Chairman of the Royal Society of Arts, should have led the RSA into establishing a major enquiry into the nature and purpose of the modern company. In December 1990 he gave a lecture at the RSA entitled 'What Is A Company For?' The lecture took up the themes of George Goyder's books: 'What is a company really for today? Do our rules and institutions reflect that purpose, or do they, perhaps, get in the way? Things do outlive their purpose, and what was once sensible may now seem crazy. We do not have to be slaves to our history.'[27] Handy went on to criticize modern institutional investors whom he compared to punters in a horse race – if they did not like a particular runner, they could easily switch their money elsewhere. 'Nevertheless, these punters have an exclusive privilege – they are, for the price of their bets, given a vote as to who should own the horse – which means that they have to be wooed.'[28]

He went on to point out that one third of all British companies were taken over in the period 1972–1982, compared to virtually none in Japan or Germany. The point is that this pushes UK companies to seek short-term profits at the expense of investing in the long-term future of the business – they have to keep their inconstant owners happy. Handy concluded by reviving Goyder's notion of stakeholders. 'I see the company as operating in a bounded space, a sort of hexagonal ring, surrounded by competing pressures for financiers, the employees, the customers, the suppliers, the environment, and the community – the so-called "stakeholders". With that ring of forces I want to see the development of the "existential corporation", the corporation whose principal purpose is to fulfil itself, to grow and develop the best that it can be . . . it is not a piece of property, inhabited by humans, it is a community which itself has property.'[29]

Following this lecture, the RSA, a charitable society set up in 1754 'for the encouragement of Arts, Manufactures & Commerce', held discussion meetings in 1991–92 with the chief executives of a number of major companies, and this in turn led to the formal establishment of the RSA Inquiry in January 1993. Called 'Tomorrow's Company: The Role of Business in a Changing World', it brought together the heads of twenty-five of the UK's top companies under the leadership of Sir Anthony Cleaver, Chairman of IBM UK. The declared aim was practical – to stimulate competitive performance by provoking business leaders to think about the sources of sustainable business success. The Inquiry had an intriguing subtext – 'the Case for the Inclusive Approach', and this was not just a philosophical theme of the Inquiry, for the RSA established the Inquiry Network in parallel for RSA Fellows and others to contribute to it. In a sign of the continuity of ideas, the Inquiry was run by the RSA Programme Director, Mark Goyder, a son of George.

In February 1994 the RSA published an Interim Report on 'Tomorrow's Company',[30] apparently designed to be open-ended and provoke discussion, rather than a flat and definitive statement of the RSA's views. It seemed to me that there was relatively little new in the Interim Report, although overall its assessment of the prospects for the UK economy was quite chilling. What was new was *who* was saying it, i.e. the leaders of such companies as Anglian Water, Blue Circle, Cable & Wireless, Cadbury, Guinness, National Westminster Bank, Unipart and leading City names such as Barings, Kleinwort Benson and Rothschild. Cadbury, of course, included Sir Adrian Cadbury whose own Committee had raised some searching questions about corporate governance. The table below shows a few key points from the Interim Report – author's numeration.

THE RSA INQUIRY

1 how to attain sustainable business success in the face of continuing and substantial changes in the nature and intensity of global competition.

2 to achieve sustainable success tomorrow's company must take an inclusive approach . . . success is not defined in terms of a single bottom line, nor is its purpose confined to the needs of a single stakeholder.

3 tomorrow's company will understand and measure the value which it derives from all its key relationships, and thereby be able to make informed decisions when it has to balance and trade off the conflicting claims of customers, suppliers, investors and the communities in which it operates.

4 the nature of competition is changing as the interdependence increases between companies and the community. In order to be internationally competitive the company requires a supportive operating environment . . . business, government and the other partners need to develop a shared vision and common agenda.

5 businesses are increasingly competing for the attention and approval of individuals, whether as customers, suppliers, employees, or members of the communities in which they operate.

6 to achieve sustainable success in the demanding world marketplace, tomorrow's company must be able to learn fast and change fast. To do this, a winning company must inspire its people to new levels of skill, efficiency and creativity, and support a sense of shared destiny with customers, suppliers and investors.

Sir Anthony Cleaver has no doubts of the *practical nature* of the Inquiry:

Of course financial figures are important, we're a group of businessmen, we are very conscious that the bottom line does matter, but, if you think about it, it's really a historic measure. It tells you where you've been. If you want to know where you're going, the questions are about your people, about your suppliers, about your customer relationships, is the community going to inhibit you because it does not like the way you do business? And they are, I think, much more capable of being predictive measures.[31]

A potential criticism of the report is that this conceptual model of the company is all very well, but empty rhetoric unless there is some way of actually measuring a company's effectiveness in the field of staff relationships, customer satisfaction, etc.. Nor, as yet, is there really any sign, apart from the relatively small ethical fund management community, that City analysts pay much attention to such indicators. Critics of the RSA report have noted that it is strong on analysis, but weak on prescriptive guidelines on how to do this. Sir Anthony again:

> I do believe that in the future we may see a standardized approach to a whole range of measures, but that I think should come because it evolves, because if we do our job properly in the companies, we will persuade the (City) analysts that's what they ought to look at, and then they will start to demand the same from other companies. Let me give you one example – the question of the environment. If I take you back just ten years ago, the average company report had no reference to the environment at all, then what happened, the pressure built up from the community, from employees, from customers. First the Chairman stood up and said that his company had a responsible policy with regard to the environment, then a couple of years later it became a paragraph, or even a page, in the annual review with a few pretty pictures and some more pious statements. That's all moved on, most of the leading companies now produce figures, they actually say 'we measured our impact on the environment last year, and we're setting targets, we're moving forward.' Ten years ago, you would have bet me that wouldn't happen.[32]

(Rover cars produces a good example of how employee involvement can increase competitiveness. By guaranteeing employment in its factories, Rover has encouraged its workforce to produce a number of ideas which have greatly reduced cost, and which the workforce would not have mentioned if the likely consequence was the loss of their jobs.) In a way Mark Goyder himself illustrates how the RSA Inquiry combines both the practical and the theoretical, as he was previously a business executive for fifteen years with such large companies as GEC and Reed International. He summed up what for him were the key points of the Inquiry:

> This report is a challenge to business, it's the product of business people themselves. And they're saying we're not going to tell you what to do, it's up to you to make sense of all these changing circumstances, we are going to tell you that we read them this way, and we think that unless you follow an inclusive approach, you look at all the relationships in a business, and you measure your success in all of them, you will be missing opportunities to be competitive. The report points out that we in the UK tend to operate under a mindset that *focuses on the shareholder to the detriment of the shareholder* because it diverts attention from other business opportunities which are available through better attention to customer, supplier, community, and people relationships.[33]

A new world-view?

Many people will find it hard to accept what has been written above, which is quite understandable. The world is undergoing a shift both in its technological potentiality and in its view of itself, its *Weltanschauung*. Older people in particular find this hard to accept. How many of us do not have computers and video recorders which our young children use quite happily, but their university-educated grandparents find impossible. Peter Drucker called his latest book *Post Capitalist Society* because he feels that the world is at one of those great shifts which divide human history into distinct segments. (Some people use the word 'discontinuity', or 'paradigm shift'; I prefer the concept of 'inflection point', but the underlying idea is the same – that human history consists of long periods of consistency interrupted abruptly by periods of very rapid change, and that generally speaking, the dynamics of this are driven by ideas and technological change rather than politics.)

In the thirteenth century the High Middle Ages began almost overnight; universities were founded, trade revived, as did urban society and the use of money for the first time in eight centuries. England in 1500 was wrapped in medieval, feudal slumber; but fifty years later Renaissance and Reformation had laid the foundations of future empire. Likewise for the first Industrial Revolution 1780–1820. Since Peter Drucker has made a number of long-range successful forecasts (for example, his 1976 book *The Unseen Revolution* predicting that pension funds would eventually own the majority of US company shares) his views demand consideration. As he put it: 'Every few hundred years in Western history there occurs a sharp *transformation*. We cross what . . . I called a "divide". Within few short decades, society rearranges itself – its world-view; its basic values; its social and political structure; its arts; its key institutions. Fifty years later there is a new world. And the people born then cannot even imagine the world in which their grandparents lived and into which their own parents were born.'[34]

CHAPTER THIRTEEN

The Social Economy

Men always work harder and more readily when they work on that which is their own . . . it is evident how such a spirit of willing labour would add to the produce of the earth and to the wealth of the community.

POPE LEO XIII, Rerum Novarum 1891.[1]

The previous chapter discussed the idea that it was time to re-examine the form and purpose of the company in view of the much greater demands on it and its scale of operation today. Some possible alternative structures are provided by the social economy, a form of economic organization not centred around money, but on a sense of shared values, which is growing rapidly at present. At the same time, in many countries budgetary constraints are forcing governments to cut back their scale of operations leaving a gap in the area of social need which in the UK is being filled by charities. This in turn is causing a transformation of the charity sector from a voluntary, part-time culture to that of a *social business*. One of the oldest and most successful forms of the social business is the cooperative, of which Mondragon in Spain is a good example.

The Mondragon Cooperative

'The Basque Country is a poor country, without its own natural resources. We have to import everything. It's also a country which traditionally has seen a lot of emigration, to other parts of Spain and other countries. Life has normally been very hard for the people who live here, and the only way they could get out of that hardship has been to work. The cooperatives grew out of this culture of poverty, of difficulty.'[2] Senor Javier Mongelos, President of the general council of Mondragon

The Basque country of northern Spain has normally felt cut-off from the rest of the country. A poor, mountainous region, it is culturally separated from its Castilian and Catalan neighbours by its incomprehensible language which is unrelated to any other in Europe. Always economically backward, it was deliberately kept so by General Franco as a punishment for fighting against him in the Spanish Civil War. (Picasso's famous painting *Guernica* represents the bombing of a Basque town during that war.) Spain has traditionally had one of the highest rates of unemployment in Europe, and even now for the country as a whole it is around 25%, which is over double the British figure. It can be imagined that life here in the 1940s and 1950s was bleak, with widespread poverty that the central government ignored.

Into this misery came Father José Maria Arizmendiarrietta, parish priest of the mountain district of Guipuzcoa from 1943. Initially he worked with the poor of the parish and established a technical training college to help men find work elsewhere. In 1956, having persuaded the local bank to provide the £2500 essential capital, he organized the local workers into a small cooperative called Ulgor to make the cookers and later refrigerators for which there was a strong demand in Spain at that time. Inspired by the encyclical *Rerum Novarum*, Father José was absolutely clear that his was a mission to put Catholic social teaching into practice: 'Salvation is achieved through community action, and involves the development of the capacity to think, to invent and to serve. I advocate the thesis (of transforming the world) by doing real work, within what is possible.'[3]

Since that time Ulgor has developed into the Mondragon Cooperative Corporation (MCC), which now coordinates 102 separate cooperatives in the Basque country. At the end of 1993 MCC employed over 25,000 employees, making it the largest company in the area, and incidentally the fifteenth largest company in the whole of Spain! Sales amounted to 4,242m pesetas (around £2.0bn), concentrated in machine tools, automotive components and all kinds of electrical appliances, as well as a rapidly growing finance division. The total assets of Mondragon were an even more impressive Pt.1992bn (£4.8bn) at the end of 1993. MCC made great efforts to ensure that all workers were informed about the business prospects of their particular company, while cooperative councils allowed anyone to discuss what was happening with the management of a particular business. Despite an increasing range of activity, no Mondragon cooperative has ever gone bankrupt in the forty years of its existence.

How did it achieve this? By following its founder's advice of community action, but also his words of developing a worker's capacity to think, rather than the usual approach of regarding him as a mere robot on a production line. Mondragon does this by carefully training workers with its own college, and is prepared to invest time (up to two years) and effort into helping new cooperatives stand on their own feet, something which the normal Anglo-Saxon capitalist simply cannot afford to do. Each new worker has to buy a share of the cooperative in which he works; normally the cooperative makes a loan to enable him to do so, which is then deducted from his pay. Likewise, on retirement the departing worker is obliged to sell his share back to the company with the value depending upon the success of the particular cooperative. It is not unusual for workers who invested £1000 some thirty years ago, to find that their share is now worth £20,000, which is a useful nest egg for retirement. In 1965 the individual cooperatives set up the central cooperative now called Mondragon to coordinate trade between them, and this encourages some cooperatives to take shares in each other.

The other key facet of Mondragon's success is the local credit union it set up in 1959, the Caja Laboral Popular. This has 140 branches, over 100,000 savers, with banking assets of £85m. This ensures that the profits of the Mondragon's success stay and are reinvested in the local community. The CLP also has an investment department, which not only lends money to individual cooperatives, but works with them to plan ahead for new developments, and since it monitors closely the individual progress of a particular company, can step in with both money and practical advice if things go wrong to nurse the cooperative back to health. It is due to CLP that no Mondragon unit has ever gone under despite the very difficult industrial climate which occurred when the Gonzalez government adopted a policy of high interest rates and a strong peseta in the late 1980s. This policy was identical in philosophy and effect to the Major policy of a strong pound in the Exchange Rate Mechanism, and just like the British experience, it plunged the country into recession.

Spain was obliged by the European Community to open its markets to foreign competition when it joined the EC in 1986, and coupled with the strong peseta policy and recession, it put a tight squeeze on

Spanish manufacturers in particular. The result was to push many companies into making losses and this in turn caused enforced redundancies. The Gonzalez Government's Socialist credentials led to good industrial relations in the 1980s, but as the 1990s progressed these became much more aggressive and confrontational. Trade unions refused to help companies restructure their operations and the number of strikes rose sharply. In contrast, Mondragon was able to overcome the poor economic background and continue to grow its sales and exports, with one result being that unemployment in the Guipuzcoa district was virtually nil compared to the gloomy situation in the rest of Spain.

Mondragon
Financial performance 1991–93

	1991	1992	1993
Sales Pt bn	357.3	397.1	424.2
exports Pt bn	51.5	52.0	61.8
Labour force	25,479	25,322	25,317

How did Mondragon manage to achieve this?

According to Senor Mongelos: 'We have certain advantages in the Mondragon Corporation, because the benefits or otherwise of productivity go directly to the person who works; the owner of the company is the same as the person who has to work there . . . We don't have strikes for example. When there is a problem then a general assembly is organized to sort it out. The future of the corporation must be one of further adaptation to this new world of international competition,'[4] he added. Many companies are finding that, too late, having alienated their workforces they cannot rely on them for the cooperation in restructuring and the general flexibility that they need to survive. Mondragon, in contrast, has found that by treating them as men and not machines and making them owners of the business, it is able to thrive in this extremely competitive modern world.

Cooperative Shopkeepers

Mention cooperative shopkeepers and most people's minds will immediately construct an image of a small corner shop, probably in the North of England. Some economists might even add that they are well-meaning, but of course they cannot compete with shareholder-owned (proprietary) companies. How many people realize that one of the UK's largest and most successful retailers is, in fact, a cooperative. Not only that, but the majority of the group's stores are in the prosperous South-East, with a *middle-class* customer base who would hardly shop in a store just because it was owned by its staff.

The company is of course the John Lewis Partnership (JLP), and its flagship department store in Sloane Square, Peter Jones, probably has a more upmarket domestic clientele than any other store in the country. Currently JLP has twenty-two large department stores and over one hundred Waitrose supermarkets. Over the last eight years Corporate Intelligence figures show that it has increased its share of the total retailing cake, putting it in the distinguished company of Marks & Spencer as the only other non-food retailer to do so. This is an impressive result as John Lewis, like Marks & Spencer, suffered from its refusal to join competitors in breaking the Sunday trading law. In 1993 the profits of the John Lewis Partnership (JLP) rose 31% to £93m on sales of £2.4bn. In accordance with the usual custom, £42.3m of the profit was ploughed back into the business, and £34.5m was paid to staff as a bonus. The bonus depends on trading conditions, but over the last twenty years has averaged 17% of pay.

The company was established as a partnership owned by its staff in the 1920s by John Spedan Lewis who had inherited and grown the family owned draper-shop business. Lewis was struck by the fact that the profit of the company, after tax and interest payments, was equal to the total staff wage bill. As the Partnership's weekly newspaper states on its back page every week:

> *The business belongs to those who work in it. All, except those engaged temporarily, are Partners from the day they join and all the ordinary share capital is held by a trustee on their behalf. Under irrevocable trusts, Partners get all the profits, after provision for prudent reserves and for interest on loans and fixed dividends on shares held outside. A large part of the distribution is made direct in the form of Partnership Bonus, shared among Partners at the end of the trading year as a percentage of their pay.*

Lewis's stroke of genius was the realization of how to combine the efficient running of the business with the workers genuinely feeling that they had *control*, and not just *ownership* as can happen in some modern ESOPs (employee share-ownership plans). This was achieved firstly by making the staff the owners in 1929; Lewis sold them the company financed from a £1m loan, interest free, provided by himself. Secondly, he split management into two: *executive* and *critical*. The executive branch consists of management as normally conceived, who run the business. Top of the tree is the Chairman who is normally appointed by his predecessor. However, the supreme body of the Partnership is the Central Council, where 80% is elected by secret ballot of all the Partners and 20% appointed by the Chairman. If two-thirds of the Council pass a motion of no-confidence in the Chairman, the trustees must dismiss him. This has never happened in practice. It is also worth noting that the share-ownership system has not been financed at the expense of other employee benefits, as has happened in the case of some American ESOPs. There is a noncontributory pension scheme amounting to 6.7% of salary.

The heart of the critical system is the thirty-three Registrars, whose function is to get to know all the Partners in their branch, to ensure that the branch works within the spirit and law of the Partnership regulations and to represent the branch to the central management. Historically, the Registrars have always been women, and despite equal opportunity, they still are. Finally, rather like the ancient Venetian Republic, any member of the Partnership is encouraged to submit critical letters to the *Gazette* which must be answered by the management. John Lewis's Chairman Stuart Hampson believes that the partnership structure has at least two distinctive advantages. Firstly that the business can invest for the long term without worrying about a takeover bid. Secondly that the fact that the staff own it gives them a distinct incentive to perform well, which is obvious to the customer. As Hampson says:

People sometimes ask whether the partnership makes the staff complacent. If that were the case I think the opposition would be beating us more than it is doing. We are distinct, not because there is nobody like us, but because it would be difficult today to start out creating our trust status. The employee is the shareholder and the shareholder is the employee. There is no question that it does work to our comparative advantage.[5]

Nor is the lack of a stock market quotation a problem.

> If we wanted £100m tomorrow there would be bankers rushing forward to lend it to us. We have no problems raising funds – in fact we are always getting clever bankers turning up with their clever wheezes finding ways for us to spend our money.[6]

Does it work over the long term? In 1986 JLP commissioned a research report by Keith Bradley of the London School of Economics. Its conclusions were that:

1) Between 1970 and 1985 retail sales at the John Lewis Partnership grew at a rate of 7.0% per year faster than its main competition.
2) Profit performance in the JLP has a long-run trend rate in excess of 4%, better than most of its competitors.
3) The Partnership has a respectable employment growth rate of 2.9% p.a. and now employs in excess of 30,000 partners.
4) With above-average turnover growth and below-average input growth the JLP has *higher productivity growth than comparable companies.*

The last item is impressive, as if there is one obvious potential weakness in employee-owned businesses, it would be that of protecting jobs at the expense of productivity.

The report concluded: 'Taken together, the figures suggest that John Lewis is maintaining a successful share of the British retail sector and performs well, particularly with respect to labour and to a lesser extent capital employed ... these findings decisively refute the view that participative organizations such as John Lewis will necessarily perform worse than their conventional counterparts.'[7]

Tales of ESOPS

Employee share ownership plans were devised in the United States, and grew rapidly in the 1980s. See table 33 below:

NUMBER OF ESOPS IN EXISTENCE IN US

1975	1977	1980	1983	1985	1990	1992
1700	3100	5000	6300	7200	9800	9600

Source: National Center for Employee Ownership

In essence an ESOP is very simple, it is a means whereby part of the profit of a company is diverted into a trust giving employees a significant stake in the company. When it works, it works very well. An oft-cited US example is the Herman Miller Company, a furniture company. Like John Lewis it was originally a family-owned business developed by Max DePree who believed in employee share ownership as a way of building what he called a 'covenantal relationship' with employees, i.e. that the work place should be a community. According to DePree such relationships 'fill deep human needs and enable work to have meaning and to be fulfilling. They reflect unity and grace and poise. They are an expression of the sacred nature of relationships.'[8] He believed that the leader should follow the New Testament example (Luke) as 'one who serves.'

DePree created an ownership structure to reflect this: 'Make certain that in every position you have both an owner and an employee. The shared sense of ownership, in turn, creates a shared sense of values.'[9] A common sense of values has been identified as the key to corporate success by such management gurus as Tom Peters and Tom Lloyd as well as many of America's top companies. 'I hope that anyone visiting our plants will come away saying "Those folks are a gift to the spirit".'[10] This ownership structure has worked very well indeed for Herman Miller. Employing 5800 employees and with sales of $800m, it is in size near the bottom of the *Fortune* 500 of the 500 largest companies in America. Yet it has won a *Fortune* poll as one of the top ten most admired companies in the US, as well as a place in the *100 Best Companies to Work for in America*, while the performance of its shares generated a 41% compound return 1976–86.

Yet it is fair to say that not all ESOPs have been so happy. In the late 1980s some were created to enable some US companies to escape the clutches of 'corporate raiders' who were taking over companies at that time. In return for pay cuts, de-unionization and job layoffs, workers were given sizeable stakes in a number of companies. Yet ownership was not always coupled with control. In some cases the ESOP was used as part of a highly indebted 'leveraged buyout' to remove the company from the stock market, and the management often needed the savings from job cuts, more flexible working conditions, etc. to keep the company alive. Yet the profits from such cuts could be used later to refloat the company on the stock exchange, making huge profits for the managements with their share options, but not necessarily for the workers.

An example of the latter was Weirton Steel, based in West Virginia, where in December 1993 the company's planned reflotation collapsed into lawsuits over the management's plan to shrink the employee stake, while the workers filed a lawsuit charging the management with gross mismanagement. A Weirton employee Frank Slanchik, a maintenance worker, described how the workers accepted lower pay, job cuts and threw away the old job demarcation rules: 'We kept the job moving. We felt what we were doing was best for the company.'[11] Weirton illustrates what can go wrong with ESOPS unless the key issues of control and of who gains if a private company is floated on the stock exchange are thoroughly sorted out before the ESOP takes place. Slanchik said how the atmosphere at the plant had totally changed. 'I won't do that today. They've taken the drive right out of my heart. The trust factor here is zero.'[12]

Shared Interest

Shared Interest (SI) is another example of a financial company based on Christian principles and yielding a 'social return'. (Technically, it is a company registered under the Industrial and Provident Societies Act with the stated aim of 'people investing together in real jobs for the poor of the world.') It was set up in April 1990 in Newcastle, in order to take deposits from British savers and lend the money on to the Third World to help finance sustainable local business there. Shared Interest's investors get little clear financial return – its 2,400 investors, with savings of £ 3.4m in 1993, get 1.5% interest on their deposit accounts. Managing Director Mark Hayes described the philosophy thus: 'We see ourselves as group of people coming together to pool our funds in a business-like manner to provide other, less fortunate people with access to business credit. We're really not surprised at the growth. The reason they join is that they want to invest in poor people. The interest is secondary. They're identifying with the social return.'[13]

How does the society use its funds? Initially it lent on most of its capital to the Ecumenical Development Co-operative Society, but by the middle of 1991 was able to lend directly with £40,000 going to Traidcraft and C$60,000 to Oxfam Canada. In each case Shared

Interest was able to make low cost trade finance available, enabling them to carry more stock and thus increase their sales of Third World products. (Traidcraft itself is described later in this chapter.) In 1993 it lent £250,000 to Traidcraft, and also made a loan of £350,00 to Oxfam Trading. This helped Oxfam to pay the producers of the Third World goods it sells in its shops an advance of part of the purchase price, enabling them in turn to buy necessary materials without borrowing the money from moneylenders at crippling rates of interests.

Like the Co-operative Bank, Shared Interest refused to speculate against the pound during the sterling crisis of 1992. 'The sort of money that was up for grabs was a very serious temptation. But we felt that the end would not have justified the means.'[14] Most people surely agree with Mark Hayes that it is not the business of a British bank or other financial institution to try to destroy the value of the pound on the foreign exchange markets in return for a quick profit. Such integrity is likely to be rewarded by Shared Interest reaching its target of £5m in assets by the end of 1994.

Conscience Foods

The 1980s saw a boom in the sales of products perceived to help the environment, such as recycled paper or enzyme-free detergents. The early 1990s has seen rapid growth in the sale of foodstuffs which appeal to the customer's sense of justice as much as his tastebuds. In October 1993 a poll by NOP found that 68% of the thousand adults polled would be willing to pay more for products that guaranteed a fair return to farmers and workers in the Third World; in fact the average consumer was prepared to pay a 25% price premium to achieve this. A similar RSPCA poll found that 30% of the population were sufficiently concerned about animal rights that they were prepared to pay up to 50% more for meat from animals which had been well treated. The RSPCA launched its own label, Freedom Food, in the middle of 1994 to guarantee eggs and meat came from animals which had been kept, transported, and slaughtered in a humane way. Like most ethical products, it is essential that the product has 'ethical integrity', that is, it not only produces what it claims, but an increasingly cynical consumer *is certain that it does so*. Of course, like the Co-op in banking, the

RSPCA has a unique tradition behind it. As its marketing manager Mike Sharp explained: 'The consumer response has been very positive because the RSPCA is trusted as an independent party.'[15]

A similar branding idea to help the Third World is called Fairtrade. Fairtrade's initial products include Maya Gold, a chocolate brand where cocoa farmers from Belize have guaranteed contracts to receive about 20% more than the free market price for their products. In terms of sales, the most important Fairtrade brand is Cafedirect, which has achieved a growing market share in the ground coffee market. Cafedirect was formed as a profit-making company by Oxfam Trading, Equal Exchange, Traidcraft, and Twin Trading, all charities which believe that just trade is the best way to help development in the developing world. Based in Edinburgh, Cafedirect has four directors who work free on secondment from the four founding organizations, and employs consultants as and when needed. It has no full-time employees as such.

The company buys coffee beans from Costa Rica, Mexico and Peru and pays the farmer twice the market rate. Despite this, it retails for little more than standard ground coffee, and Cafedirect, first stocked by Waitrose, became available from Safeway and in some stores of Gateway, Tesco, Asda and Sainsbury. The number of farmers supplying the company rose from 13,000 in 1992 to 214,000 in 1994, most of them in some form of collective. In turn the collectives were able to put their profits to use building schools, hospitals, etc. – a fact that Cafedirect successfully used in its advertising to differentiate itself from the industry majors such as Nestlé. Marketing Director Lorna Young said that: '. . . we are a profit-making company, definitely a trading organization rather than a campaigning organization . . . I think we've surprised a lot of people by how well we've done in such a short time . . . orders have tripled in the last 18 months.'[16]

Monitoring all of this is the charitable, membership-supported research group New Consumer, based in Newcastle. New Consumer describes itself as: 'Shopping for a Better World. Whilst consumerism may be at the heart of some of the world's most pressing problems, the creative use of consumer power is a powerful force for social change.'[17] Richard Adams is the Director of New Consumer and has edited or written such books as *Shopping for a Better World*[18], a guide to the environmental and social policies of 126 major consumer goods companies. It rated 2,500 brands in sixty different social and environmental categories, and found that companies with strong social policies also tended to provide value for money, and that good social environmental practice carried through into all aspects of company policy. It also produced *Changing Corporate Values*[19], an analysis of the UK's largest companies on the following criteria:

1 Disclosure of information
2 Environmental impact and action
3 Women's advancement
4 Equal opportunities
5 Community involvement
6 Industrial democracy
7 Socially sensitive products
8 Animal experimentation
9 Third World exploitation
10 Military sales.

Changing Corporate Values is a very useful source of information on what companies actually do, rather than what they say. Its 650 pages take apart 128 of the UK's largest companies, and as such it is an obvious companion to *Shopping for a Better World*. In 1992 New Consumer announced that it would be working with EIRIS to develop positive ethical investment criteria. EIRIS's Director Peter Webster said: 'We hope to develop our service to include more detailed criteria on equal opportunities and employment conditions. We also hope to cover some environmental issues. We are pleased to be able to use New Consumer's experience in drawing positive criteria from company group's responses to questionnaires.'[20] In 1994 Richard Adams announced that in his opinion the way forward for conscience products might be to group them in a separate High Street *conscience store*, and that New Consumer was conducting a feasibility study.

Traidcraft's Social Audit

Traidcraft consists of two arms: a charity called Traidcraft Exchange and a trading arm which is a company – Traidcraft plc. Traidcraft Exchange was set up by a number of Third World charities in 1979, in particular the Christian development agencies Christian Aid, CAFOD, and SCIAF. Its aim is to: 'expand and establish just trading systems which are more just and which express the principles of love and justice fundamental to the Christian faith. Its objectives arise from a commitment to practical service and partnership for change, which puts people before profit.'[21] This is implemented in three ways:

1 to provide business assistance – primarily the transfer of skills and information – to small and medium-sized enterprises in poorer countries who want to export their products but who need help in design, production, marketing or business processes in order to do so.
2 to raise public awareness in the UK about the difference fair trade can make.
3 to support initiatives pushing for fairer trade practices.

Another means of doing so is by owning all the voting shares of Traidcraft plc; the latter has some 3,900 shareholders who have invested £1.9m in nonvoting shares and where, like Shared Interest, financial reward is slight. Indeed, Traidcraft plc was deliberately set up as a company:

> . . . because of the company's wish to demonstrate the possibility of encouraging people to invest with the prime expectation of a social – rather than a financial – return. Traidcraft's Foundation Principles establish it as an organization committed to practise equity and compassion in its economic relationships . . . Traidcraft has no worth if it does not adhere to its Christian concern for social justice. However, by consciously placing itself in the social trading sphere and taking the form of a public company, Traidcraft seeks to demonstrate that such principles are compatible with sustainable economic activity. It is committed to working out, and being a working example of, more just systems of international trade between North and South.[22]

Traidcraft imports and distributes handicrafts, fashion goods, beverages and foods sourced in the Third World. It also sells recycled paper products made in the UK, and Christmas cards in partnership with Christian Aid, CAFOD and SCIAF. It does this through mail-order catalogues and a network of 2,000 voluntary 'representatives', plus through other retailers. Sales in 1992 to 1993 were £5.8m, analysed as follows: Voluntary reps 36%; other retail reps 32%; mail order 19%; Tradefair shops 7% and contracts 6%. It played a leading part in 1992 in the second Biennial Conference of the International Federation of Alternative Trade (IFAT), in the Philippines. Filipino producers, many with a very strong Christian orientation themselves, said that: 'Our relationship with Traidcraft is special in that we feel a strong sense of spiritual values in people there . . . trading with alternative trading organizations is based on principles of solidarity and compassion, not profit.'[23]

Most people would feel convinced that Traidcraft is clearly fulfilling its Foundation Principles. Yet in a quest for ethical integrity it devised a social audit to demonstrate this. Part of the introduction is shown below:

What is Social Auditing?	The Stakeholders	Why a Social Audit
The assessment of a company's social impact and ethical behaviour in relation to its aims and those of its stakeholders.	producer groups consumers staff voluntary reps public/consumers shareholders	to determine social and ethical performance. To strengthen stakeholder role in the company. To improve social impact and ethical behaviour. To encourage others to do likewise.

Hence, under producer groups, Traidcraft's social audit examined whether it was conducting a just trading system: whether wages were fair, what working conditions were like, to what extent its activities benefited workers and their communities, the continuity of business and how it prefinanced orders. Under environment, how it has tried to reduce widespread environmental degradation. The social audit is frequently self-critical – in the Philippines it noted that it did not always verify the origins of wood being offered by woodcarvers. The idea of a social or ethical audit has been around for a long time. Business ethicists have played with the theory, while critical 'ethical audits' of business groups by campaigning activists are also well-known. It would seem that social auditing is of vital importance, not least as more and more activities in the health sector and education are farmed out to market forces, and therefore the preparation by Traidcraft of a practical example by an organization for its own use as well as for outsiders is timely.

As well as its own social audit, Traidcraft produced a sixty-page book, *Auditing the Market* [24] showing in great detail how the social audit had been prepared by Richard Evans of Traidcraft and Simon Zadek of the New Economics Foundation. What was striking about *Auditing the Market* was the total commitment to honesty that runs through it; anyone with real experience of ethical investment will identify with the oft-quoted remark in it that in real life there are often no clear answers. In a secular age it was also pleasing to see a company that openly declaimed spiritual values. In fact six different themes could be distinguished within *Auditing the Market*:

a) an actual social audit of Traidcraft plc
b) an exercise in methodology of how social audits can be carried out in practice
c) a description of how the above was implemented in Traidcraft – the 'social auditing or accounting system'
d) the NEF audit in the sense of verifying the accuracy of the accounts
e) an evaluation of the results as a banker might look at an ordinary set of accounts
f) a deliberate process of involvement of as many of Traidcraft's stakeholders as possible as part of the company's policy of openness.

LETS Exchange

No discussion of the social economy would be complete without something new which threatens to do away with money! This is Local Exchange Trading Systems (LETS). LETS are simply local barter systems which enable people to trade within a local economy without money. They are fast growing. The first LETS was started in Canada in 1981, and although they only arrived in the UK at the beginning of the 1990s, by the end of 1994 there were over 250 of them here. Each uses a local unit of account, called variously 'acorns', 'bobins', 'links', etc., and just as they do with normal money, people bill each other for services and write LETS cheques in payment. One of the most recent LETS was set up in the area of South West London where I live, so I spoke to the organizer, Perry Walker, who is also Chair of the New Economics Foundation which is a great advocate of LETS:

> In Barnes the central feature is the village pond, so we've decided to call our unit of currency 'the pond'. Like the majority of LETS we allow people to negotiate what they charge (a small minority of LETS insist on the same price for each hour's work, whether it's computer programming or mowing the lawn). As a rough approximation, we suggest 10 ponds = £1. Suppose I spend two hours mowing your lawn, you write me a LETS cheque for say 100 ponds. In the central register, I get a credit for 100 ponds, and you are currently overdrawn by 100 ponds. People ask me why some people don't exploit the system and just build up a huge LETS overdraft without contributing anything, but that illustrates the beauty of LETS, that they build the sense of local community, and just like a credit union, people don't like to cheat their neighbours whom they have to meet every day. In fact, since we started the LET, we have developed quite a good social life among members. Another advantage, although it's not so important in a rich area like Barnes, is that it gives purchasing power and a sense of activity to people like pensioners and the unemployed who feel excluded from normal financial life.[25]

Anyone joining a LETS gets a members' directory as well as a LETS chequebook. Services offered can be simple things like baby-sitting or pet care, to skilled services or in some areas taxi rides or clothes in a shop. The following is an extract from the Barnes Directory:

SERVICES OFFERED	SERVICES REQUESTED
Book-keeping	P.C. Marketing
Business Planning	Software Installation
Database/ Spreadsheet	Decorating
Public Speaking	Pet care
French translation	Baby-sitting
Baby-sitting	German lessons

Gardening	Gardening help
Carpentry	DIY
French Conversation	Clothes alterations

For the unemployed, as long as they declare it to their local benefit office, are still available for work and do not exceed the 16 hour limit, working for LETS should not affect their entitlement for benefit. For the employed, a small amount of work in LETS outside normal work will probably have a blind eye turned to it by the Inland Revenue, but if it is part of normal work should be declared. For example, if a plumber earned a few ponds a week baby-sitting, that would probably be ignored, but any LETS income earned as a plumber would have to be declared and would be taxed in hard cash!

The average size of a LETS is 100 to 150 members according to Liz Shephard of LETS LINK UK, the national coordinating body, run as a non-profit agency and which has received over 27,000 inquiries. According to Liz Shephard: 'LETS helps develop and free markets, providing local goods and services not otherwise available. Business can benefit from the increased local trade and help to hold wealth in the local community,'[26] Some people envisage that LETS should be tradeable across different communities, creating a kind of alternative money. This seems doubtful, since the essence of the LETS system is the common bond of a local community. Liz Shephard agrees: 'We have taken tentative steps towards setting up a national system, with reciprocal arrangements between groups in different parts of Britain. But to be honest, the whole essence of a LET is that it should operate on a local basis, with all the members being within easy reach of each other.'[27]

Voluntary Sector – or Social Company?

'Charities are not the sticking plaster on the welfare state. The activities of volunteers are part of the cement that binds our society together.' John Major, Charities Aid Foundation Conference 1991[28].

'The Left has for too long misunderstood (the voluntary sector's) role as nineteenth century charity, whilst the Right uses it as a convenient way to relieve government of its own responsibilities.

In fact, the voluntary sector can often provide services more efficiently and more creatively than either public or private sector . . .
people who volunteer to give service to our community should be
praised for the work they do.' Tony Blair, Arnold Goodman Charity
Lecture. 1993.[29]

Clearly the charity sector is regarded as 'a good thing' by both sides
of the political spectrum. Charities are of course the ultimate form
of the 'social company', since they exist only to benefit society, and
historically have been run on social, rather than financial guidelines,
i.e. on a voluntary basis. Most people are probably aware that things
which used to be done by the Health Service or by local government
have been 'contracted-out' to a charitable trust. They are probably
less aware of the momentous changes in the sector itself. Like
industry and commerce itself, technological and social change are
causing a sea change in the way charities work and the public's
perception of them. In the last ten years professional fund-raisers
have literally revolutionized the way charities raise funds.

Henry Drucker was brought in to head Oxford University's first
ever fund-raising campaign. 'I regard the old "hair shirt view" of
the voluntary sector as a self-inflicted piece of nonsense . . . One
needs to employ a certain professional service, one needs to employ
a certain professional attitude, and if the sector is constantly manned
by people who are underpaid and overworked, doing too many jobs,
then they're not going to do their job properly, which is going to lead
to inefficiencies *and poor service to the client.*'[30].

The Campaign for Oxford was set up in 1988 and had raised
£282m by the end of 1993. Fund-raising became accepted as an
integral part of the university's core function and it used modern
marketing techniques to do so. Drucker again: 'We don't rattle tins.
We strategically analyse each "prospect", each one is different, each
one has to be thought about uniquely in a systematic way. My job is
to organize that kind of solicitation. We solicit, we woo, we establish
long-term, stable, mutually rewarding relationships.'[31] Interestingly,
Drucker was not a professional marketer, but a don in politics at
Edinburgh University.

Professional fund-raising is not just about the sort of sophisticated marketing that the commercial financial world does all the
time, such as targeted letters of solicitation etc. It is about expensive
high-profile publicity campaigns, affinity cards, endorsement of

commercial products, etc. There is also increasing use of 'celebrities', and media events to increase awareness of the particular cause as well as to raise money, even if the extensive media telethons such as *Live Aid* have declined in popularity. From the point of view of most charities this is, in fact, a big problem. All these glossy techniques do not appear actually to have raised an increased amount of money going into the sector, but, like the activities of big business generally, they have enabled large charities to gain 'market share' at the expense of small ones. These commercial techniques are also changing the very nature of the charity sector. Increasingly, professional managers are being hired to bring 'commercial' disciplines to charities, and the paid staff they hire make the term 'voluntary sector' less and less relevant.

The Charities Aid Foundation (CAF) and the National Council for Voluntary Organizations (NCVO) are the leading bodies monitoring developments in the voluntary sector. Every year CAF produces a review of resources and giving in the sector, which is normally released at the same time as its annual November Conference. November 1993 was called 'The Resource Crisis', and showed that the largest 200 fund-raising charities saw their voluntary income increase by 4% in the previous year, but the medium-sized ones suffered a 9% reduction. An increasing amount of charity revenue comes from government, normally in contract fees rather than outright grants, so it was worrying that government grants showed an identical pattern. The biggest 200 saw total government-derived income rise by 5%, but for the middle-ranking 200–400 size, it declined by a shocking 16%!

As Executive Director of the Charities Aid Foundation, Michael Brophy is one of the most respected commentators on the voluntary sector, and on the rapid changes happening in it:

Now if one imagines the resources of the sector as a pond, out of which the animals drink at nightfall, then there are some new big animals barging their way to the edge of the pond and drinking enormous amounts of water. I'm thinking about things like the opt-out schools, the National Health Service trusts, and all the other agencies the government sets up and gives charitable status. Because all these organizations can go to the public and to business, and they are drinking out of the same pot. And that is going to make some of the smaller animals go thirsty! I did think that it would be possible using promotional techniques to raise the level of contributions from the public to charities by something, something substantial. To raise it up to something like the levels we see in the United States. So instead of the 0.6% of people's income being devoted to the support of charities it is here, it might be nearer the 2% level you see in America. Despite the rhetoric of government, despite the efforts of the Council for Charitable Support, despite the promotions of individual charities, the exhortation hasn't had much effect, and that in a sense, leaves us with a real conundrum. Because everybody expects the voluntary, charitable sector to be doing more, but it isn't getting any more, or much more, resources. So something has to give sooner or later.[32]

What has to give is the medium-sized charity, which has neither the financial resources to use sophisticated fund-raising techniques nor the small-scale of operation to operate on a local voluntary basis. CAF itself however illustrates that this turmoil is not without its positive side. It appears to be turning itself, at least in part, into a social investment bank. At the same time, it is also making people think about what is happening to the charity sector. At the end of 1993 CAF commissioned the radical think-tank DEMOS to look at the vast subject of the future of charities, their structure and funding. The first DEMOS briefing paper: 'The future of the charities – themes and issues' noted the current and rapidly increasing blurring of the old clear distinction between the voluntary sector, the corporate sector and the governmental sector.

The previous chapter argued that the whole world is at an inflection point, when the traditional models which have worked well for hundreds of years become obsolete almost overnight. If that chapter demonstrated it happening in the corporate sector, the DEMOS study shows it happening in the charity field. To quote Charles Landry and Geoff Mulgan, the authors of the second DEMOS paper on funding, 'Rethinking Charity Finances':

Making these issues more problematic is the rise of community enterprises and more entrepreneurial charities which are blurring the lines between charities and for-profit enterprises. In the long run some would even argue that we will see a convergence: private firms will be increasingly membership based, as well as shifting from a base in financial capital towards human capital, while charities will evolve from philanthropy towards more associational and mutual forms . . . fewer could be accused of the main failure that Charles Handy described in his famous report on voluntary organizations: strategic delinquency, where ethos is put before strategy and the 'servant syndrome', which makes virtues of parsimony and shabbiness, and eschews the possibilities of modernity.[33]

It is not just DEMOS which sees the charity sector in a major transition phase. One of the UK's leading management writers, Tom Lloyd, devoted his 1993 book, *The Charity Business*, to showing how rapidly it is changing: 'One of the signs of maturity in an industry, a profession or a society is an increase in the number of institutions that serve it . . . By this token, the charity sector is maturing rapidly. There are already a host of dedicated institutions specializing in particular charity-related areas, and more are being set up all the time.'[34]

DEMOS and Lloyd are surely right. Just as socially responsible investment is migrating from a one-dimensional 'exclusive' mind set to multi-factor analysis, so the charity sector is looking at means as well as ends. The 1993 Centris Report was rightly criticized for suggesting that charities should lose their nontaxable status, but this controversy overshadowed a sensible point the Report made about how the concept of 'the charity' was being stretched ever wider. The largest are increasingly turning into social companies, with turnover, resources and a level of sophistication comparable to most ordinary companies. Few people probably realize how big the charity world is; total turnover in 1991 was £ 17bn, making it larger than agriculture in the UK. Whether the old system of trustees is adequate for the task of running these social companies is a vitally important question which the DEMOS study is also addressing.

Notes

CHAPTER ONE
1. Richard Harries, speech to CEIG/EIRIS seminar, 'Ethical investment – an idea whose time has come', October 1990.
2. Quoted in 'Ethical Investment and the Third World' Eiris 1991.
3. 'BAT unit accused of boosting nicotine in tobacco', *Financial Times* 22 June 1994.
4. R.Bertell. *No Immediate Danger*, The Womens Press 1985.
5. *Ethical Investing* by Amy Domini and Peter Kinder, Addison Wesley 1984.
6. Quoted in EIRIS Newsletter May 1992.
7. 'Ethical Views', *Charities Management*, Spring 1994.
8. *The Green Capitalists* by John Elkington with Tom Burke, Gollancz 1987.
9. 'The issue is the environment', *Professional Investor* February 1994.
10. Quoted in 'Ethical Investment, an idea whose time has come'. Christian Ethical Investment Group/EIRIS 1991.
11. Tessa Tennant 'The Ethical Issue' *Planned Savings Magazine*, February 1991.
12. Printed in full in *The Tablet* January 1991.
13. Charles Rubin, 'The Green Crusade', quoted in *Wall Street Journal*, 28 March 1994.
14. HRH the Prince of Wales, quoted in Anne Simpson, *The Greening of Global Investment*, Economist Books 1991.
15. Domini Kinder op cit.
16. 'The Ethical Investor', EIRIS Nov 1993.
17. Domini Kinder op cit.
18. Quoted in *The Nice Company* by Tom Lloyd, Bloomsbury 1990.

CHAPTER TWO
1. 'The Ethical Investor', November 1993.
2. 'Our Best Interest – Guidelines for Ethical Investment.' £6. Christian Ethical Investment Group, 90 Booker Avenue, Bradwell Common, Milton Keynes, MK13 8EF.
3. *Investors Chronicle* – 'Beginners Guide to Investment' Bernard Gray, Century Business, 1993.
4. Peter Lynch, *One Up on Wall Street*, Simon & Schuster, New York 1989.
5. 'Body Shop shows recovery with £29.7m', *Financial Times*, 6 May 1994
6. 'Anita Roddick', *Evening Standard* Letters Page, 25 May 1994.
7. 'Roddick's new age business school', *Sunday Times*, 1 May 1994.

8. *The Times*, 6 May 1994.
9. *Today*, 18 May 1994.
10. *Financial Times*, 20 July 1994
11. EIRIS Research into the Body Shop Stories, 6 September 1994.
12. 'The Ethical Investor', August 1993
13. 'The Ethical Investor', May 1992.
14. 'Ethics spotlight on Salesmen', *The Observer*, 3 April 1994
15. 'The Ethical Investor', August 1994.

CHAPTER THREE

1. Joan Bavaria, speech to UKSIF Conference, London, May 1991.
2. Charles Jacob, Initial Proposals for the Formation of a Stewardship Trust, 1973.
3. *The Greening of Global Investment*, Anne Simpson, Economist Books, 1991.
4. 'Investing with Conscience', *Money Observer*, May 1994.
5. 'The Rewards of Virtue', *Professional Investor*, March 1994.
6. 'Ethical investors point to a betrayal of trust', *The Times*, 9 October 1993.
7. Quoted in 'Green Goes Global', *Money Management*, August 1993.
8. Robert Taylor, letter to the author.
9. Chris Holmes, conversation with the author
10. ibid
11. Charles Jacob, conversation with the author.
12. Lord Clinton-Davis, conversation with the author.
13. Steve Burkeman, speech to CEIG Conference October 1991.
14. Chris Holmes, conversation with the author.
15. 'A Look at Ethical Funds', *Sunday Times*, 14 May 1989
16. Quoted in 'Ethical Investment', *Financial Times*, 24 July 1993.
17. 'Green Goes Global', *Money Management*, August 1993.
18. Quoted in 'How Ethical Funds have performed', *Daily Telegraph*, 14 November 1993
19. 'Insurers accused for poor surrender values', *Financial Times*, 18 June 1994.
20. Peter Silvester – letter to the author
21. CIS Environ Brochure.
22. Robert Taylor, letter to the author.
23. NPI Press Release, 20 May 1994.

CHAPTER FOUR

1. *Financial Adviser*, May 1994.
2. 'How charges reduce returns', *Daily Telegraph*, 2 April 1994.
3. *Financial Times*, 24 March 1994.
4. Lee Coates – letter to the author
5. 'Attack on appalling life policy advice', *Financial Times*, 4 November 1993.
6. 'MPs question PIA's standing', *Financial Times*, 16 March 1994.
7. 'A Question of Disclosure', *Financial Times*, 20 April 1994.
8. Lee Coates in conversation with the author.
9. Giles Chitty in conversation with the author.
10. Pat Meehan in conversation with the author.

CHAPTER FIVE

1. Foreword to 'Managing the Environment', Trudy Coe, British Institute of Management, 1992.
2. 'Sheep And Trees Are Acting Strangely At "End of World".' *Wall Street Journal*, 15 January 1990.
3. Jonathan Porritt, *Sunday Telegraph*, 4 June 1994.
4. 'This Common Inheritance' – The Third Year Report, HMSO 1994.
5. 'A pale green blockbuster', *Financial Times*, 26 January 1994.
6. 'Environmental Europe', Ecofin Financial Services, March 1994.
7. Pope John Paul II, Speech, 22 October 1993.
8. Letters page, *The Times*, 14 March 1994.
9. John Davis, *Greening Business*, Basil Blackwell 1991.
10. *Costing the Earth*, BBC Radio June 1994.
11. *For the Common Good, Redirecting the Economy towards Community, the Environment and a sustainable future*, Herman E. Daly and John Cobb, Green Print 1990.
12. Merlin Research Unit – Survey of ethical and environmental funds in Europe, February 1993.
13. 'Managing the Environment', Trudy Coe, British Institute of Management, 1992.
14. 'Investing in the Future', *Investors Chronicle*, 20 September 1991.
15. '"Green investment", what does it mean to the ethical investor?', EIRIS 1991.
16. 'Green issues sway fund managers', EIRIS newsletter, Summer 1991.
17. 'Investing in the Future', *Investors Chronicle*, 20 September 1991.
18. 'Pirc wants companies to turn green', EIRIS Newsletter, Spring 1994.
19. ibid
20. 'Accounting for the Environment', Professor Rob Gray. Paul Chapman in association with the Chartered Association of Certified Accountants 1993.
21. 'Companies yet to give the green light', *Financial Times*, 20 April 1994.
22. 'The issue is the environment', *Professional Investor*, February 1994.
23. Advisory Committee on Business and the Environment, Report of the Financial Sector Working Group February 1993.
24. 'Wanted: greater environmental disclosure', Mark Campanale, *Professional Investor*, May 1994.
25. 'Looking for life beyond the green paint job?' David Owen, *Professional Investor*, April 1994.
26. *Merlin Research Bulletin* No 5. November 1990.
27. 'Environmental Europe', Ecofin Financial services, February 1994.
28. *Merlin Research Bulletin* No 4, May 1990.
29. Environmental Investment Company – listing particulars.
30. 'Looking for life beyond the green paint job?', *Professional Investor*, April 1994.
31. ibid
32. ibid
33. Kidder Peabody Research Report, September 1994.
34. 'A freight train out of control', *Financial Times*, 13 April 1994.
35. 'Balance Sheet Poison – environmental liability comes to Europe', *Institutional Investor*, August 1993.

36. 'Finance with green strings', *Investors Chronicle*, 20 September 1991.
37. 'Greening of Industry', *Sunday Telegraph*, 18 June 1994.
38. 'Balance Sheet Poison – environmental liability comes to Europe', *Institutional Investor*, August 1993
39. 'Greening of Industry', *Sunday Telegraph*, 18 June 1994.
40. Elisabeth Holtzman, speech to CEIG conference, Windsor, May 1994.
41. 'Exxon guilty of oil spill recklessness', *Financial Times*, 14 June 1994.
42. 'Wanted: greater environmental disclosure', Mark Campanale, *Professional Investor*, May 1994.
43. 'Green goes Global', *Money Management*, August 1993.
44. 'Greening of Industry', *Sunday Telegraph*, 18 June 1994.
45. Serge Lourie – conversation with the author.
46. BBC Radio – author's transcript.
47. 'Top pension firms speed destruction of the rainforests', *The Observer*, 3 April 1994.
48. *Merlin Research Bulletin* No 10, May 1993.
49. 'Balance Sheet Poison – environmental liability comes to Europe', *Institutional Investor*, August 1993.
50. 'Rivers and Seas suffer grisly death by ecocide', *Sunday Telegraph*, 12 June 1994.
51. 'Ripple Effect – Forecast by Munich Re puts added pressure on Europe's Insurers', *Wall Street Journal*, 26 April 1994.
52. 'Greening of Industry', *Sunday Telegraph*, 18 June 1994.
53. 'Balance Sheet Poison – environmental liability comes to Europe', *Institutional Investor*, August 1993.

CHAPTER SIX

1. 'The Implications of Ethical Constraints on Investment Returns', The WM Company, World Markets House, Crewe Toll, Edinburgh EH4 2PY1.
2. Robert Hazell, Speech to 'Working for a Charity' Seminar, January 1994.
3. Gerald Loeb, *The Battle for Investment Survival*, Simon & Schuster 1965.
4. Burton Malkiel, *A Random Walk Down Wall Street*, 6th ed 1986.
5. Barra International – Survey of ethical investment performance 1983–1988, available from EIRIS.
6. 'Socially Responsible Investment: the American Experience'. GLC 1984.
7. Quoted in Simpson, *Greening of Global Investment*.
8. ibid
9. Russell Sparkes, 'The Rewards of Virtue', *Professional Investor*, March 1994.
10. *Sunday Times*, 20 April 1989.
11. 'Friends unveils investment trust', *Daily Telegraph*, 9 December 1993.
12. The Implications of Ethical Constraints on Investment Returns, The WM Company, World Markets House, Crewe Toll, Edinburgh EH4 2PY.
13. The Central Finance Board of the Methodist Church 1993 Annual Report, 1 Central Buildings, Westminster, London, SW1H 9NH.
14. Friends Provident press release 6 June 1994.

CHAPTER SEVEN

1. *Ethical Investing*, Amy Domini with Peter Kinder, Addison Wesley 1984.

2. *Socially Responsible Investment: the American Experience*, Dr Robert Schwartz, GLC 1984.
3. Quoted in *Ethical Investing*, Amy Domini with Peter Kinder, Addison Wesley 1984.
4. Rev Timothy Smith, the Corporate Examiner 1984, quoted in Sue Ward, *Socially Responsible Investment, Directory of Social Change*, 1984.
5. Rev Timothy Smith, speech to ECCR Conference, London March 1992.
6. Quoted in Domini/ Kinder.
7. 'A Friedman Doctrine – the social responsibility of business is to increase its profits', *New York Times Magazine*, 13 September 1970, quoted in Domini/ Kinder, op cit.
8. Quoted in Anne Simpson, 'Greening of Global Investment', Economist Publishing 1991.
9. Franklin Research Screening Questionnaire, quoted in Simpson, op cit.
10. Quoted in Simpson, op cit.
11. ibid
12. 'History of ethical investment in the UK', Charles Jacob, speech at Friends Provident Investment Conference, November 1993.
13. 'Ethical Investment Origins in the UK', Charles Jacob, speech at UK Social Investment Forum, July 1991.
14. 'CFB Practice Regarding Ethical Investment', Bill Seddon, October 1991.
15. Jacob – July 1991 op cit.
16. Bill Whiffen, speech to CEIG/EIRIS seminar, 'Ethical investment – an idea whose time has come', October 1990.
17. CEIG – Investing for the Future.
18. *Our Best Interest*, published by the Christian Ethical Investment Group 1992.
19. ECCR Policy Statement.
20. *The Greening of Industry*, ECCR 1992.
21. 'Benchmarks' – ECCR.
22. Pat Conaty – address to UKSIF AGM, June 1994.

CHAPTER EIGHT

1. Martin Luther King, quoted in Richard Harries, *Prayer and the Pursuit of Happiness*, Fount 1985.
2. *Financial Times*, 4 May 1994.
3. Quoted in Anne Simpson, *The Greening of Global Investment*, Economist Publications 1991.
4. *Business Week*, June 1987.
5. Quoted in Simpson, ibid.
6. *Guardian*, 7 October 1985.
7. Quoted in 'International Banking Campaign Against South Africa' (IBCASA) *Bulletin* No 6, spring 1988.
8. Quoted in Simpson 1991
9. ibid
10. R. Harries: *Is there a Gospel for the Rich?*, Mowbray 1992.
11. W. T. Seddon: South Africa, A report on a visit. February 1992. Unpublished.
12. Sr Margaret Kelly, Secretary of Justice and Peace Commission of SACBC, *Catholic Herald*, 8 October 1993.

13. Community Growth Fund Report, June 1994.
14. 'CGF flexes its muscles', *Weekly Mail and Guardian*, 22 July 1994.
15. Community Growth Fund Report, June 1993.
16. (ICABA) *Bulletin* No 9, Autumn 1989.
17. ibid
18. SACC. Statement on the Lifting of Sanctions, 24 September 1993.
19. Statement by Joint Advisory Council on Ethics of Investment, October 1993.
20. ELSTA Briefing, 'Financial Sanctions: Have They Worked?', December 1991.
21. ibid
22. ibid
23. Letter to the 'Nation', June 21 1993.
24. ibid
25. Responsible Investment – The Fruit of Anti-apartheid Action. Joint Statement by Methodist Church Overseas Division and Methodist Church Division of Social Responsibility, 1 October 1993.

CHAPTER NINE

 1. Terry Thomas, letter to the *Financial Times*, 14 September 1993.
 2. 'Freshers urged to shun the Big Four', *The Observer*, 18 September 94.
 3. John Willcock, 'Small firms hit out at bank charges', the *Guardian*, 3 November 1992, quoted in 'Bankwatch, New Economics Foundation', October 1993.
 4. 'Tireless Thomas the Bank Engine', *Marketing Week*, 24 September 1993.
 5. ibid
 6. ibid
 7. *An Introduction to the Co-operative Bank*, The Co-operative Bank 1993.
 8. 'Ethical Banking – a modern concept and a true reflection of our roots.' Terry Thomas, speech to CEIG 11 July 1993.
 9. Conversation with the author, May 1994.
10. 'Terry Thomas in Conversation', UK Social Investment Forum, January 1994.
11. 'Tireless Thomas' ibid.
12. Quoted in *Catholic Herald*, 8 October 1993.
13. ibid
14. ibid
15. Catholic Building Society, Directors' Report, 22 March 1994.
16. Quoted in *Ethical Investor*, Winter 1990/91.
17. 'Sound finances and sound principles', the *Independent*, 28 April 1993.
18. Quoted in 'Reformed Banking', Bankwatch.
19. Author's notes from speech given by Glen Saunders to UK Social Investment Forum Conference, 'Social Investment and the Voluntary Sector', May 1994.
20. *Outside the Banking System*, HMSO 1994.
21. 'Life-savers for the poor', the *Tablet*, 23 February 1991.
22. Michael Brophy, *CAF Newsletter*, June 1993.
23. *The Charity Business*, Tom Lloyd, John Murray 1993.
24. ibid.
25. *CAF Newsletter*, July 1993.
26. *The Charity Business*, ibid.

CHAPTER TEN

1. Robert Reich, quoted in 'Pension funds take on watchdog role', *Sunday Telegraph*, 10 July 1994.
2. Socially Responsible Investment: A strategy for local authority pension funds. PIRC 1993
3. 'A costly investment strategy', *Investors Chronicle*, 17 July 1992.
4. 'Church and Estate', *Wall Street Journal*, 27 April 1994.
5. 'Carey warns on Church finances', *Financial Times*, 12 December 1993.
6. 'Unravelled cloth', *Financial Times*, 12 August 1994.
7. Unpublished speech to Christian Ethical Investment Group, Windsor Castle, May 1994.
8. Supporting the Church's Ministry – Report & Accounts of the Church Commissioners 1993.
9. The Central Board of Finance of the Church of England, CBF Annual Report & Accounts 30 November 1993.
10. Quoted in *Charity Magazine*, June 1993.
11. The Central Finance Board of the Methodist Church,1993 Annual Report.
12. 'CFB practice regarding ethical investment', Bill Seddon, speech to CEIG seminar, Westminster 30 October 1991.
13. ibid
14. ibid
15. *Money – the Christian Dilemma*, Patrick O'Mahony, Catholic Truth Society, 1981.
16. Rev Timothy Smith, speech at ECCR Conference March 1992.
17. 'the era of no-commitment capitalism', Louis Lowenstein, *Financial Times*, 22 January 1993.
18. PIRC services for local authority pension funds – socially responsible investment. PIRC 1993.
19. ibid
20. 'Rowntree shuffles pension fund team', *Financial Times*, 3 May 1994.
21. *PIRC Intelligence*, July/August 1993.
22. 'Power of the shareholder vote', *Financial Times*, 10 April 1994.
23. Quoted in 'Pension funds take on watchdog role'.
24. 'Growing corporate governance from George III to George Bush', speech by Bob Monks to National Association of Pension Funds, Eastbourne 1990.
25. 'Putting investors back in power', Dale Hanson, *Professional Investor*, April 1993.
26. Growing corporate governance – op cit.
27. Quoted in, 'A fairer slice of the pie', *Financial Times*, 14 February 1994.
28. 'City slams "low-calibre" non-executive directors', *Financial Times*, 4 July 1994.
29. Capital choices: changing the way America invests in industry. Michael Porter for the Council on Competitiveness.
30. *The Comparative Advantage of Nations*, Michael Porter, Macmillan 1986.
31. Quoted in 'The City and Manufacturing Industry', speech by Howard Davies, October 1993.
32. ibid
33. ibid
34. Quoted in 'Let's be friends', *Global Investor*, May 1994.

CHAPTER ELEVEN
1. Anna Kelly, 'A Matter of Trust', *Pensions World*, January 1994.
2. Sir Robert Megarry, Investing Pension Funds, quoted in Simpson, *Greening of Global Investment*, Economist Publications 1991.
3. Lord Halsbury – Learoyd vs Whitely 1886.
4. Kelly – ibid.
5. Ian Gault, Partner Herbert Smith; The Legal Background for Ethical Investment in the UK – unpublished contribution to Friends Provident Ethical Investment Conference October 1993.
6. Lord Halsbury – ibid.
7. *Pension Law Reform* – the report of the Pension Law Review Committee HMSO October 1993.
8. Quoted in Simpson, *Greening of Global Investment*.
9. Vice Chancellor Megarry – Judgment in Cowan vs Scargill 1984.
10. ibid
11. ibid
12. Megarry, Investing Pension Funds
13. Underhill and Hayton, *Law of Trusts* – quoted in Simpson, op cit.
14. Martin – vs City of Edinburgh District Council 1988.
15. Vice Chancellor Nicholls – Judgment Bishop of Oxford and others vs the Church Commissioners Oct 1991.
16. ibid
17. ibid
18. Andrew Phillips, Partner Bates, Wells & Braithwaite, unpublished memorandum on Bishop of Oxford et al to CEIG November 1991.
19. Nicholls – ibid.
20. *Solicitors Journal*, 20 November 1992.
21. Charity Commissioners, Annual Report 1987.
22. Charity Commissioners, CC3: *Responsibilities of Charity Trustees*, HMSO August 1993.
23. *Investors Chronicle* – Charities Annual Review, 5 November 1993.
24. ibid
25. *Financial Times* – Charities Investment and Finance, 14 December 1993.

CHAPTER TWELVE
1. Peter Day – In Search of the Good Company, *In Business*, BBC April 1994.
2. Adam Smith, *The Wealth of Nations*, Everyman Classics 1960.
3. ibid
4. George Goyder – *The Just Enterprise*, Adamantine Press 1994.
5. G. Goyder – ibid.
6. Sir Owen Green, 'Why Cadbury Leaves a Bitter Taste', *Financial Times*, 9 June 1992.
7. G. Goyder – op cit.
8. *The Economist*.
9. Peter Drucker, *Wall Street Journal*.
10. 'The Post Capitalist Executive, An Interview with Peter Drucker', *Harvard Business Review*, May–June 1993.
11. ibid

12. George Bull, 'Morality in Management', the *Tablet*, 21 May 1988.
13. Andrew Stark, 'What's the Matter With Business Ethics?', *Harvard Business Review*, May–June 1993.
14. ibid
15. Laura Nash, *Good Intentions Aside*, Harvard Business School Press, 2nd Ed 1993.
16. Nash – ibid.
17. Nash – ibid.
18. Nash – ibid.
19. John Drummond & Andrew Wilson – 'The Importance of Being Ethical', Ashridge Management College, 1992.
20. John Drummond, conversation with the author.
21. John Drummond, 'Values For Money', *The Observer*, 24 April 1994.
22. John Drummond, 'Values For Money', *The Observer*, 24 April 1994.
23. John Drummond & Bill Bain, *Managing Business Ethics*, Butterworth Heinemann 1994.
24. *Corporate Reputation: Managing the New Strategic Asset*, Smythe, Dorward and Reback, Century 1993.
25. Neil Shaw, Chairman Business in the Community, 'A Social Side to Business', *Financial Times*, 14 September 1993.
26. Charles Handy, *The Empty Raincoat*, Hutchinson, 1994.
27. Charles Handy, 'What is a Company for?', *RSA Journal*, March 1991.
28. ibid
29. ibid
30. *Tomorrow's Company: the role of business in a changing world.* Interim Report – RSA February 1994.
31. Sir Anthony Cleaver – *In Business*, BBC April 1994.
31. ibid
33. Mark Goyder, author's lectures notes.
34. Peter Drucker, *Post-Capitalist Society*, Butterworth Heinemann, 1993.

CHAPTER THIRTEEN

1. *Rerum Novarum*, Official translation, the Vatican Polyglot Press, included in 'The Social Teachings of the Church', ed Anne Freemantle, Mentor-Omega 1963.
2. Quoted in Mondragon Cooperative Movement, *Financial Times*, 24 November 1993.
3. Quoted in Guy Dauncey, *After the Crash*, Green Print, 1988.
4. Quoted in Mondragon Cooperative Movement.
5. Quoted in 'Upturn boosts Middle England's Shopkeeper', *Sunday Telegraph*, 5 June 1994.
6. ibid
7. 'The Success Story of the John Lewis Partnership' – A Study of Comparative Performance. Keith Bradley and Saul Estrin, London 1986.
8. Max DePree, 'Leadership is an Art', quoted in New Economics Foundation briefing note, 'Denationalization and Employee Stock Ownership' by Jeffrey Gates.

9. ibid
10. ibid
11. Quoted in 'ESOP Fables', *Wall Street Journal*, 28 December 1993.
12. ibid
13. 'Sensible finances and sound principles', the *Independent*, 29 April 1993.
14. *Ethical Investor*, Summer 1991.
15. Quoted in 'The Cost of a Fair Deal', *Financial Times*, 17 March 1994.
16. Quoted in 'Care in a Coffee Cup', *Financial Times*, 29 March 1994.
17. New Consumer.
18. *Shopping For a Better World*, Richard Adams, Kogan Page 1991.
19. *Changing Corporate Values*, Richard Adams, Jane Carruthers and Sean Hammill, Kogan Page 1991.
20. 'EIRIS teams up with New Consumer', *Ethical Investor*, November 1992.
21. Traidcraft plc, Social Audit 1992/93.
22. ibid
23. ibid
24. Auditing the Market – a practical approach to Social Auditing, Richard Evans and Simon Zadek, Traidcraft/NEF.
25. Conversation with the author.
26. Quoted in *Ethical Investor*, August 1993.
27. Quoted in 'Greenlets – the car boot', *Sunday Telegraph*, May 1994.
28. John Major, speech at Charities Aid Foundation Conference, November 1991.
29. Tony Blair, 'New Community – New Individualism', Arnold Goodman Charity Lecture, quoted in Charities Aid Foundation Newsletter, August 1993.
30. Henry Drucker, 'The Gift Horses', Analysis – BBC, October 1993.
31. ibid
32 Michael Brophy, 'The Gift Horses', Analysis – BBC, October 1993.
33. The Future of Charities : themes and issues. Charles Landry and Geoff Mulgan, DEMOS 1994.
34. Tom Lloyd, *The Charity Business*, John Murray 1993.

Green and Ethical Investment Funds

FUND	Tel
Abbey Ethical Abbey Life Investment Services Ltd P.O. Box 33 80 Holdenhurst Road Bournemouth BH8 8AL	0202–292373
C.F. Acorn Ethical City Financial Unit Trust Managers 1 White Hart Yard London Bridge London SE1 1NX	0171–407 5966
Abtrust Ethical Abtrust Unit Trust Managers 99 Charterhouse St London EC1M 6AB	0171–490 4466
Allchurches Amity Allchurches Investment Management Services Ltd Beaufort House Brunswick Road Gloucester GL1 1JZ (a subsidiary of Ecclesiastical Insurance Group)	0452–305958
CIS Environ CIS Unit Managers Ltd P.O. Box 105 Manchester M4 8BB	061–837 5060
Clerical Medical Evergreen Clerical Medical Unit Trust Managers Narrow Plain Bristol BS2 0JH	0275–554711

Commercial Union Environmental Inv Tr   0171– 283 7500
Commercial Union Investment Management Ltd
St Helen's 1 Undershaft
London
EC3P 3DQ

Credit Suisse Fellowship   0171–247 7474
(formerly Buckmaster Fellowship)
Credit Suisse Asset Management Ltd
Beaufort House
15 St Botolph Street
London EC3A 7JJ

Eagle Star Environmental   0242–221311
Eagle Star Unit Trust Managers
Eagle Star House
Bath Road
Cheltenham Road
Glos GL53 7LQ

Ecofin Environmental Financial Services   0171–839 5944
19 Buckingham Street
London
WC2N 6EF

Equitable Ethical Trust   0296–386386
Equitable Unit Trust Managers Ltd
Walton Street
Aylesbury
Bucks
HP21 7QW

Fidelity UK Growth Trust   0732–361144
(Fidelity Famous Names)
Fidelity Investment Services Ltd
Oakhill House
130 Tonbridge Road
Hildenborough
Kent
TN11 9DZ

Fiona Price Opp 2000 PEP   0171–430 0366
Fiona Price & Partners
35 Great Queen Street
London
WC2B 5AA

Friends Provident Stewardship   0722–413366
Friends Provident Unit Trust Managers
72–122 Castle Street
Salisbury
SPI 3SH

Henderson Green PEP   0171–638 5757
Henderson Unit Trust Managers Ltd
3 Finsbury Avenue
London
EC2M 2PA

Homeowners Green Chip   0423–567355
Homeowners Friendly Society
P.O. Box 94
Homeowners House
Springfield Avenue
Harrogate
N. Yorks HG1 2HN

Merlin Research Unit   0171–412 0703
Jupiter Tyndall Merlin
Knightsbridge House
197 Knightsbridge
London
SW7 1RB

MI Environmental   0171–495 1511
Medical Investment Ltd
10 Queen Street
London
W1X 7PD

NM Conscience
(from December 1993, same as Friends Provident)

NPI Global Care   0171–623 4200
National Provident Investment Managers Ltd
P.O. Box 227
48 Gracechurch Street
London
EC3P 3HH

Scot Equitable Ethical   031–556 9101
Scottish Equitable Fund Managers Ltd
28 St Andrew Square
Edinburgh
EH2 1YF

Sharp Ethical Pep   0272–260051
Albert E. Sharp
2 Trinity Street
College Green
Bristol
BS1 5TE

Sovereign Ethical   0202–298422
Sovereign Unit Trust Managers
12 Christchurch Road
Bournemouth
BH1 3TS

TSB Environmental   0264–346794
TSB Unit Trusts Ltd
Charlton Place
Andover
Hants
SP10 1RE

Ethical Bankers

Banking Group	Tel
Chris Smith Group Public Affairs Manager **The Co-operative Bank** 1 Balloon Street Manchester M60 4EP	061–829 5436
Susan Jenkins Publicity Manager **Mercury Provident plc** Orlingbury House Lewes Road Forest Row East Sussex RH18 5AA	0342–823739
Mr Francis Higgins Managing Director & Secretary **Catholic Building Society** 7 Strutton Ground Westminster London SW1P 2HY	0171–222 6736
Bob Lowman General Manager **Ecology Building Society** 18 Station Road Cross Hills Keighley West Yorks BD20 7EH	0535–635933
National Federation of Credit Unions Meadow Well Resources 35 Avon Avenue Meadow Well North Shields NE29 7QT	091–257 2219

Association of British Credit Unions Limited (Abcul)   0171–582 2626
Unit 307
Westminster Business Square
339 Kennington Lane
London
SE11 5QY

Leading Ethical IFAs

(IFA's doing a minimum of £100,000 in ethical business in 1993, and
who have at least 25% of their business in this area).

	Tel
Giles Chitty **Barchester Green Investment** Barchester House 45/49 Catherine Street Salisbury Wilts SP1 2DH	0722–331241
Louise Kennedy **Bromige & Partners** 1 Hobart Place London SW1W 0HU	0171–245 1234
John Crowe **Crowe Money Advice** 69 Jamestown Road London NW1 7DB	0171–485 9738
Kate Nathoo **Daniels Holt Investment Managers** Tunsgate Square 98 High Street Guildford Surrey GU1 3QZ	0483–304183
David Martin **Earthwork Financial Planning** 1–7 Princess Street Albert Square Manchester M2 4DD	061–839 3218
Lee Coates **Ethical Investors Group** 16 Carisbrooke Drive Charlton Kings Cheltenham GL52 6YA	0242–522872

Brian Spence   0446–421123
Ethical Financial
31b House
7 & 8 TY Verion Business Park
Barry
South Glamorgan
CF6 3BE

Brigid Benson   061–434 4681
Global & Ethical Investment Advice
13A Heaton Road
Manchester
M20 9PX

John Glavey   0491–832278
Glavey & Co
22 St Mary's Street
Wallingford
Oxon
OX10 0EW

Holden Meehan (London)   0171–404 6442
Amanda Davidson
55 High Holborn
London
WC1V 6DX

Holden Meehan (Bristol)   0272–252874
Patrick Meehan
Top Floor
40 Park Street
Bristol
BS1 5JG

Mike Daniels   0869–252545
Kingswood Consultants
68 Sheep Street
Bicester
Oxon
OX6 7LD

Alex Farrow   061–491–5199
Independent Insurance Consultants
53A Church Road
Gately
Stockport
Cheshire
SK8 4NG

Mike Woolley   0737–225552
Priory Investment Management
5 Belmont Road
Reigate
Surrey
RH2 7ED

IFA Promotions
28 Grenville St
London
EC1M

Research/Campaigning Groups

GROUP	Tel
UK Social Investment Forum Mr Pat Conaty Executive Director 318 Summer Lane Birmingham B19 3RL	021–359 3562
The Ethical Investment Research Service (EIRIS) Mr Peter Webster Executive Director 504 Bondway Business Centre 71 Bondway London SW8 1SQ	0171–735 1351
Christian Ethical Investment Group (CEIG) Hon Secretary Canon Bill Whiffen 90 Booker Avenue Bradwell Common Milton Keynes MK13 8EF	0908–677466
Ecumenical Committee for Corporate Responsibility (ECCR) Secretary Rev Crispin White 11 Burnham Wood Fareham Hants PO16 7UD	0329–239390

Index